79/16

JACOB NEUSNER

Jacob Neusner

An American Jewish Iconoclast

Aaron W. Hughes

NEW YORK UNIVERSITY PRESS

New York

NEW YORK UNIVERSITY PRESS
New York
www.nyupress.org

References to Internet websites (URLs) were accurate at the time of writing. Neither the author nor New York University Press is responsible for URLs that may have expired or changed since the manuscript was prepared.

Library of Congress Cataloging-in-Publication Data
Names: Hughes, Aaron W., 1968– author.
Title: Jacob Neusner : an American Jewish iconoclast / Aaron W. Hughes.
Description: New York : New York University Press, [2016] | "2016 | Includes bibliographical references and index.
Identifiers: LCCN 2016011141 | ISBN 978-1-4798-8585-5 (cl : alk. paper)
Subjects: LCSH: Neusner, Jacob, 1932– | Rabbis—United States—Biography. | Jewish scholars—United States—Biography. | Jewish college teachers—United States—Biography. | Rabbinical literature—History and criticism.
Classification: LCC BM755.N474 H84 2016 | DDC 296.092—dc23
LC record available at http://lccn.loc.gov/2016011141

New York University Press books are printed on acid-free paper, and their binding materials are chosen for strength and durability. We strive to use environmentally responsible suppliers and materials to the greatest extent possible in publishing our books.

Manufactured in the United States of America

10 9 8 7 6 5 4 3 2 1

Also available as an ebook

B
NEUSNER
JACOB
H

Jennifer

now and always

CONTENTS

Everyone in the field of Jewish studies knows the name "Jacob Neusner." Many of us employ, perhaps without attribution, the categories he pioneered. Despite his commanding presence, however, I worry that we have largely forgotten him. This concern was reinforced several years ago when a session devoted to his work at the annual meeting of the American Academy of Religion, an organization that Neusner helped to pioneer and that could count him as one of their first presidents, was woefully underattended. That event would, unbeknownst to me at the time, precipitate this biography. In the weeks that followed that session I was surprised to discover that rather than respect the herculean efforts of Jacob Neusner and acknowledge the battles he fought to make what we do today possible, we minimize them by telling jokes about how much he wrote or how difficult he could be. He did write too much, and he was notoriously mercurial, but this tells us only part of the story. This book's goal is to tell the other part. Rather than engage in muckraking or innuendo, I spent several years with Neusner—the individual, his family, his friends, and most important his archives and his written corpus. The more I read, the more fascinated I became. In this one character we can isolate the story of the study of Judaism in this country. After I casted the net even wider, it became apparent that Neusner's story is also the story of American Jews who came of age in the second half of the twentieth century.

Not only did Neusner redefine the academic study of Judaism, he changed the larger frame of religious studies by forcing that field's categories to expand to include postbiblical Judaism. Even those who disagreed with his interpretation of rabbinic texts had to engage his pioneering methods. But, the more I read, the more I realized that

Neusner was so much more than a scholar of rabbinic Judaism. He was also a journalist, a social commentator, a post-Holocaust theologian, and an outspoken political figure during the height of the cultural wars of the 1980s. Indeed, his legacy, as I define it, may well be in these other fields.

This project has been several years in the making, and I would like to thank many individuals and institutions for making it possible. The Jacob Rader Marcus Center of the American Jewish Archives located on the campus of Hebrew Union College–Jewish Institute of Religion (HUC-JIR) in Cincinnati awarded me a Bernard and Audre Rapoport Fellowship for the 2014–2015 academic year that greatly aided my research. Kevin Profitt, Dana Herman, and Jason Kalman facilitated my time there, and made my stay both productive and enjoyable. I would also like to thank Vardit Samuels, the library assistant for the Judaica Division at the Widener Library, for facilitating my time at Harvard. The American Academy of Religion and its executive director, Jack Fitzmeier, permitted me access to the transcript of an interview between Neusner, a former president of the AAR, and Barbara DeConcini, a previous executive director of the organization, which I found to be very helpful.

In terms of individuals, I would like to thank, first and foremost, Jack and Suzanne Neusner, who opened their home to me in the summer of 2013 to talk with them at length about a life and career in scholarship. Although he liked to be called Jacob in print, in person he preferred Jack. For the sake of consistency, I use Jacob throughout. This project has also benefitted from talking to many others (in alphabetical order): Alan Avery-Peck, Kalman Bland, Bruce Chilton, James A. Diamond, Bonny Fetterman, William Scott Green, Jennifer Hall, Susannah Heschel, Jason Kalman, Laura Levitt, Shaul Magid, Russell McCutcheon, Noam Neusner, Norbert Samuelson, Richard Sarason, Jonathan Sarna, Michael Satlow, Rona Sheramy, and Donald Wiebe. I would also like to single out my friend and colleague, Elliot R. Wolfson, with whom I spoke regularly about Neusner, and the larger field of Jewish studies.

My editor at NYU Press, Jennifer Hammer, has taken an interest in my project from the moment I "pitched" it to her. She went over the entire manuscript and gave me many helpful suggestions to "tighten up" my prose in the service of "flow." I hope I have done so and, if I have, I thank her. I also appreciate the work of Joseph Dahm, who copyedited the entire manuscript.

Introduction

Jacob Neusner is one of the most important scholars in the history of Judaism. He was instrumental in transforming the study of Judaism from an insular project conducted by, and primarily of interest to, religious believers into a dynamic field of study at home in the secular setting of the modern university. He was also a public intellectual who became increasingly critical of what he considered to be the watering down of academic standards in American higher education, and he frequently and vociferously critiqued the system he believed to be responsible for its diminution. He became a household name in the 1970s and 1980s, when Ronald Reagan appointed him to the National Council on the Arts as a conservative voice in an era of debate around the public funding of controversial artists such as Robert Mapplethorpe and Andres Serrano. To this day, he is the only scholar to have served on both the National Endowment for the Arts and the National Endowment for the Humanities. On top of all this, he is one of the most published figures in history. He is the author of over a thousand books, and probably ten times as many book chapters, articles, and op-eds. Later years saw him become a proponent of ecumenical dialogue, and it is in this capacity that he developed a friendship with Pope Benedict XVI, who awarded him a papal medal in 2010. He received over ten academic medals, in addition to nine honorary degrees from institutions such as the University of Chicago and the University of Bologna. Yet in his relations with others he was often cantankerous and controversial, and he garnered a great deal of animosity over his long career.

Unlike other great American Jewish thinkers, such as Abraham Joshua Heschel, Joseph B. Soloveitchik, and Mordecai Kaplan, Jacob Neusner was born in the United States, and his Judaism was informed from a very young age by an American ethos. He wrote profusely on this topic, both academically and for a more general reading audience. For him, Judaism was to be open, informed by, and informing the world. Judaism should have an American inflection, enabling American Jews—the freest in history—to be fully American and fully Jewish.

Jacob Neusner was immensely influential both in shaping the study of Judaism, and in shaping American Jewish life. Yet, although Neusner was the author of so many publications, his legacy risks being lost, or at least muted, by the sheer multitude of his published works. Who was Jacob Neusner? What motivated him not only to write, but to write so much? What did he accomplish? What is his lasting legacy? Which book does one examine when wanting to know what he said about a particular topic? This intellectual biography provides answers to these and related questions for the reader who possesses neither the time nor the energy to read even a fraction of Neusner's diverse corpus. Furthermore, it offers an assessment of Neusner's contributions to the fields in which he wrote. What did the study of Judaism look like before he arrived? And, perhaps just as important, what does it look like now, after Neusner? What did he change? Between these two bookends resides an intellectual life, one full of creativity, rapacious energy, and contention. Each, not surprisingly, fed the others.

Neusner's vision was motivated by the desire to make the study of Judaism respectable and inclusive. It was not to be an insider's club, as it was in the traditional Jewish seminary, but an academic and intellectual endeavor that simultaneously informed and was informed by rigorous theoretical and methodological frameworks that were external to the tradition. Many, both Jews and non-Jews, objected to such an approach. Many Jews believed that the study of the timeless and sacred texts of Judaism belonged in the yeshiva, where they would be scrutinized in the same manner that they had been for centuries, with little or no engagement with critical historical questions, let alone a methodology that had the potential to deprive these texts of their intrinsic sacrality. At issue was history. If the traditional approach to rabbinic texts involved a deep philological and historical appreciation, Neusner contended that this approach possessed an uncritical way of construing history.

Others in the secular academy also objected, but for different reasons. Many had very little interest in Judaism after the time of Jesus, and the study of rabbinic texts was largely unheard of because such texts were thought to be either too technical or too irrelevant. By the 1960s, however, both the Jewish and the non-Jewish academic status quos were on the precipice of being undermined. Divinity schools were giving way to departments of religious studies, and now other religious traditions—Buddhism, Hinduism, Islam—were slowly entering the academy to be studied alongside Christianity. Although Protestantism still largely inspired the categories used to study religion, change was inevitable. Neusner benefitted from this change as he simultaneously helped to facilitate it.

Prior to Neusner, traditional, postbiblical Jewish texts were studied and taught in a variety of places and institutional contexts. There were traditional yeshivas or seminaries in Eastern Europe before World War II, with those that survived relocating to Israel and America after the war. There was also the more technical approach found in academic settings, particularly in Israel, such as the Hebrew University in Jerusalem. There were, in addition, the seminaries associated with the various Jewish denominations in the United States, such as the Jewish Theological Seminary of America (JTS; associated with the Conservative movement), Hebrew Union College–Jewish Institute of Religion (Reform), and the Rabbi Isaac Elchanan Theological Seminary associated with Yeshiva University (Orthodox). There also existed several private nondenominational institutions, for example, Dropsie College for Hebrew and Cognate Learning, which was founded in Philadelphia in 1907, the Baltimore Hebrew College and Teachers Training School (1919), and the College of Jewish Studies in Chicago (1924). In addition, a small handful of European-born scholars were already embedded within universities, such as Harry Austryn Wolfson at Harvard and Salo Wittmayer Baron at Columbia, who were scholars of Jewish philosophy and history, respectively.[1]

Into this milieu came the American-born Neusner. Neusner grew up in a Reform house, had very little formal Jewish education, had probably never even heard of a yeshiva, and could barely read a line of Hebrew. Paradoxically, if not surprisingly, only such an individual could transform the study of Judaism. Not bound by traditional canons of rabbinic study, and unwilling to defer to "Old World" ways of doing things, Neusner was perfectly poised to open the study of rabbinic texts to all—male and female, Jew and gentile—using new methodologies. As the chapters that follow show in detail, it would be neither a straightforward nor a simple task, to be sure.

"The holy books of Judaism (or any other books) are important not in themselves," Neusner wrote in 1984, "but because of what they tell us about what is important: they answer urgent questions of humanity."[2] With such a bold and potentially heretical statement, Neusner signaled his approach. Judaism and Jewish texts are not unique. They differ little from Buddhist texts, Hindu texts, or Muslim texts. Just like the texts from other religions, the sacred texts of Judaism represent localized reflections on timeless and universal human questions. As such, they must be studied using well-established disciplinary methods in order to speak beyond a particular ethnos. Neusner did not want to join the narrow conversation of the yeshiva, wherein men become holy by studying holy books taught to them by holy masters. Indeed, he spent his entire life fighting to open up the study of Judaism, specifically rabbinic texts, to a larger intellectual audience. Today we may well take this for granted. One can now go to college and take a course on Jewish texts taught by someone with a PhD in religion and with a specialization in Judaism, as opposed to being taught by the local rabbi. However, this required real intellectual battles. Neusner was the instigator of many of these conflicts, and he was in the thick of many others. In this way, he created an intellectual space for the scholar of Judaism:

So although we spend our lives studying Jewish holy books and there is no more particularly Jewish activity than what we do, yet it is accurate to describe us as standing outside of the community of Judaism. Among the available categories, rabbi or "professional" or lay leader, there is no place for us. True, there *is* room for learned Jews. But they are perceived as eccentrics or turned into Hebrew teachers. There is no room in Jewry for a learned Jew who makes a living by teaching what he or she knows, on the one side, but who is paid for doing so by secular, neutral institutions, on the other.[3]

Since Neusner did not have the authority of the yeshiva world behind him, he had to create his own. This he did by establishing a space for the study of Judaism in the American humanities, by translating the entire rabbinic corpus into English, and by helping to establish a press, Scholars Press, to disseminate this translative activity to a potentially large reading public. In so doing, he sought to create a curriculum that would transmit Judaism to a generation of Jews like him—Jews who were American, were Reform, and did not grow up in the yeshiva world.

Neusner divided his lifework in rabbinic literature into four distinct phases, each occupying roughly a decade—history, literature, religion, and theology—with each successive stage building upon the previous. Historically, Neusner asked us to be aware of the specific times and places in which rabbinic texts were created, as opposed to assuming that they exist in a timeless vacuum. Following this approach, he examined the literary character of these texts, such as genre, arguing that how something is said is as important as what is said. In his third phase, focused on religious study, Neusner demonstrated the religious nature of rabbinic texts and how they were received by subsequent generations of religious followers. The final phase, the theological, saw Neusner discern the inner structures of the ideas that have been received as religious, and outline their coherence as they formed the details of religious belief and expression.[4] These four phases loosely structure the intellectual biography that follows. They provide the points around which I have constructed Neusner's life and shown the intellectual contributions he made to the academic study of both Judaism and religion.

Yet personal narratives, when framed properly, open up onto much larger social and intellectual landscapes. Neusner's biography is not simply reducible to that of an academic life mired in technical discussions that have little or no relevance. Neusner's story is the story of what happened as Jews migrated to the suburbs, creating new lives for themselves as they successfully integrated into American society. It is the story of how American Jews tried to make sense of the world in the aftermath of the extermination of European Jewry. It is the story of the transmission of Judaism to a postwar generation, and of trying to define what it meant to be an American Jew in light of the tragedy of the Holocaust and the subsequent creation of the State of Israel in 1948. And, finally, it is the story of trying to find new ways and institutional frameworks to study Judaism. These much larger stories form the context of Neusner's life and career. The story of Jewish studies in America, framed slightly differently, mirrors the story of American Jews. Both of these can be told through the prism of Jacob Neusner's life and career.

Neusner made the academic study of Judaism possible in this country through his refusal to ghettoize Judaism. His was not solely an academic enterprise, however. He also imagined a new Judaism, one beyond the ethnic pride of the nonreligious and the parochialism of an observant tradition that masqueraded as authentic. It is here that Neusner the American Jewish thinker meets Neusner the academician. Judaism, as both a religion and an object of study, offered much to illumine eternal human questions. The problem was, however, that too often these questions were not entertained in either the secular university or the yeshiva. Neusner forced Judaism to enter much larger conversations. This is his lasting legacy.

To define Neusner solely as a scholar of early Judaism and rabbinic texts, however, would be too limiting. In addition to his work on rabbinic Judaism, Neusner published on a host of other academic topics, from the Ancient Near East to Zionism. He was also much more than a scholar. He was a journalist, a post-Holocaust theologian, and a commentator who was never afraid to take an unpopular position on any given issue. Before Neusner could read a line of Talmud, he was writing regularly for the *Jewish Ledger*, a weekly newspaper that his father had founded in West Hartford in 1929. By his early teens, he was reviewing for the *Ledger* every book published on Jewish topics in the English language, in addition to writing opinion pieces on the state of American Jewry that were syndicated throughout the country and beyond. Neusner's analyses, more often than not, put him at odds with Jewish leaders, many of whom he accused of being out of touch with reality.

At the height of his career, Neusner was never far from the headlines. He wrote about current affairs as much as about rabbinics. What should Jewish education look like? Who should be charged to carry it out? Where did Jewish studies—or, as he preferred to call it, Judaic studies— fit in the university curriculum? All of these questions he raised and attempted to answer, not only in academic books for his colleagues, but also in newspapers, magazines, and other popular venues. The paradox, however, is that although Neusner saw himself as transmitting Judaism to a postwar American Jewish audience, he was very far removed politically from that audience.

Despite this paradox, one of many in Neusner's narrative, the story that follows is, among other things, an attempt to make the case for Neusner's inclusion in the pantheon of great American Jewish thinkers.

1

Afloat in a Sea of Words

The religious study of sacred texts has a long and ancient history in Judaism.[1] The secular study of such texts, however, is a much more recent affair that dates to nineteenth-century Germany.[2] There, young Jews, many alienated from the faith of their ancestors, began to apply the critical historical methods that they had learned at university to texts previously encountered only in the synagogue. This application provided an important impetus for the rise of the various denominations of Judaism that were only then beginning to take shape. Those associated with the more liberal denominations, such as Reform, used scholarship to show how changes could be made within Judaism, which included jettisoning aspects of the *halakhah* believed to conflict with modernity. Many critical of this enterprise sought to keep what they perceived to be Judaism's essence far removed from history.[3]

For those who began to apply historical methods to Judaism, the results were revolutionary. Judaism now entered history, and vice versa. Things would never again be the same. Leopold Zunz (1794–1886), one of the leading architects of this transformation, summarizes as follows: "when all science and all of man's doings have been illumined in brilliant rays, when the remote corners of the earth have been reached, the most obscure languages studied and nothing seems too insignificant to assist in the construction of wisdom, how is it possible that our science [namely, the study of postbiblical Jewish texts] alone lies neglected?"[4] This project of illumining the texts of Judaism using history and philology was an apologetic enterprise, to be sure. In many ways it had to be. It was the attempt to remap Judaism as the foundation of Western civilization as opposed to the embarrassing law-based tradition of a pariah people.[5]

Whereas the traditional approach to Jewish texts took place in a vacuum and was largely mistrustful of secular learning, the young German scholars stressed context, sometimes even at the expense of the texts themselves. Scholarship was used in the service of inclusion.[6] If Jews could be shown to have a history, people like Zunz reasoned, then surely they were worthy of political and legal emancipation. Even better: if Judaism could be shown to be the "midwife" of later monotheisms, both Christianity and Islam, then their own religion resided at the epicenter of the civilized world. This new type of scholarship had two objectives. One was to show non-Jews that Judaism was a religion in light of critics like Immanuel Kant who had argued that it was not; and the second was to show Jews that their tradition was, when properly understood, a spiritually and aesthetically edifying religion, just as they imagined Protestant Christianity, their lodestar, to be.[7] Their project proved untenable. The German academy, not surprisingly, was uninterested. When Zunz petitioned the state for a chair in Jewish history and literature at the University of Berlin, the disingenuous reply came back that neither the university nor the state was in the business of training clerics.[8] To be a professor in a German university at this time meant that one had to be a Christian. The only options for a Jew were either to convert to Christianity, and many did, or to teach in the parochial seminaries associated with the new denominations. The latter option, for all intents and purposes, created a shadow or pariah academy.

It was an initial attempt to normalize the academic study of Judaism, to be sure. But it was one that would have to wait for another time and another place to be realized.

* * *

Fast-forward to West Hartford, Connecticut, and July 28, 1932, the birthplace and date of Jacob Neusner. America was not Germany. The case no longer needed to be made that Jews could be productive and loyal citizens. The unpleasant odor of anti-Semitism still filled the air, but its acridity was slowly diminishing as America would soon emerge from the Great Depression and rise to prominence.[9] However, if one wanted to study Judaism's traditional texts in 1932, the primary place to do this was within the context of the yeshiva world. There were, as we have seen, several other options: seminaries associated with the various Jewish denominations in the United States, such as the Reform Hebrew Union College–Jewish Institute of Religion in Cincinnati, the Conservative Jewish Theological Seminary of America in New York, and the Orthodox Rabbi Isaac Elchanan Theological Seminary associated with Yeshiva University, also located in New York; or private nondenominational institutions, such as Dropsie College in Philadelphia and the Baltimore Hebrew College and Teachers Training School. The one place where it was virtually impossible to study Jewish postbiblical texts was in the secular context of the university. It was most certainly impossible to do so in departments of religious studies, today the primary place to study Jews and Judaism in a secular setting. To study rabbinic texts, even academically, it was assumed that one would have to receive years of technical training at a yeshiva. One certainly would be neither a woman nor a non-Jew.

Neusner was to change all of this. His story is uniquely the product of America. Only a suburban Jew and a second-generation American with no formal Jewish education outside of Reform Sunday school could have taken Jewish texts out of the yeshiva and into the mainstream academy where they could be studied and appreciated by Jew and non-Jew alike. Neusner's background enabled him to ignore the status quo and its regnant approach to Jewish texts. Compared to someone like his future undergraduate advisor at Harvard, the great Harry Wolfson (1887–1974), the quintessential outsider, Neusner never had to acclimatize to American culture. He was a consummate insider, one who knew how to work the system to his own advantage. As his wife, Suzanne, once remarked, "he feels lucky to have been born in his particular time and circumstances."[10]

* * *

Although Neusner was born on the cusp of the Great Depression, his formative years would be on the other side of the Second World War. He spent his early years during a time that witnessed the rapid expansion of the middle class, which demanded, and received, unprecedented access to higher education, all of which was precipitated by the G.I. Bill. Politics tended to be moderate; unions were strong; and Americans, who were increasingly enjoying the fruits of prosperity, moved out to the suburbs in the search of bigger houses and yards, a symbol of the better lives that they hoped to enjoy. Jews, of course, were no different. Experiencing unheralded freedom, they sought access to all that had been denied to them in Europe. The search for the illusive American Dream motivated many to make the great migration from cityscape to suburban landscape.[11]

At the time of Neusner's birth, West Hartford was a small, incorporated town, slowly becoming one of several growing suburbs for the much larger city of Hartford, one of the oldest cities in the United States. West Hartford, roughly 100 miles (160 km) southwest of Boston and 120 miles (190 km) northeast of New York City, had a population of around 25,000 inhabitants in the 1930s. The town, on the verge of being the epicenter of Greater Hartford's Jewish community, was soon to have the largest per capita Jewish population of any other in the state, including places such as Stamford and New Haven. Although prior to the 1930s the majority of Hartford's Jews had lived in the city's North End, the 1930s witnessed a shift in demographics, not unlike Jewish populations in other large urban environments, from city to suburb. It was a major time in the development of American Jewry as many began to enter middle-class professions and increasingly to identify as "Jewish Americans," that is, as equally Jewish and American. West Hartford became a convenient place for those Jews who desired to leave the "tight Jewish atmosphere of the city" in search of cheaper and what was considered to be more middle-class housing.[12] This "westward migration" to the suburbs also witnessed the movement of Jewish businesses out of Hartford and into their new places of residence. This small town became increasingly larger and larger, and Jewish Americans increasingly interacted with other Americans in schools, in the marketplace, and in other places.

The specter of nuclear annihilation loomed on the horizon for a generation of men and women who had been too young to fight in the Second World War and who were increasingly aware of the military threat from the so-called Iron Curtain. Although Neusner would, in 1960, write his doctoral dissertation on Yohanan ben Zakkai, the first-century rabbinic sage, it is perhaps no coincidence that he gave it the subtitle "The Day after Doomsday: Jewish Palestine after the Destruction of the Temple in 70."[13] Writing in the preface to the second edition of the published version of the dissertation, *A Life of Yohanan ben Zakkai, Ca. 1–80 CE*, Neusner made this explicit:

> Perhaps a personal word may not be out of order. Many years ago, when I began my studies of Yohanan ben Zakkai, I was drawn to him out of the deepening gloom of the Cold War. Day by day one looked to the skies, fearful of sighting that single plane bearing a single bomb to end the life of the city. What struck me then was the challenge of "the next day," the 10th of Av in Yavneh, or who knew what date the stars then would designate. He who passed through that awful time would bear witness that life could go on, in new forms to be sure, and that men confidently might look beyond disaster.[14]

Against the backdrop of the Cold War, Neusner would spend his formative years. The Holocaust and the destruction of European Jewry seemed like a distant event since it had not touched the Neusner family personally, whereas the threat of nuclear annihilation seemed much more tangible. Although anti-Semitism certainly existed, the Neusner family chose not to see it.[15] Despite its omnipresence, the Neusners, like many Jews in the 1940s, enjoyed the unprecedented possibilities associated with access to American institutions that had been denied to previous generations of Jews—these formed the cornerstones upon which Neusner would build his career.

At the time of his entry into Harvard as an undergraduate, there was, for all intents and purposes, no such thing as Jewish studies within the American academy. Certainly the sacred texts of Judaism had been studied and were still studied in the context of the yeshiva world. Therein, texts such as the Bible, the Mishnah, and the Talmud were read according to the rhythms of Jewish life with very little, if any, concern for integration into the higher criticism associated with the university. Although the Mishnah and the Talmud would increasingly find their way into the curricula of American institutions of learning, they still tended to be examined using traditional methods. This approach would prove anathema to the young Neusner, who sought to integrate Jewish texts with the themes and issues that were of concern to others working in the humanities in general and the academic study of religion in particular. If Jacob Neusner could be both proudly Jewish and proudly American, why, he wondered, could there not be a Jewish American way of examining these texts?

Prior to the 1970s the major place in the United States where Judaica was taught from a nondenominational perspective was in departments of Semitics. The texts studied, however, were in the Old Testament, rarely if ever the Mishnah or the Talmud. Those who taught courses in such departments were often Jews funded by local Jewish communities. They were more like scholar-rabbis than scholars. They enjoyed the largesse of American Jews, many of whom perceived university recognition as the pathway to attain social and cultural inclusion. University campuses and the academic study of Jewish topics, they hoped, would become one of the primary institutional spaces for Jewish normalization. The teaching of Jewish subjects within American universities would help to establish, in the words of sociologists Paul Ritterband and Harold Wechsler, "university-based Jewish learning that could serve both a parent discipline and the Jewish community."[16] This was a delicate balance to be sure. How can academic study be critical while simultaneously serving the local Jewish community?[17]

An example is illustrative.[18] Felix Adler (1851–1933) was the son of one of the leading figures of Reform Judaism in America, Samuel Adler, rabbi of Temple Emanu-El in New York City. In 1874, after it had become clear that the young Felix would not follow in his father's footsteps and enter the rabbinate, members of his father's congregation funded a professorship in Hebrew and Oriental literature at Cornell University, and nominated the younger Adler for the position. Writing of the appointment in the same year, the *Jewish Messenger*, a weekly periodical that was published out of New York City, proclaimed,

> It is significant of the progress of culture in this country, when a thriving educational institution—such as Cornell University—adds to its faculty a young and talented Israelite to fill the professorship of Hebrew and Oriental Literature. . . . We hail the appointment of a Hebrew professor as a grand concession to the liberality of the age, and congratulate the faculty of Cornell University in having thus demonstrated their freedom from prejudice. . . . [Adler's supporters who financed the position] have the satisfaction of having not only placed their friend-protégé in an honorable position, but elevate the Jewish name and Jewish interests in the opinion of the world, again demonstrating that the Jew has higher ideas that mere moneymaking.[19]

In this passage we see how Adler's religious and ethnic identity means as much to the editors of the *Jewish Messenger* as his scholarly potential or capabilities. Although Adler's position would eventually not be renewed, and his vision of Judaism alienated many of his initial supporters, this quotation reveals just how important it was that these positions in Jewish subjects be held by individuals who embodied what was generally perceived to be a positive Jewish identity.

Although Neusner, from a very young age, knew that he wanted to spend his life dealing with Jewish texts, he thought at the time that this meant life as a rabbi. It was not until graduate school, however, that he began to realize what rabbinic texts were, since he had never encountered them until he arrived at the Jewish Theological Seminary. In his desire to integrate Jewish texts with non-Jewish contexts, he had to blaze a trail that many of us today take for granted. Indeed, before he encountered rabbinics, he was well on his way to becoming a rabbi and a public commenter on contemporary American Jewry through his work with his father's paper. In this respect he was a journalist quite literally before he was a scholar. This journalistic impulse never left him, however, as he would frequently turn the theses of books into op-eds or articles for both Jewish and non-Jewish papers.

The towering figures of Jewish studies in the mid-twentieth century—for example, Gershom Scholem at the Hebrew University of Jerusalem, Harry Austryn Wolfson at Harvard, Salo Wittmayer Baron at Columbia, and Alexander Altmann at Brandeis—were products of the Old World. None of them were particularly interested in the academic study of religion or the place of Judaism within this fledgling field. They instead represented a different ideological world, epitomized perhaps by the adjective "European," in which Jews were discriminated against, and that meant that Jewish topics were insular and, for the most part, "ghettoized" in the non-Jewish academic world. The natural reaction was to engage in apologetics or to show, as Wolfson and Altmann did, the filiations between Hebraic and other Western-inflected rationalisms.

Harry Wolfson, who would eventually be Neusner's undergraduate advisor at Harvard, wrote in 1921, prior to his appointment to the Harvard faculty, about the importance of rabbinic texts. He also noted, however, that they tended to be studied in ways that removed Jews from others. Writing in the *Menorah Journal*, he remarked,

> For I believe, just as our pious ancestors believed, though for different reasons, that the Talmud with its literature is the most promising field of study, the most fertile field of original research and investigation. But I believe that medieval Jewish philosophy is the only branch of Jewish literature, next to the Bible, which binds us to the rest of the literary world. In it we meet on common ground with civilized Europe and with part of civilized Asia and civilized Africa. Medieval philosophy is one philosophy written in three languages, Arabic, Hebrew, and Latin, and among these

Hebrew holds the central and most important position. In it we have the full efflorescence of Arabic thought and the bud of much scholasticism.[20]

This privileging of Hebrew and, by extension, Judaism is not unlike what we saw among a generation of earlier German Jewish scholars. What is important, though, is less this rather obvious genealogy than in noting that while Wolfson acknowledged the importance of the Talmud and other rabbinic texts, he seemed to think—perhaps because of his own yeshiva background—that they had very little to contribute to larger questions. For Wolfson, it was the Bible and medieval philosophy that showed Judaism at it most universal. Neusner would spend his career showing how Wolfson's remarks were incorrect and that the dense arguments found within rabbinic texts had much to contribute to universal human questions.

When the young Neusner eventually went off to college as a young undergraduate there were no exemplars or prototypes of what it meant to be an American scholar of Judaism or someone who wanted to work with Jewish data within the discipline of religious studies.

* * *

There exist two narratives concerning the origins of the Neusner family in this country. The first is what the family always told itself, namely that Samuel Neusner, Jacob's father, was born in 1896 in Korets, Poland. He came to the United States in 1906 at the age of ten, and settled in Beverley, Massachusetts. Samuel's father, also Jacob Neusner, and after whom Jacob was named,[21] was one of the founders of the synagogue there.[22] The second narrative is that a nineteen-year-old Jacob Neusner, trained as a blacksmith, boarded the S.S. *Palatia* in Hamburg, Germany, and landed in New York Harbor on October 13, 1898. On the passenger list the young Neusner is listed as single, which would have meant that he started his family in the United States, not Poland.[23]

At any rate, Samuel—or, as he liked to be called, Sam—would go on to serve in the U.S. Air Corps in World War I. After the war he lived in

Texas for a few years working in the newspaper industry, before return-ing home to Beverley and then moving to Springfield. From 1924 to 1929 he was the Western Massachusetts representative of the *Boston Jewish Advocate*, in whose pages he wrote about community affairs, trying to visualize for Bostonian Jews something of the "spiritual and cultural de-velopment" of Jewish communities outside of the Boston area.[24] By 1928, Sam Neusner had so established himself in the Springfield area that he asked the *Advocate* for more space and a better layout so that he could de-vote more attention to reporting about Springfield's Jewish community. When they refused, he offered to buy the *Advocate*'s assets for Western Massachusetts, as well as for its *Connecticut Hebrew Record*. In April 1929 he began to publish a monthly, the *Springfield Jewish Ledger*, to cover the events in Western Massachusetts and Hartford, Connecticut.[25] Reflecting on the origins of this newspaper, Jacob, his son, would later write,

> It was the height of the boom, and the lowest point of Jewish religious spirit in this century. Pessimism was the dominant note in the writings of Jewish intellectuals. Jews were apathetic toward their faith. Zionism and Israel had not yet captured their imagination, nor had the terror of Hitlerism—foreign and native-bred—aroused as yet any sense of Jewish loyalty. Sam Neusner, describing this twilight in Jewish life, says, "Strange as it seems to me today, Jewish life at this time was more tranquil than at any time in my memory."[26]

For Sam Neusner, the interwar years witnessed a calm and a consolida-tion. The First World War had seen a set of restrictive quotas to stem Jewish migration to the United States. The majority of Jews in this coun-try were soon, like the young Jacob, native-born. If an earlier generation had been interested in the absorption of Jewish immigrants, this new generation focused more on entering the middle class and creating new institutions—synagogues, Jewish centers, Hebrew day schools—to reflect their new status.

Sam Neusner would speak indefatigably about the newspaper at, among other places, local chapters of B'nai B'rith, whose members he would sign up at meetings for a one-dollar subscription. The first advertisers were some of the leading non-Jewish firms of Springfield and surrounding towns. The elder Neusner would speak fondly of these firms, saying, "Up to this day our most generous and liberal advertisers are non-Jews because in most cases the leading firms in each community are owned by these people. These firms have always recognized the need for a Jewish newspaper printed in English. Our paper has tried to show its gratitude by filling the void—from the Jewish side—that exists in Christian-Jewish understanding. So we have followed the principle of publishing a newspaper that would place the Jewish citizen in a dignified, respectable position, and that would project the position of the Jewish community before the general community."[27] As was typical of Jews of this age, the creation of a positive image in the eyes of non-Jews was of paramount importance. At a time when the potential for anti-Semitism seemed omnipresent, Sam Neusner, the young newspaper editor, did all that he could to show the normalcy of Jews and their ability to fit into American life.

As the monthly newspaper transformed into a weekly, Sam Neusner changed its name to the *Connecticut Jewish Ledger*, a Jewish newspaper that to this day continues to serve the Connecticut region in addition to Western Massachusetts.[28] As the Second World War broke out, the elder Neusner used the *Ledger* as a Zionist publication. He would travel the state, organizing mass meetings and telling his readers that political action was needed to allow the immigration of German Jews to Palestine. He even visited Washington as an unofficial representative of Connecticut Jewry. When Senator Brian McMahon, who later referred to the elder Neusner as "Mr. Zionist," was running for the Senate in 1944, Sam Neusner secured from him a promise to help the Jews in Palestine. When McMahon became a member of the Senate Foreign Relations Committee, he kept his promise by keeping the issue of Palestine before the Senate, the president, and the State Department. Even a heart attack in October 1945, the result of overwork, did not stop Neusner from ensuring that the paper was published in a timely fashion.

Sam Neusner also saw his paper as a vehicle for Jewish education. It not only provided a forum to keep Jewish readers informed about local, national, and international issues, but also created a positive space wherein Jewish ideas and books could be discussed. In an era of increased assimilation, these Jewish newspapers helped to keep Jewish readers Jewish. Sam was also a founder of the American Jewish Press Association, and in 1956 received its Award of Merit. He published the *Connecticut Jewish Ledger* until he passed away from the complications of Parkinson's disease in 1960. His obituary in the *Hartford Times* of December 16 reads, in part, as follows:

> Mr. Neusner was a dynamic and unifying force in the state-wide community. His newspaper is a strong and respected voice for the Jewish population. . . . He was dedicated to the cause of Zionism, and his work for various philanthropic organizations was widely recognized. One of his proudest moments was his visit to the White House as a representative of the Jewish press when President Truman posed for a photograph with him. The sense of loss caused by his death is tempered for his friends by a realization of the services he performed.[29]

Neusner's mother, Lee B. Neusner (née Green), was born on June 12, 1901, in New York City, but her grandmother came from Odessa. Writing to his friend Klaus in November 1997, just after Lee's death, Neusner said that his maternal grandmother had died around the age of twenty from a botched abortion, leaving her three children homeless. The children were left in a Catholic orphanage until Lee's own grandmother located the children and took them to Holyoke, Massachusetts. When Lee's father remarried, he brought the children to Springfield, Massachusetts, where Neusner's mother was raised. Neusner said of her that she "got herself more of an education than was usual for Jewish girls at that time."[30] Lee Green married Samuel Neusner in 1924, at the age of twenty-three. Her eldest son, Fred, later referred to her as "an unhappy bride" due to Samuel's overwork and organizational activities, in addition to the hypercritical presence of her mother-in-law.[31]

Lee took over the publishing business after her husband's death, and remained in charge until she sold the paper in 1966. Jacob rarely talked about his parents. He was not particularly close to his mother. At the death of his elder sister, Sandra, in 1986, Jacob was upset that neither his mother nor his sister's family had informed him of her death (he was told by an aunt) nor invited him to the funeral.[32] His memories of his mother were primarily negative. Neusner wrote that "as she grew older, she developed anti-Semitic views of Judaism."[33] Jacob's brother, Fred, commented that "[a]s far as Mother and her 'hobby' of hating everyone is concerned, I attribute it to her upbringing. It was like a form of mental illness that she seemed to share with her sister."[34] Lee would tell others that the family kept kosher, by which she meant that she bought kosher meat, yet she did little else to follow the complex rules that went into the establishment of a kosher kitchen. Neusner claimed that Lee's desire to say she had a kosher kitchen was only out of deference for her husband's mother. On special occasions, Neusner later wrote, she would take him to G. Fox and Company in downtown Hartford for a bacon-lettuce-tomato sandwich and a strawberry milkshake. He was also furious when, as an adult with children of his own, and as someone who would eventually keep his own kosher kitchen, his mother would visit and take his children, against his wishes, out to places such as McDonald's.[35]

In a letter written to Marvin Fox after her death, Jacob lamented, "I tried to think of one pleasant memory about her over the past forty years, from the time I left West Hartford in 1950, and I was unable to think of a single one—something nice she did or said, some satisfaction she gave. I'm sure there was something to be remembered, but I could not think of what it might be; and of the period from 1964, when [Suzanne and I] were married, there was nothing. It suffices to say, I tried to think of something lost, something to be mourned for, but failed. So much for the mourning period."[36] His brother, Fred, wrote to him years later, saying, "We come from a line of people who never got off the boat when it arrived, but carried it on their backs all their lives and passed it onto the children. Now let's forget all about them for a while as we go on with our lives."[37]

Samuel Neusner was, according to Jacob, a "self-taught Jew."[38] Jacob's parents spoke only English, and they attended the century-old Reform synagogue in West Hartford, Temple Beth Israel. What the young Jacob wanted most of all was that which no one could provide him: knowledge of Hebrew and a Jewish education. Although he knew from a young age that he wanted to be a rabbi, in these early years he had no formal education in Judaism and only a rudimentary knowledge of the Hebrew alphabet. It is also worth noting that "being a rabbi" did not necessarily mean that this is what he really wanted to become. Rather, it seems to have functioned as a trope for a life immersed in Jewish learning. Today someone might easily say "I want to be a Jewish philosopher" or "I want to be a Jewish historian." This, however, would have been unheard-of for a ten-year-old in 1940s America. It is worth noting also that, despite the fact that he grew up as a suburban and largely assimilated Jew, Neusner never contemplated a more secular profession, such as law or medicine.

He held up as his role model the rabbi of his synagogue, and the young Neusner knew of no other pattern for Jewish life than Reform. When for his sixteenth birthday his parents asked him what he most wanted, he responded: Hebrew lessons. So for the next two years he learned the ancient language from a young woman who had recently graduated from Boston Hebrew College. This encounter was tantamount to his first with Jewish education.[39]

Jacob was the youngest of three children. His two older siblings were Frederick D. Neusner (1924–2014), who would go on to distinguish himself as an assistant attorney general of the state of Connecticut before becoming an administrative law judge of the U.S. Department of Labor in Washington, D.C., and Sandra D. Neusner Friedman (1929–1986), an assistant dean at the University of Hartford. Jacob seems to have been closest to Fred, especially in later years when they corresponded with one another frequently to make sense of what they both considered to be their dysfunctional family and their cold upbringing. The elder sibling accused the youngest of being the favorite of his parents. "All in all," Fred would later write to his younger brother, "my life in the house of our parents gave me capacity for empathy with Esau, when I encountered him in the parashas about Jacob, Rebecca, and Isaac."[40]

Many remember Jacob, even at a young age, as a stubborn child who never wanted to do what other kids were doing. Writing in 1981, when Richard Lyman, then chair of the National Endowment for the Humanities, encouraged the younger Neusner to resign due to "irregular attendance," Fred remarked, ". . . you are a feisty, trouble-making rascal, and you have always been one since the time you were able to walk."[41] This attitude is confirmed by his third-grade report card in 1940–1941, in which his teacher remarked, "He prefers not to do as the others are doing which causes many difficulties."[42] Little did she know that such comments would prove to be a leitmotif that functioned as a constant throughout Neusner's long career. Corresponding with Jacob in 2007, Fred sought to give him encouragement. "Your enemies," he wrote,

> were right to envy you and hate you for what you had done. They had reason to feel diminished because they were diminished. What was wrong was that they were small men and could not defer to you for what you had accomplished. It is hard to give recognition to someone whose work outshines everything you have done and one which you based your career. On the other hand, acting out their anal retentive feelings by mistreating you was not sufficient to hold back history. Your time had to come because you were right and stubborn enough to continue onward. And you kept on your path long enough to urinate on the reputation of those who had envied and hated you.[43]

Neusner and his siblings attended public school rather than Jewish day school. "Along with everyone else," he writes in a rare autobiographical moment, "young Jewish Americans were taught Connecticut history in the setting of Puritan Christianity, and drew pictures of Congregational Churches, celebrated our forefathers' Thanksgiving with the Indians, observed Christmas in school, recited the Lord's Prayer, and, in general, thought of ourselves as perfectly normal Americans, for everybody did these things."[44]

In these early years, Neusner described himself as "a typical suburban yokel, able to see the horizons that stretched only to Bloomfield and Wethersfield and as far as my father's newspaper's printing plant in Southington."[45] Neusner worked frequently at his father's paper, where he became mesmerized from a young age with words and the writing process. At the paper, for example, he learned how to work, how to write and type quickly, and, of course, how to meet deadlines. He received his first typewriter at age twelve, and his later students and colleagues would remark that they had never seen anyone type as quickly and as accurately as he could. He ran errands for the paper every afternoon after school, five days a week. Stringers, or freelance journalists, from the *Hartford Times* taught him how to write news stories, develop headlines, and engage in news editing layout and makeup. By his junior year in high school, the young Neusner could do all the jobs associated with a newspaper except sell advertising. By the age of thirteen he was writing book reviews in the paper, and soon thereafter he became the main editorial writer when the editor was away. He could, in sum, run a newspaper on his own.

Naturally, his work at the paper shaped him. Not only did it teach him technical skills about deadlines and writing, it also gave him a ready forum to express his views about Judaism, America, and American Jews. By the 1950s, the young Neusner would serve as acting editor when its permanent editor, Rabbi Abraham Feldman, was out of the office. In 1951, he started a regular column, "Speaking of Jewish Books," later renamed "On the Book Shelf." He wrote of his rationale in an early column:

A reviewer of Jewish books has a unique responsibility. He must not only give his considered opinion of a book, but he must also keep in mind the needs of Jewish book publishers and must, consequently, treat many mediocre books with a gentle tolerance. The reading public for Jewish books is small; the publisher is often publishing books at a loss, for the service which he renders to the cause of Jewish culture. The reviewer, then, cannot afford to drive away possible readers; while he must warn them of mediocrity, he cannot afford to be snide, pithy, and sophisticated in cases where he is tempted to slam a book.[46]

One of the earliest reviews that Neusner wrote was of Abraham Joshua Heschel's *Man Is Not Alone* on November 8, 1951.

In our daily life we are constantly beset by problems with which, as sensitive people, we must grapple. . . . Dr. Heschel, as a philosopher, is developing possible solutions to these problems of which this book is the first glimmering. We see in these beginnings a rational approach, leaning on what has been said and brought before. We see in this book, however, something vastly more original than any of the "philosophies of religion" produced by those who would express their Judaism in something more than ritual. This is not interpretation of writings and dogma. Dr. Heschel starts with life and his answers end in life.[47]

Neusner subsequently sent the review to Heschel, one of the great American Jewish figures of the twentieth century and a professor at the Jewish Theological Seminary, where Neusner would eventually study. He received a very gracious reply from Heschel: "I read your review with a great deal of pleasure. You have indeed emphasized an important aspect of the book."[48] It was around this time that the young Neusner decided to buy a scrapbook to save this and other copies of his articles. Thus began his tradition of saving everything that he wrote, something that would continue throughout his life.[49] Indeed, he might have been inspired to do so at this particular time because of an article he wrote to commemorate the sixth anniversary of the founding in 1947 of the American Jewish Archives at the Hebrew Union College–Jewish Institute of Religion in Cincinnati. The Archives were created with the aim of collecting materials to document the history of American Jewry. "The Archives," he wrote, "seeks old records, minute books, etc., for its expanding collection. Photographs of great Jews of our generation and earlier ones are of value. . . . Families seeking to preserve memoirs in the Archives building are assured of their privacy."[50] Neusner went on in the article to note that American Jewry was the leading, and largest, Jewry in the world and that the American Jewish Archives not just was a story about the past, but also would serve as a guide for the future.

Neusner's childhood, in sum, was cold, revolved around his father's paper, and was filled with an awareness of his lack of Jewish knowledge.

Harvard: The Undergraduate Years

Writing in 1997, Neusner described himself: "I was a smartass kid from West Hartford who always got As without trying because things came naturally and without much effort—[I] never understood that other people would be angry and jealous on that account."[51] After graduating from William H. Hall High School in the spring of 1950, the young Neusner had a choice between attending his local college, Trinity, or Harvard. He chose between these two because he had never heard of any other place. In his own words: "What about Yale or Brown or Columbia or Chicago or Stanford? As a Connecticut boy, I knew only 'Yankees' (descendants of early settlers) went to Yale, and they were all anti-Semitic so I didn't want to go there. The only other college that I'd ever heard of which seemed a cut better than whatever we had in town was Harvard."[52] The other distinct advantage of Harvard, as he later told me, was that it offered Hebrew.

That June, the eighteen-year-old Neusner made his way from West Hartford to Cambridge, Massachusetts, to begin a new chapter of his life. If the threat of nuclear annihilation formed the backdrop of the young Neusner's life, the idyllic charms of Harvard Yard now reminded him that he was far from home, both literally and metaphorically. In addition to the fact that he did not particularly get along with his parents, Neusner was also afraid to return to West Hartford in case, Brigadoon-like, his new world would disappear. As a result, Neusner remained at Harvard throughout most of his undergraduate years, even attending summer school in 1951 and 1952, in order to graduate in three years. His undergraduate advisor, as we have already seen, was Harry A. Wolfson—an individual who never fit or, perhaps better, was never allowed to fit within the waspy corridors of Harvard.[53] Neusner remembered him as full of grace, and having a good sense of humor. It was unusual at that time for senior and well-known Harvard faculty to advise freshmen. Perhaps because there were so few Jewish students there, Wolfson seems to have known that the young Neusner was coming to Harvard and had asked to advise him. Wolfson was one of the first holders of an endowed Jewish studies chair (the Nathan Littauer Professorship), and was an expert in Jewish philosophy, one of the few fields in Jewish studies to which Neusner himself never contributed.[54] The young Neusner, however, never took a course with Wolfson since he was not particularly interested in philosophy; and Wolfson, to whom Neusner would grow close only years later when he had a postdoctoral appointment at Brandeis, was resigned to the fact that Neusner was interested in American Jewish history and in becoming a Reform Rabbi. Neusner once told me that the senior Wolfson even discouraged him from going on in Jewish studies since he did not have a yeshiva background or possess proper training in traditional Jewish texts.[55]

Neusner, perhaps not surprising given his early life in the newspaper business, became the editor of the Harvard freshman newspaper. In the cold world of 1950s Harvard, Neusner—although feeling no ill will directly from anyone—nevertheless felt marginalized, and out of the mainstream of college life. Non-Jewish students were rarely interested in friendships with Jews, so Neusner spent the majority of his time in the library, studying. He majored in American history because, as he puts it, "he knew the language." Jewishly, Neusner still seems to have been cognizant of the fact that there was much more to learn, both academically and religiously. He occasionally attended Friday evening services at a local Reform temple, in which he also occasionally taught Sunday school.

Although Neusner was attracted to the ivy-covered buildings of Harvard, the intellectual environment on campus nevertheless proved to be cold for him. He felt that many students were there not to learn, but to begin their careers as socialites, to make the necessary business connections, or to earn the grades to enter Harvard Law School or Medical School. Among his fellow classmates—the class of 1954—a few stood out, such as the novelist John Updike, with whom he maintained a lifelong friendship.[56] He subsequently lobbied for a National Arts Medal for Updike after Lynne Cheney, the chairman of the National Endowment for the Arts (NEA), appointed him to serve on the Selection Committee in 1988.[57] In an interview with Barbara DeConcini, he recounted how the young Updike would bring him poems to publish in the freshman newspaper that he edited, and that he was always envious of Updike's use of language.[58] He also befriended the late social theorist Christopher Lasch, and the late historian of ancient science David Pingree. Neusner, reflecting upon his own life as an educator years later, did not have much good to say about the Harvard professors of that time. In all his time there, he could not recall a classmate ever telling him about talking with a professor outside of class. Neusner was also critical of the fact that it was teaching assistants, only a few years older than the students, who taught the majority of his classes. Neusner complained that they were often ill equipped to teach, instead offering summations of the textbooks from which they taught and which they had probably read only the night before. Eventually Neusner would dismiss this type of undergraduate education as he constantly sought to develop new and better ways to impart analytic thinking and problem solving to undergraduates. Indeed, so aloof was the faculty at Harvard that the young Neusner did not even know that professors maintained regular office hours. The only time he ever walked into the office of a professor was to see Wolfson when he first arrived on campus and, once, to talk to his senior honors thesis advisor. "I cannot claim to have excelled at learning, only at getting As," he once remarked. He was proud of the fact that he received these grades from the beginning of his education until he completed his PhD.[59] His senior thesis was on the Jews of Boston from 1880 to 1914.

The one class that did stand out for the young Neusner was taught by the late Thomas S. Kuhn and Leonard Nash on the history of laboratory science. Forming the foundation of Kuhn's pathbreaking *The Structure of Scientific Revolutions* (1962), this course dealt with the very notion of knowledge and how it is produced. This course conveyed to Neusner what was at stake in knowledge and knowledge production, and what we do when we learn. In an interview with William Novak, years later, Neusner invoked Kuhn's book to explain the difference between his own scholarship and that produced in Israel. "You've read *The Structure of Scientific Revolution*?," he asked Novak and then explained that "Kuhn talks about changes in paradigms. When the evidence is different, the questions shift completely. One of the things that makes a difference is *who does the work*. In Israel they do a lot of articles about *pintelach*, little points about this and that. . . . There's no critical program, no method and no system."[60]

If the other professors at Harvard seemed aloof and indifferent, Kuhn and Nash not only had an intellectual problem that they tried to solve systematically, but also were interested in the intellectual lives of their students. Indeed, decades later when Neusner, now the world-renowned scholar of rabbinics, met the elder Kuhn, the latter remarked that he could still remember the young Neusner standing by the lectern after class and arguing about a scientific idea that had been presented or discussed in class that day, even though the older Neusner had no such memory.[61]

In the fall of 1950, during his freshman year, Neusner became increasingly aware of the discrepancy between Judaism and the secular academy. Although previously he thought that the only way to proceed with Jewish learning was through the rabbinate, his time at Harvard, time spent in the mainstream of American intellectual life, led him to seek to meld these two distinct and, to many at the time, mutually exclusive spheres. Recall that even Wolfson tried to dissuade Neusner from such a life due to the paucity of his Jewish education. The assumption was that one had to have been an ex-yeshiva student, like Wolfson, to be even a secular scholar of Jewish texts. Yet, Neusner's love of learning and his intellectual interest in all things having to do with Judaism further contributed to his desire to nudge Judaism into an intellectually respectable field. Indeed, it is precisely this desire that would drive Neusner's work for the rest of his life. If the university provided a new set of methods to open up Jewish texts, the latter also provided a new way of thinking to address age-old problems.

Neusner the undergraduate continued his publishing. In 1953, for example, he published in the B'nai B'rith Hillel Foundation newspaper at Harvard a brief article titled "The Dreyfus Affair and *der Judenstaat*."[62] It was, not surprisingly, the work of an undergraduate still on the path toward finding his intellectual voice. It is important to note, however, that even as an undergraduate Neusner was publishing constantly both on academic topics, though not yet on rabbinics, and on issues relevant to American Jewry. Many of the more popular articles that he published in his father's paper were syndicated throughout other Jewish publications in North America, making Neusner one of the leading Jewish public intellectuals of the time even as an undergraduate at Harvard.

Within this context, Neusner was always interested in addressing what he, and many others, considered to be the intellectual paucity of American Jews. How, he would always ask, is it possible to thrive as a people in America when all that Jews have to hold onto is the Holocaust and Zionism? He remarked on what Zionism meant to him: "I am a Zionist because I am a Jew, and Judaism is incomplete without Zionism. . . . Because I am a Jew, a child of Abraham, Isaac, and Jacob, of the prophets of Israel, I have a stake in the land. A part of it, some stone in the Galil, or a clod in the Sharon, or a speck of Negev dust, belongs to me, and I to it. If all is not well with it, the world is off its center, because that is the land which men have to earn, to merit, and on whose account men have suffered punishment."[63] Yet, while a Zionist, he was opposed to American Jewish migration to the land of Israel. In an address to Hillel at MIT on March 7, 1952, "Israel's flag is not mine," he argued, "my homeland is America." Even at this age he seemed to have been acutely aware of the problems besetting American Jewry. He continued, "The challenge of building a vibrant and living American Jewry cannot be met by annual trips to the synagogue and annual checks to the UJA. The problem is to build the communities, the congregations, the cultural life, and the means for community expression."[64] Indeed, Neusner would spend much of the next sixty years trying to accomplish this building. His popular writings, his "American translations" of all of the classics of rabbinic Judaism, and his subvention of a press to carry out the dissemination of such works to an American reading public contributed to this vision. However, his irascible personality meant that he was largely unsuccessful in his attempts to build a bridge between the academy and the community. As he would remark in 1964, "I favor, therefore, more Judaism and less 'Jewishness.' . . . I do not participate in any Jewish organization . . . because I do not find personally relevant or socially significant any of the societies available to me."[65]

Since Neusner had graduated from Harvard in three years, he decided to apply for a Henry Fellowship that would permit him to continue his education in England for an additional year. The fellowship, for unmarried seniors, permitted students of Harvard and Yale to spend a year at Oxford or Cambridge (and vice versa) and had a cash value of five hundred pounds sterling (roughly one thousand dollars). The terms of the fellowship were that he neither get a degree nor undertake formal studies, but "rather read books, travel, talk to people, and, in general, learn and grow."[66]

So in July 1953 Neusner set sail on the *Queen Mary* for England, his first trip outside of the United States.

Oxford

On the passage, the purser responsible for seating assignments asked the young Neusner if he had any special dietary restrictions. Uncertain, he asked the purser what he meant, to which the purser responded, "Well, for example, are you Jewish and do you want kosher food?"[67] Although he had never kept kosher, protestations of his mother to the contrary, he decided that he would do so onboard and see what it was like. As it turns out, he was seated next to a young American rabbinical student and his wife, both of whom were traveling to Israel for a year of study. At breakfast one day, the rabbinical student asked Neusner if he wanted to study *blatt gemara* (that is, a page of the Talmud). He had no idea what the student was talking about and asked him to explain. Neusner had heard of the Talmud, having read Abraham Cohen's *Everyman's Talmud* (1931) the year before.[68] However, he had never heard of anyone who actually studied the Talmud, nor, at this age, even why anyone might want to. Somewhat interested, he spent the rest of the day in the company of the young student who explained to him what rabbinic Judaism was about. Despite this initial lesson, the young Neusner would not spend any further time studying the Talmud until he entered rabbinical school himself the following fall. His goal, that year abroad, was to see the world and not get stuck, ostrich-like, in the Jewish past.

The ship landed in Southampton, on the southern coast of England, and Neusner made his way by train to Oxford, where he would study at Lincoln College. Perhaps not realizing the gloom of postwar Britain, he had high expectations for the famed cloisters of Oxford University, and had romanticized what it might be like to live in a medieval college town renowned for its lengthy and celebrated history of higher learning. Instead, he found Oxford a "dull backwater," and a place that, not unlike Harvard, was very cold to Jews, especially American Jews. Within a very short time, he got to know every single American in Lincoln College, and they all formed their own clique. Among those he encountered was his fellow student from Harvard and subsequent important social historian Richard T. Vann, who encouraged him to apply for a fellowship from the National Council on Religion in Higher Education, which he subsequently would receive and that supported him both financially and intellectually over the course of his graduate education in New York City. This fellowship would become the catalyst for introducing the young Neusner to the field of religious studies.[69]

His tutor in Jewish history was Cecil Roth, a well-respected historian of the Jews, and an observant Jew in an intellectual and theological environment that was not particularly hospitable to them. Roth had convinced the university to allow Jewish students to take exams on Sunday instead of Saturday. Since these students had an extra day and the potential to learn what was on the exams, they would have to spend the Sabbath sequestered in the Roth home. Like Neusner, Roth wrote a tremendous volume of work on all aspects of Jewish life, from the Dead Sea Scrolls to the Jewish communities in Renaissance Italy. He also had a journalistic side and wrote for newspapers and other popular outlets.

Roth gave Neusner an assignment on English Jews in the United States in the nineteenth century. Although Roth had meant it to occupy Neusner over the course of the eight-week fall term, Neusner mistakenly thought it was his homework for the following week. So he handed it in and then decided to spend the rest of the academic year studying other things, many of which had nothing whatsoever to do with Jews or Judaism. These subjects included Italian, the history of art and architecture, and European history.

In addition to such subjects, the young Neusner also became aware of his own nationality while abroad. Though he had long considered himself a proud American, for the first time in Oxford he encountered individuals who genuinely detested America and who blamed the United States for the Korean War. Many of these students were youth members of the Labour Party in Britain, and Neusner thought that they "stood for a world-view different from any I had ever known."[70] In response, Neusner joined the only pro-American party in Oxford, the Conservative Party. He wrote articles for their magazine, the *Oxford Tory*, about life in America and about subjects such as the role of America in the British press. He went regularly to their meetings not because he understood anything of British politics, but because, he admitted, he knew who America's friends were.[71] Although he considered himself a Democrat, and went on to work on Edward Kennedy's 1962 senatorial campaign, he eventually became disillusioned with what he considered to be the culture of entitlement of the Democrats and switched allegiances to the Republican Party, where he would remain for the rest of his life and for which he worked tirelessly.[72] At this point, though, Neusner seems to have gravitated to the Conservative Party in Britain less for political than for personal and social reasons.

At Oxford, the young Neusner also discovered Orthodoxy and the Orthodox liturgy. Since Reform Judaism was largely unheard of in Britain, the majority of Jewish students whom he met at Oxford were Orthodox, and he would attend their *Kabbalat Shabbat* services and eat Sabbath meals with them. He, thus, began to experience Judaism as a foreign tradition. He reflected upon how little he knew about Judaism and about the major lacunae in his own Jewish education back in West Hartford. While he found this, for him, hitherto unknown world of Judaism interesting, the tradition primarily remained a hobby for him in Oxford, something that competed with all the other new things that he was learning there, including the operettas of Gilbert and Sullivan.

That cold, dark autumn in England also gave Neusner his first real encounter with what would eventually come to be called the Holocaust. While he had certainly been aware of the events surrounding the massacre of European Jews while in West Hartford, only now did he begin to both realize and think about the magnitude and systematization of these events. In the famed Oxonian bookstore, Blackwells, Neusner noticed a stack of *The Final Solution: The Attempt to Exterminate the Jews of Europe, 1939–1945*, an acclaimed work by the English art historian Gerald Reitlinger. Reading about the extermination of European Jewry at great length, the young Neusner was initially pleased that his own maternal great grandparents and paternal grandparents had come to America when they did. These feelings, however, were quickly eclipsed by the sheer carnage and inhumanity of the events in question. How, the young Neusner asked himself, as thousands of others have and would subsequently, could people have committed such atrocities against others? If the mass murder of European Jews had previously formed a part of the more general history of the Jews for Neusner, after reading Reitlinger's book it now became part of his own, personal life story. The mass murder of the Jews of Europe would, from this moment on, form a critical part of both his personal and intellectual life. Although in the weeks following his reading of the book, he tried to avoid the company of non-Jews, he became increasingly interested in what Christianity was and what role, if any, it played in the tragic events of the Second World War.

The Britain of 1953 was a bleak place, still in postwar recovery. The chill of those years was pervasive, especially with the cold and rainy weather. It was also the time of austerity, when meat was scarce, and one still needed ration cards for foods such as bananas and sugar. The Henry Fellowship provided Neusner with the funds, and the lengthy six-week breaks between terms in Oxford with the time, to engage in travel to further his education and expand his horizons. Escaping the gray of an English winter, he traveled south to Italy, in a desperate search for the sun. Neusner was certainly not the first traveler to find in Italy everything that England was not. Its climate, its people, and their mannerisms showed the warmth that he found so wanting in England. The world of light and shadow, architectural majesty, beauty, and food left an indelible mark on the young man. "Italy from then on," he recounts, "formed one boundary of my life."[73]

From Italy, Neusner made his way to Germany, to Frankfurt, to visit a friend whom he had met while at Harvard. This trip enabled him to witness firsthand—only eight years after the end of the Second World War and the closing of the gas chambers—Germany, the German people, and something of the attitudes that had brought about the Holocaust. It was a difficult visit. Meeting his friend's father for the first time, he was asked if he was a Protestant or a Catholic. Afraid to speak the truth, he said he was Protestant, reckoning that this rubric could include Reform Judaism. For the next ten days his friend's family introduced him to the German upper-middle class, individuals who had worked for and supported Hitler. Although critical of Hitler's "excesses" with the Jews, they nevertheless deplored them. One man told Neusner that the Jews "even took our names."

As disturbing as the visit was, Neusner realized that Germans were not unlike Americans, the only difference lay in their anti-Semitism.[74] This trip would, it would turn out, be the first of many for Neusner. Years later, his critical and formative work on rabbinics and its relationship to the academic study of religion would find a very positive hearing in that country (often when it was heavily criticized at home). He would go on to be awarded honorary doctorates from German universities, the same universities that had turned against Jewish students and faculty during the war, and to enjoy many good relations with Germans, perhaps the most famous being Cardinal Ratzinger, also known as Pope Benedict XVI.

His third major trip that formative year was to the newly formed State of Israel in the summer of 1954. Traveling with an Anglo-Jewish group on an eight-week tour, Neusner saw firsthand the fulfillment of the Zionist dream. What struck him was not, as he initially thought it would be, the specialness of the country, but its sheer normalcy. He also noticed how few of the people on his tour, to the consternation of the many Israelis he met, did not see migration there as an option. Far from being the final solution to the Jewish problem, the State of Israel was, then and now, not a viable option for many Jews. For Neusner, personally, he saw no contradiction whatsoever in being Jewish and being American. This fact certainly did not infringe or impinge upon his Zionism, it simply realigned its focus.

Return to the United States

Oxford had been a formative experience for the young Neusner. Not only did he expand his horizons, as he had intended, he also made an important decision that would prove pivotal for his subsequent development as a scholar. As we have seen, since the age of twelve, Neusner had wanted to be a rabbi. Whether this actually meant becoming a pulpit rabbi or simply formed part of a vague idea of wanting to surround himself with Jewish learning for the rest of his life is uncertain, though it was likely the latter more than the former. Since Neusner had grown up in a Reform home and, as he made clear, the only Judaism that he really knew existed, at least until he got to Oxford, was that of the Reform tradition, it was assumed that he would simply go on to Hebrew Union College, the Reform seminary, in Cincinnati.

In conversation with Cecil Roth at Oxford, however, Neusner decided instead to go the seminary associated with the Conservative moment, the Jewish Theological Seminary (JTS) of America in New York City. Here it is important to note that in the 1950s the Conservative movement was aligned much more closely with Orthodoxy than it is today. JTS, its leadership hoped, would function as the go-to place for all traditional Jews, including Orthodox, and not just reflect the ideology of a specific denomination. In a period before, among other things, the ordination of women, which JTS began to do in 1985, this was indeed much more possible than it would be after. Roth reasoned to Neusner that he would presumably get a better Jewish education at JTS. At that time, the young Neusner did not really know the difference between the two denominations. However, it was clear to him that he wanted to know more than he did as a Reform Jew and to move beyond what he thought that he already knew about Judaism.[75] Why go to a Reform seminary if this were the case? With this decision, Neusner's "self-conversion" was complete. He had gone to Oxford as a Reform Jew and returned to the United States as a Conservative Jew or, at least, a young man who was training for the Conservative rabbinate.

In the meantime, he had applied to JTS, which at that time, according to Neusner, would admit anyone who applied. The young Neusner departed England in the summer of 1954 with fond memories, an increasing awareness of the world, and the further realization, on the verge of actualization, that he would devote the rest of his life to the study of Jewish topics. Rabbinic literature, however, was still only a distant blip on his horizon.

Thirty years later, on August 18, 1983, Neusner—never afraid of controversy and of airing it in a public forum   complained in London's *Evening Standard* that Oxford "has become a mediocre place. It has a certain lethargy, a sleepiness. It is common knowledge among American academics that most of the important scholarship going on today is not happening in Oxford." Instead he claimed that the University of Chicago, in addition to other American universities, "is what Oxford claims to be—a serious place where intellect pure and simple is the only criteria."[76] Interestingly Neusner used as his comparison Chicago, a university where he had never taught. Since Neusner had by this later point fallen out with colleagues at Brown, where he was then teaching, he must have reasoned that the University of Chicago was that illusive perfect university. It should come as no surprise to learn that this critique caused considerable scandal among professors at Oxford. John Macquarrie, the Lady Margaret Professor of Divinity, retorted in the *Oxford Times* that "I have a student with me at the moment from Chicago and he has not heard of this chap. So we are not dealing with a major figure."[77] He further argued that "[t]here is a saying which you might like to include in your article that goes: 'Theology is created in Germany, corrected in England, and corrupted in America.' I think there is a certain amount of truth in that."

* * *

Returning to the 1950s, we see that by the time that Neusner departed Oxford, still an undergraduate, many of the sources of his academic interests were in place. The obvious exception was rabbinics. While this would come soon enough, almost immediately from the time that he entered JTS the coming fall semester, his interests in Judaism, the Holocaust, pedagogy, and the relationship between Israel and America were all beginning to take shape in his young mind.

2

From Rabbi to Scholar

By 1954, after he had graduated from Harvard and having just spent a year in Oxford, Jacob Neusner was determined to pursue a life in Judaica. He had, however, absolutely no idea either how to go about this or indeed even the contours of what such a life might resemble. He had traveled to England, Continental Europe, and Israel, but with the exception of his experiences with the young rabbinical student on the boat to Southampton, he had barely read a Jewish text. Today, a young scholar interested in Judaism but lacking a traditional immersion in Jewish texts simply applies to an established and well-known graduate program in Jewish studies. As Neusner contemplated his future, this option did not yet exist. If one wanted to be a scholar, especially of rabbinic texts, one went to a yeshiva and spent years mastering what the ancient sages said. Issues of theory, method, and disciplinarity were largely marginalized at the expense of a reverential treatment of the textual canons of Judaism. Another option was to enter a rabbinic program associated with one of the more liberal streams of Judaism. Neither of these career trajectories, however, appealed to Neusner. He initially thought that the latter might provide him with what he was seeking. It did for a time, but he soon realized that although he wanted to read Jewish texts, he did not want to do so religiously or as a pulpit rabbi. Though he could not have known it then, he would have to forge his own path—a path that subsequently made it possible for all those who came after him who wanted to study the texts of Judaism in a nonpartisan and unapologetic manner.

As he prepared to enter JTS, the young Neusner, as we have seen, had very little training in Judaism and absolutely no familiarity with the technicalities of rabbinic texts. He was also a smoker, and the thought of spending one day a week without indulging in his nicotine habit seemed daunting. Since incoming students had to sign a pledge saying they would abide by traditional Jewish law, which included being *shomer Shabbat*, he mailed in his application only when he was certain that he could spend an entire day without smoking. This lack of tradition or, perhaps better, this lack of respect for tradition, I submit, was what made Neusner's revolution possible. Since he was not confined by the parameters of tradition, he was free to apply methodologies that he had learned in other contexts to the sacred texts of Judaism. He did not know what he did not know, as he always put it. The result would be a new way of looking at texts, a way that he most likely would have overlooked had he had the traditional education that many criticized him for lacking. "I had the advantage of seeing everything fresh because I didn't know anything," he remarked once, "often someone who comes in fresh can completely restructure the field because he has not prior commitments."[1] In order to restructure the field, however, he first had to learn the methods of the status quo. Only then would he be in a position to critique them. Although he would go on to produce an award-winning dissertation on the life of Yohanan ben Zakkai, it was a work that he would soon thereafter repudiate as too simple and uncritical. He later realized and publicly admitted that his early work simply accepted sources at face value, as accurate historical transcripts as opposed to later additions. Had his early work, especially his dissertation, not conformed to this old-fashioned model, however, his teachers who belonged to that status quo and whom he would soon criticize as naïve never would have passed it.

The travels and auto-didacticism that defined his year at Oxford would now give way to a defined structure that is characteristic of an intensive graduate program. First and foremost, he had to learn the languages—Hebrew and Aramaic.

Jewish Theological Seminary of America (JTS)

When Neusner entered JTS in the fall of 1954, the Seminary was an institution at the height of its glory. Founded in 1886 to combat the rise of

Reform Judaism in America, the Seminary saw itself as an "orthodox" response to the perceived excess of the Reformers, whom the more traditional referred to as practicing a "bastardized Judaism."[2] In many ways, then, the Seminary sought to train traditional, American-born rabbis with the aim of shaping traditional Judaism in this country. Although JTS began as a seminary without a denomination, it would subsequently become the epicenter of the Conservative movement.[3] It is, however, worth noting that the line separating "Conservative" from "Orthodox" was a very fine one at the Seminary for most of the first half of the twentieth century, before the rise of hot-button issues like the ordination of women as rabbis firmly and irreparably established the boundary. The Seminary saw itself as leading a renaissance in Jewish scholarship in America during the first decades of the twentieth century. In addition to its creation, this period also witnessed the growth of Hebrew Union College's library in Cincinnati, the creation of the Jewish Publication Society of America in Philadelphia, and the establishment of the American Jewish Historical Society in New York City.

In the years following its establishment, JTS quickly became one of the world's leading centers of Jewish learning and scholarship. This primacy was aided by the arrival from England of the charismatic Solomon Schechter, whose desire to transform JTS into the major place "for Jewish scholarship and Jewish learning" helped to cement further the Seminary's success.[4] Whereas the majority of JTS faculty carried on the study of Jewish texts in the classic European tradition, it is important to remember that the Seminary was also a place where young rabbis were trained. There was, and still is, a tension between the faculty who saw themselves as scholars and the students, many of whom were destined to be pulpit rabbis. Many of the faculty in the first half of the twentieth century—Louis Ginzberg, Israel Friedlander, Alexander Marx, and Schechter himself—saw themselves as scholars first. Since most had been born in Europe, they had—with few exceptions, such as Abraham Joshua Heschel and Mordecai Kaplan—little interest in the problems besetting American Jewry.[5] Although JTS would eventually establish a graduate program in Jewish topics in 1970, Neusner remembers the majority of the faculty taking very little interest in their students.[6]

When Neusner entered the Seminary, the president (later to be renamed chancellor) was the formidable Louis Finkelstein (1895–1991). Finkelstein was a scholar of the Pharisees, the precursor to the rabbis at the time of the Second Temple. He also wrote a biography of Rabbi Akiba in a way that Neusner—although he would also adopt this genre for his own dissertation—later characterized as naïve. Finkelstein's goal was to make JTS into *the* institute of Jewish higher learning in America and, as such, the voice of American Jewry.[7] He envisaged JTS as a place for all traditional Jews as opposed to a seminary that reflected a specific denominational ideology.[8] Because of this goal, he was, like his predecessors, reluctant to make too explicit the relationship between the Seminary and the Conservative movement. As the leader of the Seminary, one of Finkelstein's top priorities was public outreach. He created a radio and television show called "The Eternal Light." The goal of these programs was to engage the general American public by drawing on history, literature, and social issues to explore Judaism and Jewish holidays in an accessible and nondenominational manner for both Jews and non-Jews. Finkelstein also recognized the importance of interfaith dialogue, and he regularly brought together Protestant, Catholic, and Jewish scholars for theological conversation.

Finkelstein's most significant academic appointment occurred in 1940 when he hired the prominent Talmud scholar Saul Lieberman as professor of Palestinian literature and institutions. Lieberman was born in Motol (modern-day Belarus), and studied at the famed Knesset Yisrael yeshiva of Slobodka, before immigrating to Palestine in 1927. Although he would attend the Hebrew University of Jerusalem, he was mistrustful of the scientific-like style of scholarship produced there. Instead of continuing the secular study of Talmud at the university, he served as the dean of the Harry Fischel Institute for Research in Talmud, which was founded in 1932 with the enthusiastic support of Rav Kook, the chief rabbi of Israel. Although he also taught courses in Talmud at the Hebrew

University in Jerusalem, a permanent position eluded him. These two positions did not pay Lieberman particularly well, and by the late 1930s he was looking to relocate, even to America if necessary, to gain appropriate employment.[9] Prior to his departure, he was regarded by many as a rising star in the traditional scholarly world in Israel.

Finkelstein had enticed Lieberman to New York to teach at the Seminary, where he joined Louis Ginzberg, another émigré from Europe, to create a formidable team of expertise in rabbinic Judaism. Lieberman represented the authentic Lithuanian *talmid hakham* (scholar) and lent legitimacy to JTS as it sought to be one of the premier homes of Jewish learning in the world. Lieberman, in the words of his biographers, stressed "the study and the implementation of the ethical values of the Talmud, that is, how to engage in a systematic study of Talmudic ethics and make these available to the public, and how to deal with contemporary moral issues in such a way that the decision-making processes are exemplified for others to follow."[10] For Lieberman, anyone who wanted to study rabbinic texts had to have a yeshiva-style education. His introductory lectures to JTS Talmud students were, again in the words of his biographers, "frequently characterized by advocacy, if not apologetics. . . . He not only taught texts, but a positive and reverential attitude toward the texts."[11] In his own work, Lieberman, as a product of the traditional Lithuanian yeshiva system, emphasized a conservative style of textual study, and was rarely interested in large, synthetic questions.

It came as a shock to many that the traditional Lieberman would take up a position at a non-Orthodox institution, even though the Seminary may well not have perceived itself as such. Lieberman did not go to the Seminary out of any change in ideological conviction, but rather to take up a position that would provide him with the economic security to devote himself to his scholarship. Again, though, it is worth noting that in the 1930s, the distinction between "Conservative" and "Orthodox" congregations was very fine. It was not uncommon, for example, to find graduates of JTS in Orthodox synagogues, or to find graduates of the

Rabbi Isaac Elchanan Theological Seminary (RIETS), the main modern Orthodox seminary, in addition to other Orthodox yeshivas, ad-
ministering Conservative synagogues. Nevertheless, the time at which
Lieberman came to the Seminary was one of increased tension between
the Orthodox and Conservative movements as the latter increasingly
asserted its independence when it came to matters of legal decision
making. This came to head over the Conservative movement's approval
to end the *agunah* (divorce) problem, namely, the status of a married
woman who no longer lives with her husband, but who has not yet been
formally released from the bonds of matrimony by him.[12]

In 1948, Lieberman became dean of the Rabbinical School. Although
he still regarded himself as an Orthodox Jew, his imprimatur now stood
behind every rabbi the Seminary produced. In 1958, he was named rec-
tor of the Seminary, making him responsible for the general tenor and
direction of the Conservative moment in America. His relation to the
Orthodox world began to come under increased strain. He was accused
of betraying Orthodoxy and of violating a principle of the *Shulhan
Arukh*, the primary code of Jewish law: "Whoever appoints to the office
of judge one who is unfit for it or one whose knowledge of the Torah is
inadequate to entitle him to the office, though the latter is otherwise a
loveable person, possessing admirable qualities, whoever makes such an
appointment transgresses a negative commandment."[13] When Lieberman passed away on a flight from New York to Tel Aviv on March 23,
1983, his death was not even announced in major Orthodox journals,
and his name and many of his works have been "blacked out" in the
ultra-Orthodox world.[14]

As Neusner prepared to enter the Seminary in 1954, it is certain that
he had never heard of Saul Lieberman. As a young rabbinical student,
Neusner had arrived at JTS shortly after the 1953 death of Louis Ginzberg, who had been the primary teacher of Talmud at JTS for much
of the first half of the twentieth century, leaving Lieberman as the primary scholar of rabbinic literature. Although Lieberman and Neusner
would eventually be extremely critical of one another, Neusner spent

two years studying rabbinic texts with him. Neusner referred to him in a 2013 interview as an "unimpressive teacher," but it is not clear how much of this is a projection onto the past in light of Lieberman's subsequent criticisms.[15] Neusner, for example, thanks Lieberman in the preface to his 1962 *A Life of Rabban Yohanan ben Zakkai, ca. 1–80 CE*, but this acknowledgment mysteriously disappeared from the second edition in 1970. Their early relationship seems to have been cordial. Writing to Neusner on December 4, 1972, Lieberman gave the young Neusner the following advice in a handwritten letter: "You highly exaggerate the hostility towards you and your work. You must get reconciled to the fact that in our *olam sheqer* [vain or lowly world] there is such a thing as envy and jealousy, and nothing can be done about it except in diligently pursuing your work."[16] In a December 10, 1981, letter, Neusner wrote to Lieberman, despite the fact that he had taken out the acknowledgment to him in the aforementioned book, that "I am enjoying *Hayerushalmi Kifshuto* so much, that I wanted to tell you so. . . . It reminds me of why I have long ago concluded you are the greatest exegete of rabbinic texts of the twentieth century and among the true greats among the ones I have studied and used—of all times."[17]

Things would change, however. In a review article of Neusner's Talmud translation published shortly after Lieberman's death in 1984, Lieberman strongly criticized what he perceived to be Neusner's lack of scholarship and ignorance of the canons of rabbinic scholarship. In a private letter to Neusner, Rabbi Bernard Mandelbaum, president of JTS between 1966 and 1971, suggested that Lieberman had penned the nasty review as a way of getting back at Neusner because of a nasty footnote about Ginzberg and Finkelstein in an article that Neusner had published in the collection of *Sam Friedland Lectures* that were delivered at JTS.[18] Neusner never forgot this review, and it seemed to haunt him throughout his career. In response, Neusner criticized Lieberman's work as lacking any valid methodological or coherent theoretical framework. It was, to be sure, an intractable debate between two generations of scholars, between the Old World of Europe/Israel and the New World of America, and between two modes of Jewish scholarship—the one done solely for its own sake, and the other to show how Jewish data illumined larger questions in the academic study of religion. It was also a one-sided debate because Lieberman's review had been published posthumously, so Neusner could not defend himself. The tense relationship between Lieberman and Neusner irreparably undermined Neusner's relationship not only to JTS, but also to the Conservative movement more generally.

Neusner at JTS

To return to 1954: Neusner had no idea why he was admitted to JTS. He possessed no qualifications and had very little educational preparation that would have been appropriate for their course of study.[19] He claimed to have never given up the values of Reform Judaism with which he had grown up, and that he instead adapted these values to his new denominational home. Once again, though, it is difficult to ascertain if this was actually the case or if it was the older Neusner lashing out at the Conservative movement, which he felt never treated him with the respect he deserved. Harold White, a fellow student and friend of Neusner, and later chaplain and director of Hillel at Georgetown University, admitted that Neusner did not have the strongest background when he began at the Seminary. White felt that people like himself and Neusner "were regarded as lower-class citizens because we were not products of Jewish day schools or yeshivas."[20] Although Neusner was completely unprepared for a seminary education, he was an extremely hard worker with an incredible ability to focus solely on what he needed to do. Within a few short months he was able to pass his entrance exams and be considered as a rabbinical candidate. "What might have taken others twelve years to accomplish," White reminisced, "he did in three months."[21]

It turns out that Neusner and White were not alone. That incoming class at JTS had more alumni of Harvard than of Yeshiva University, a modern Orthodox institution that had been among the traditional feeder schools of the Seminary. Neusner believes that the change in makeup was the direct result of the Seminary wanting to broaden the kind of rabbis that the Conservative movement produced. Rather than ordain "Orthodox heretics" to serve as Conservative rabbis, the Rabbinical School of the College was making a conscious effort to produce leaders who were firmly committed to the ideological tenets of the movement. This change of core constituency led increasingly to new students who were in need of remedial study in languages and texts with the hope that, after the remedial work had been done, they would be uniquely qualified to serve in pulpits across the country and beyond.[22]

Neusner maintained that of all the students in his incoming class no one was in a worse situation than him. His interests, his training in American history, and his commitment to Reform Judaism put him firmly at odds with his classmates. He claimed that it took him three years to master what the majority of his fellow students already knew. Although he came in knowing little if anything about rabbinic Judaism, within days of his arrival at JTS he encountered the Talmud, the work that would form the cornerstone of his life's work. Since this text would come to play such an important part in his life, it is worth quoting the older Neusner reflecting back on this early encounter:

> From the opening lines of the first chapter to which I was exposed, I found myself in a strange and wonderful world, a world of question and answer, thrust and parry, tradition and innovation, persistently fresh and original perspectives and modes of thought. I never doubted that I would struggle on that front until I could stand on my own. And there would be no other front, no other struggle. Nothing could afford so immediate a challenge of intellect and wit—but also of spirit. For at stake in the Talmud, I would find out, are the critical issues of shaping a just and holy social order.[23]

In order to get there, however, he first had to learn the languages. His Talmud teacher had determined that Neusner would need a tutor to work line by line through the text. In addition to learning Hebrew and Aramaic, Neusner also had to memorize all the texts he was reading because, if he did not, nothing made any sense to him. This would be one of the methodological principles that would stick with him throughout his life. His engagement with the Talmud and other texts combined Neusner's love of history and mathematics. If the former was about context and human meaning, the latter was about establishing logic and order. These two trajectories would coalesce in Neusner's later use of the concept of "system" to refer to the inner structures of the various Judaisms of late antiquity.

The young Neusner put these two loves together and proceeded to work through the texts of rabbinic Judaism. He claimed that at the end of his first year, the faculty of the Seminary entertained a motion not to allow him to return the following year. It is not clear if this was the result of his outspokenness or his continual desire to write articles in the Jewish press and even other academic journals. Many seemed to have felt that students should publish only after they had graduated and established their scholarly credentials. Needless to say, Neusner did not agree. The Seminary was on the verge of dismissing him, which would have been done if not for the objections of Abraham Joshua Heschel. Neusner had served as Heschel's research assistant, which included his typing up Heschel's well-known monograph *God in Search of Man*. Neusner always spoke fondly of Heschel, and was critical of how poorly the Seminary treated him, perhaps finding an affinity with the elder philosopher. In a review of Heschel's biography by Edward Kaplan, Neusner wrote of the former's mistreatment, noting the disconnect

> between Heschel's accomplishments and the way he was treated by the Jewish Theological Seminary of America, where he was dismissed with contempt by the principals on the faculty and in the administration. Even after Heschel's heart attack in 1969 the Seminary authorities did not permit him, though weakened, to sit in the front row in the synagogue, where he could use a reading stand for holding his Siddur and

Humash. He was not asked to give the teaching of the Torah on a festival day. None of those who abused him competed with him in the very sciences they prized: text study above all. Heschel's theological achievements enjoyed no celebration and his academic studies in the history of Jewish thought in Rabbinic and Kabbalistic and Hasidic sources brought him no glory among men who claimed to represent those documents and to make sense of them. So one dominant motif in Heschel's life and work takes shape in the conflict between Heschel's greatness and his reception among small-minded and envious colleagues at JTSA. The one mitzvah they carried out to perfection is the one that says *ain navi be-iro*, a prophet is not without honor except in his own village. That mitzvah they kept.[24]

Neusner remained at the Seminary, and by the end of his third year he had read, in the original, the Mishnah, several tractates of the Talmud, and numerous Midrash compilations. This combination of memorization and textual study would serve him well over the coming years as he moved systematically through the entire corpus produced by the rabbinic sages of late antiquity.[25]

Neusner spent six years in rabbinical school. For one of these years, he was in Jerusalem studying at the Hebrew University of Jerusalem and at a yeshiva. While he was quite happy with his training in the United States, he complained, at least after the fact, about the way rabbinics in particular and Judaism in general was taught in the State of Israel. This criticism would form a leitmotif throughout his career. Even in these early years, he found the learning that went on there "dull and intellectually moribund."[26] He was critical of the Israeli system of "servile students and dogmatic teachers" that "produced little."[27] It is unclear if this criticism was leveled after his own run-ins with the Israeli academy, which he isolated to 1984, when he was invited to a conference and then uninvited when the organizers read the paper he planned to give.

Neusner realized fairly early on in his career at JTS that he wanted to be a scholar and that he did not have the temperament to be a pulpit rabbi. The time he had spent in the elite institutions of Harvard and Oxford, combined with his love of academic learning, would make it virtually impossible for the young Neusner to become a modern rabbi, someone who is defined more by social work and counseling than anything resembling intellectual activity. However, at the time there was little alternative for a young scholar interested in Jewish texts and traditions to gain exposure to them outside a seminary type of environment. Whereas the majority of his colleagues prepared to graduate and enter pulpits in Conservative synagogues throughout the country, the young Neusner decided to enroll in the PhD program at Columbia University. He would, however, give the occasional sermon at local congregations in Vermont and Upstate New York.[28] An example of such a sermon comes from his Yom Kippur address from September 24, 1958, in Oneonta, New York:

> There are two men who give to the UJA. One gives because of income tax, and that's all. The other gives because in his heart, he wants to help the refugee Jews of all the world to make a new beginning in Eretz Yisrael. Both have done a mitzvah, tsedakah, but one has profaned his mitzvah, and the other has not. I believe this is the meaning of the verse from Ecclesiastes, "For there is not a righteous man upon the earth, that does good and sins not."[29]

Also exhibited in the sermon were a number of features that would preoccupy Neusner for much of the rest of his life: the intersection of Jewish values and American society, and the poor state of contemporaneous Jewish education. He concluded,

> Our purpose is not to search for truth, but to investigate truths we have in our traditions. To find out what kind of human beings emerge from Torah. What kind of society ought to result? To share our values with other Americans, but to be sure our values are Jewish values to begin with. [This is followed by his assessment of various educational institutions:]

Hillel–Lehrhaus

Sunday Schools—worse than nothing

Hebrew Schools—disastrous

Day Schools—not so good as reputed, my friend—[this leads to]
shallow Judaism.[30]

It seems that Neusner was certainly not a good candidate for the pulpit. Neusner's relationship to JTS and to the Conservative movement—
indeed to Judaism itself—was always complicated. His rabbinic study
certainly provided him with the ability to learn the languages of rabbinic Judaism, which he would not have learned anywhere else at this
time. The Seminary also enabled him to interact with some of the towering intellects of twentieth century, such as Abraham Joshua Heschel,
Mordecai Kaplan, and, though the post-1984 Neusner might object, Saul
Lieberman. Yet JTS, and by extension Conservative Judaism, also provided Neusner, as a reactive individual, with something against which
he could define himself. If the scholars at JTS were aloof and passive
aggressive, Neusner was very engaged and aggressive. If the type of approach to scholarly activity at that institution was dry and traditional,
he would break that mold. If those at JTS were not interested in contemporary Jews, Neusner would be and would write about these concerns
in the national Jewish press. The Seminary, Conservative Judaism, and
Saul Lieberman thus all became symbols for Neusner that represented
the "old" way of doing things. His relationship to all three remained tor-
tured throughout his career.

Yet, in hindsight, the Seminary offered him quite a lot. In addition
to the language training, it gave him rabbinic ordination and the institutional bona fides to carry on with his assessments of American Jews
and American Judaism, and his subsequent redefinition of the field of
rabbinic studies. Although it would soon be clear to Neusner that he
wanted an academic as opposed to a rabbinic career, he could not have
known this without having spent six years at the Seminary. He seems to
have wanted an education from the Seminary that was impossible in the

late 1950s. Moreover, if he had received the type of education that he had wanted in retrospect, he never would have had the career that he did. As we shall witness shortly, he would have the exact same problem with Columbia, the institution from which he received his doctorate.

His Subsequent Relationship to JTS

Although Neusner seems to have spent six very productive years at JTS, his relationship with the Seminary and its leadership quickly soured as he prepared to graduate. There was little he could do as a young rabbinical student, but as his academic and journalistic career flourished, he became increasingly frustrated by what he regarded as its major shortcomings—and frequently criticized them both in private and in public. His disapproval seems to have stemmed from two major areas. First, he was critical of what he considered to be the noncritical and unsystematic nature of the JTS curriculum. This would only be exacerbated in the coming years. The JTS faculty—Lieberman, then David Weiss Halivni and Shaye Cohen—came to symbolize, for Neusner at any rate, the holdouts to full acceptance of his own critical method. Since he defined his own method against that of JTS, the latter and all those who worked there were thus guilty by association and had to be wrong on all counts. Second, he grew increasingly frustrated with the Conservative movement—epitomized by its poor treatment of people like Heschel and Kaplan—and its desire to try to situate itself as the definer of American Judaism. He seems also to have put himself in this category of creative minds alienated by the Seminary. JTS and the Conservative movement, then, became emblematic for Neusner of all that was wrong with American Jewry on intellectual and ideological grounds.

Neusner later complained that Louis Finkelstein, the chancellor, had forbidden his work to be cited among faculty at the Seminary. In Finkelstein's own work devoted to the Pharisees, *The Pharisees: The Sociological Background of Their Faith* (1966), there was no mention at all of Neusner's work on the subject. When Neusner was invited, years later in 1979, to give the Samuel Friedland Lecture at JTS, virtually no faculty members attended. To get back at his perceived enemies at the Seminary, Neusner donated a copy of every single book that he published to their library. This meant that although the faculty there might ignore him, young graduate and rabbinical students researching rabbinics would most certainly come across his books and ideas, although he believes that, despite his efforts, the faculty and students at JTS still largely ignored his work.[31]

In 1987, to commemorate his inauguration as the sixth head of JTS, Ismar Schorsch granted a doctor of Hebrew letters, *honoris causa* to Neusner and "all graduates of the Seminary who have distinguished themselves and brought merit to their *alma mater* by virtue of their contributions to the study of Judaica within the university world." Schorsch's letter of invitation continued by noting that the Seminary sought to provide "recognition of these contributions at the joyous and historic occasion of the inauguration [by] emphasiz[ing] the importance we place in furthering the study of Judaica in American colleges and universities."[32] The invitation seems to have been a way for the Seminary to finally acknowledge all those who had graduated from the rabbinical program but who had opted not to go into the pulpit, but instead had devoted their lives to scholarship. Many of these individuals, Neusner noted, had felt alienated by the Seminary's treatment. In addition to acknowledging the scholarship produced by Neusner and other JTS graduates, Schorsch and the Board of the Seminary proposed to award honorary doctorates to Harvey Cox, a Baptist minister and professor of theology at Harvard, Hans Küng, a Catholic theologian, and Geoffrey Hartman, a Jew and literary critic based at Yale. Neusner accepted the invitation and prepared to travel to New York to receive his honorary degree. Just four days before the inauguration, which was due to take place on Monday, September 14, 1987, however, Neusner published a damning indictment of the Seminary in an op-ed titled "The Next Chancellorship at JTS: Some Hopes" in the *Washington Jewish Week*. Perhaps to respond to what he considered to be decades of mistreatment by the administration and faculty, he began as follows,

The Jewish Theological Seminary of America is not a university and has no reason to pretend to be one. It is a Jewish seminary, it exists to celebrate the Torah. When it honors people like myself, who are identified with universities and with the academic study of religion, including Judaism, and when it seeks the message of Professors Harvey Cox, Geoffrey Hartman, and Hans Küng, it makes a statement that I do not think it should make. And in putting together the twin facts of the invitation to Ismar Schorsch's coming inauguration as the sixth chancellor of JTSA—the forum, the honorary degrees—I think we all hear the message that Chancellor Schorsch plans to make next week.[33]

Neusner then asks rhetorically, "Where is the Torah in this inauguration?" He continues, stating that the "least-informed persons in the room [that is, Cox, Küng, and Hartman] will be those who are asked to give a message—to the rabbis invited to listen to them and learn from it." He then concludes,

I should have celebrated receiving my degree still more, if it stood for appreciation, also, for fellow-students of mine who, nearly thirty years ago, entered pulpits, and made their lives for three decades in the service of Jewry, as I have made my life in a different realm altogether. They are the ones who should be celebrated on this happy occasion, because they are what the school exists to accomplish—they, not I. . . . Instead of teaching of Torah by JTSA teachers and students, masters and practitioners of the Torah, rabbinic alumni, we have a forum on "the reemergence of the sacred" by great professors of the secular world (Hartman) or of the Protestant and Catholic world (Cox, Küng). . . . Instead of honoring pulpit rabbis, for whom the school exists, they choose alumni who do what the school did not educate them to do, and whose entire careers derive their substance from using what they learned at JTSA in ways not contemplated by their teachers at JTSA. . . . All of this makes for a very puzzling way of celebrating the new chancellorship of JTSA next week. But I'll be there, grateful and thankful for the invitation.[34]

This is vintage Neusner. He complained when the Seminary did not acknowledge his accomplishments, then when they tried to, he complained that they should not do so. It is also further evidence that Neusner never missed an opportunity to critique JTS publicly.

It is not difficult to imagine the response to this article. The specter of Lieberman was not far from the surface. Neusner commented in private that he was offended that this recognition from JTS occurred only after Lieberman's death. Schorsch and JTS were then worried that Neusner would use the honorary doctorate to show others that he was right and Lieberman was wrong. In a letter that Neusner obtained because someone had sent it to him anonymously, Schorsch had informed a benefactor of the Seminary that it would publicly repudiate any attempt by Neusner to use his honorary doctorate as a vindication of his ad hominem attack against Professor Lieberman.[35] Two days before the inauguration Neusner was struck with a recurrence of chronic gout.[36] He sent a message to the Seminary saying that his colleagues, Ernest Frerichs and Thomas Tisch, someone whose father was on the JTS board, would be there in his stead. The Seminary, however, refused to grant the degree in absentia, saying it had never done so in the past. In effect, they rescinded it despite the fact that Abraham Karp, a scholar of American Judaism at the University of Rochester, pointed out that the Seminary had in fact awarded an honorary degree in absentia to Chaim Weizmann in 1948. Schorsch later wrote Neusner, informing him that to award the degree on a different occasion would require reapproval by both faculty and board, which would not be forthcoming.

Neusner blamed the entire affair on his relationship with Lieberman and viewed it as revenge for "my critical comments on [Schorsch's] inaugural program, which seemed to me very unJewish and so set the wrong priorities for JTSA for the future."[37] Edward Greenstein, a colleague of Neusner who worked at the Seminary, confirmed this in a letter the following year.[38] In his final years Neusner's relationship to JTS was somewhat more sanguine. He read in the *Jewish Week* that the Seminary had had a reunion for the class of 1960, the year in which he graduated, to which he had not been invited. Neusner, as was customary, wrote a letter to the new chancellor, Arnold Eisen, calling this latest slight "another small chapter in a long pointless narrative."[39] Eisen wrote back to him apologetically, and acknowledged the intellectual debt he owed to Neusner.[40] Neusner believed his omission from the reunion was the result of his formal break from Conservative Judaism the year before. In an opinion piece in the *Forward*, based on his 2009 Dr. Fritz Bamberger Memorial Lecture at HUC-JIR in New York, Neusner announced publicly that he had returned to Reform Judaism, reverting to his original childhood commitment. In the opinion piece/lecture, he spoke of the "sorry state of Conservative Judaism," and criticized the movement as little more than a "sorting house" for Jews who moved to either Orthodoxy or Reform.[41] Reform Judaism, he argued, "has intrinsic strengths that should enable it to resist the self-defeating tendency toward reversionism. From the very beginning, Reform Judaism has presented itself as the Judaism defined by the American condition."[42]

Yet, the story of Neusner at JTS tells us only half of the story of his years in New York. In 1958, he enrolled in the PhD program in religion at Columbia University. The study of religion in these years was undergoing major changes, and Jacob Neusner would, in many ways, find himself the beneficiary thereof.

Academic Study of Religion in America

When Neusner entered the PhD program in religion at Columbia in 1958, the academic study of religion, or religious studies, was taught in a handful of private universities, but primarily in divinity schools—for example, Harvard Divinity School, Yale Divinity School, Princeton Theological Seminary—associated with various Protestant denominations. When "Jewish" texts were studied, they tended to be relegated to the "Old Testament," namely, that which formed the first part of the Christian Bible and that foreshadowed the coming of Jesus.[43] Postbiblical Jewish texts were rarely entertained. Judaism, it was assumed, ended as Christianity began. All of this was about to change, however. As Neusner sought new arenas for the study of Judaism beyond the parochial confines of places like JTS, a monumental event that would forever change the landscape of the academic study of religion in this country was playing out in the courts.

In 1963, Edward Schempp, a Unitarian Universalist and a resident of Abington Township, Pennsylvania, filed suit against his local school district in order to prohibit the enforcement of a state law that required his children to hear and read portions of the Bible as part of their public school education. According to that law "[a]t least ten verses from the Holy Bible [be] read, without comment, at the opening of each public school on each school day."[44] Schempp argued that this law violated his and his family's rights under the First Amendment to the Constitution, which prohibits the making of any law respecting an establishment of religion. The district court ruled in Schempp's favor, and subsequently struck down the Pennsylvania statute. The school district appealed, however, and while the appeal was pending, the Pennsylvania legislature amended the statute to allow children to be excused from the exercises upon the written request of their parents. Not satisfied, Schempp continued his action against the school district, charging that the amendment of the law did not change its nature as an unconstitutional establishment of religion.

The case eventually made its way to the Supreme Court as the *School District of Abington Township, Pennsylvania v. Schempp*. The Court ruled eight to one in favor of the respondent, and declared school-sponsored Bible reading in public schools in the United States to be unconstitutional. Justice Clark's concurring opinion distinguished between "teaching religion" and "teaching about religion," which can be seen in the following:

> We agree of course that the State may not establish a "religion of secularism" in the sense of affirmatively opposing or showing hostility to religion. . . . It might well be said that one's education is not complete without

a study of comparative religion or the history of religion and its relationship to the advancement of civilization. It certainly may be said that the Bible is worthy of study for its literary and historic qualities. Nothing we have said here indicates that such study of the Bible or of religion, when presented objectively as part of a secular program of education, may not be effected consistently with the First Amendment. But the exercises here do not fall into those categories. They are religious exercises, required by the States in violation of the command of the First Amendment that the Government maintain strict neutrality, neither aiding nor opposing religion.[45]

This case would revolutionize the academic study of religion in this country. Since religion could now be taught *about*, many state universities (e.g., Florida State, Indiana, Iowa, Virginia) opened up departments of religious studies that would now teach religions of the globe as opposed to the Old and New Testaments. Prior to the Supreme Court case, the organization that was primarily responsible for the study of religion in the United States was the National Association of Bible Instructors, which went by its acronym, NABI, Hebrew for prophet. The following year it reinvented itself as the American Academy of Religion (AAR), an organization of which Neusner would be president in 1969, becoming the first scholar of postbiblical Jewish texts to hold this position in either the AAR or NABI. Virtually overnight, the AAR switched its mandate from the study of pre-Christian Judaism and Christianity to one that would now study the world's religions, including post–Second Temple Judaism, based on a comparative model.

Although this newly transformed academic study of religion would still exhibit a Protestant bias, there was nevertheless a desire to present other religions of the globe to American undergraduates. In terms of Judaism, this would have major intellectual repercussions. Judaism now migrated out of Semitics departments, where it had largely been taught, and into departments of religious studies.[46] Whereas some relished the thought of studying and comparing Judaism to other religions—what we can call the universalist vision—others believed that a disinterested approach to Judaism was out of sync with traditional norms: "For university teachers of Judaica to fail to inculcate in their students the notion of study as a mitzvah [i.e., commandment] is to be as unfaithful to their discipline as for teachers of physics to fail to inculcate an acceptance of the scientific method."[47]

As someone who pursued his undergraduate and graduate studies in the 1950s, Neusner prepared for an academic career in the very decades in which not only the academic study of religion, but the academy more generally, was undergoing major reorganization and reformation. Neusner, more than anyone, seems to have been aware of the possibilities that this would have for the study of Jewish texts, and he began, from a relatively early age, to integrate the study of Judaism within religious studies. Rather than keep Jewish texts on the margins of the academic world, a place where many scholars—both Jewish and non-Jewish—would have liked them to remain, Neusner sought to show how such texts had the potential to transform the traditional intellectual categories, just as these categories had the simultaneous potential to transform the ways in which Jews thought about their texts.

Columbia University

In 1958, while in the midst of his rabbinical studies, Neusner also enrolled in the graduate program in religion at Columbia University. He received his rabbinical degree in June 1960, and his PhD in November of the same year. His training in the academic study of religion would prove beneficial to his understanding of Judaism, and, indeed, this cross-pollination of his rabbinic and secular studies would distinguish virtually all of his later work. In his own words, the study of religion "marked the first time that I saw Judaism as not particular but exemplary, and Jews as not special but (merely) interesting."[48]

The academic study of religion opened Neusner to a new understanding of Judaism. Rather than describe the religion on its own terms and using its own insular language, he began to frame Judaism both more universally and more analytically. He was aided in this task by his reading of some of the major theorists of religion during the 1950s. These included Émile Durkheim, Max Weber, and, most important of all, the Rumanian Mircea Eliade (1907–1986), who taught at the University of Chicago. Reading Eliade around the time of the Jewish New Year in his first year of graduate study, Neusner appreciated the author's concept of the "eternal return" and the "repetition of the sacred." The eternal return, the conception of sacred time as cyclical and repetitive as opposed to linear, allowed Neusner to see similarities between Judaism and other religious traditions. Works by Eliade and other such theorists encouraged Neusner, at a formative moment in his intellectual growth, to think about the nature and function of religion in ways that he simply could not in the predominantly ethnic setting of a place like JTS. This enabled him to think about religion in more general and theoretical terms. At the same time he was able to connect such theories and analyses to a particular set of data, that is, Judaism and Jewish texts that he had been studying in the time-honored way at the Seminary. These texts—the Mishnah, the Talmud, and other rabbinic works—now began to take on an importance that, again in his words, "transcended their own setting."[49]

If Neusner had always sought for ways to reconcile the particularism of Judaism with the more universal concerns of the mainstream academy, the academic study of religion provided him the conceptual tools to begin this process. The study of religion was what would ultimately allow Neusner to take the study of rabbinic texts, a rather obscure field as far as the academic study of religion was concerned, out of the yeshiva world, which hitherto had no interest whatsoever in secular religious studies (and which, for the most part, still does not). The academic study of religion, framed somewhat differently, provided Neusner with the conceptual framework to normalize the study of Judaism within the academy instead of having it remain on the margins.

By studying the very texts—namely, the rabbinic corpus—that the academic study of religion had always ignored as either too legalistic or too arcane, Neusner was able to show that Judaism did not end as Christianity began. Instead, Judaism provided its own unique set of responses to the aftermath of the Second Temple's destruction in 70 CE, a set of responses that Neusner would spend his life documenting and analyzing in great detail. Certainly he was not the first to undertake this endeavor. His predecessors included the non-Jewish George Foot Moore (1851–1931), who, among other efforts, spent considerable time examining the dynamic and rich thought produced by the rabbis between the third and fifth centuries CE.[50]

Neusner—or at least the older Neusner looking back at these events—was highly critical of the mode of education at Columbia, much like he had been critical of Harvard, Oxford, and JTS. But the intellectual stimulation of the books that he read on his own and for various seminars made up for the lack of pedagogical stimulation of his teachers. He was particularly critical of the chair of his doctoral dissertation committee, Salo W. Baron (1895–1989), generally considered to be among the greatest American Jewish historians. Of Baron, Neusner complained that he "contributed nothing, being himself, intellectually vacuous. He made his books by paraphrasing sources he never troubled to criticize and by paraphrasing the opinions of other scholars he never fully understood."[51]

The person whom Neusner learned the most from at Columbia was Morton Smith, whom Neusner described as "the best teacher I ever had," someone who read and corrected every line of his dissertation.[52] If the other members of his dissertation committee provided little or no guidance, Smith offered him in-depth constructive criticism on both substantive and stylistic grounds. Neusner located Smith's scholarship as "somewhere between the early me and the later me."[53] Indeed Smith's own doctoral dissertation on "Palestinian Parties behind the Old Testament" provided Neusner with a model for how to write his own doctoral project on Yohanan ben Zakkai. Although Smith and Neusner would eventually clash, the young Neusner was grateful to Smith; as he writes in the second edition of the revised version of his dissertation, "My be-

loved teacher and friend, Professor Morton Smith, not only devoted un-
limited time and effort to the successive drafts of my dissertation, but
since that time read and further criticized every line of the 1962 edition.
His kindly encouragement, expressed not through praise but through
serious, penetrating criticism, has sustained me."[54] When the dissertation was published in book form, Smith sent Neusner a handwritten
note on January 21, 1963:

> *Yohanan* is really a beautiful book, and, what is better, a good book. I'd
> forgotten how much there was in it. I'm proud to have had a part in it
> and thank you very much for your acknowledgment, and for the copy.
> Comments in detail will follow—I'm rereading it with pleasure—but I
> wanted to congratulate you right away on the completion of a piece of
> work which is an important contribution to the field.[55]

The Dissertation: Yohanan ben Zakkai

Neusner had gravitated to the topic of Yohanan ben Zakkai because
the latter represented the first generation after the destruction of the
Second Temple in 70 CE, just as Neusner saw himself as part of the
first generation that had survived the horrors of the Second World War.
In this work, what he would later call his "pre-critical" phase, Neusner
sought to create a snapshot—what he called a conventional historical
construction—of the life of this first-century CE sage by examining and
summarizing all the extant sources, both early and late, that mention
him. Although Neusner would eventually repudiate this approach, char-
acterizing it as "gullible, conventional, and unoriginal,"[56] he remarks in
the preface to the book that his goal at the time was to ascertain who
exactly Yohanan ben Zakkai was:

> He was one of the leaders of the Pharisaic communities in Jerusalem
> before the destruction of the Temple, and afterward he undertook the
> work of reconstruction. Who he was, what he taught, and how he met the

perplexities of religion in his time—all this needs to be recovered from the rather scanty remains of his life, scattered throughout Talmudic and midrashic literature.[57]

Neusner's goal in this work, stated differently, was to recover as much of Yohanan ben Zakkai's intellectual biography as he could. Rather than focus on the forms of the traditions that relate to this rabbinic figure—for example, how, when, and why they took shape and were transmitted—Neusner instead focused on the actual contents of these traditions and assumed that they could tell us something real and objective about this first-century rabbi's life and times. He had no idea of the sorts of critical questions that would become formative to his later approach to rabbinic literature. He took it for granted that his work would be a conventional biography, and that all the sources were historically accurate. He admitted later that at this time he had no idea of what he was getting into, and did not ask the primary questions that would characterize his subsequent work, such as, "How do we know this happened?"[58]

The reviews of the work were mixed. Commenting on the first edition, Ezra Spicehandler (1921–2014) of Hebrew Union College in Cincinnati wrote in the *Journal of the American Oriental Society* that Neusner's "major achievement is that he presents a balanced summary of extant knowledge about Rabbi Yohanan for the first time in the English language."[59] Despite this assessment, he was quick to point out that, on occasion, Neusner "takes great liberties with his translation,"[60] a criticism that would continue to be leveled at his other works over the ensuing years. Spicehandler, nonetheless, concluded by saying that his "critical remarks are made out of regard for a promising scholar who has written a very interesting monograph."[61]

In an extensive review of the second edition, appearing in the *Jewish Quarterly Review* in 1972, Solomon Zeitlin (1886–1976), professor of postbiblical Judaism at Dropsie College in Philadelphia, echoed Neusner's later assessment of his early work.[62] Zeitlin remarked that "I must regrettably state that the book is a great disappointment. While Dr.

Neusner demonstrates his ability to present his ideas in good form and writing, he did not utilize proper Rabbinical literature. He did not differentiate between legend and history. Thus, we must say that his book on the life of Yohanan ben Zakkai is not an asset for the proper understanding of the Jewish history of the period."[63] We again witness in Zeitlin's critical review of the work a leitmotif that we will encounter throughout Neusner's career: the liberties he took when it came to the translation of his sources. As we will see, this criticism would culminate in the damning review by Saul Lieberman. Suffice it to say here that Zeitlin found fault with Neusner's choice of translating Hebrew into English: "A translator must be scrupulous in rendering a text."[64]

These criticisms reflect the larger tension between the academic study of religion and area studies. In his desire to connect rabbinic texts to a larger set of questions supplied by the disciplinary perspective of religious studies, Neusner was destined to step on the toes of those trained within the tradition of rabbinics and who spoke only to other specialists in a narrowly defined field of study, one that tended to be governed primarily by philology as opposed to any other recognizable methodology. As this book argues, the genius of Neusner was that he sought not to join this narrow conversation, but to open up the study of Judaism, specifically rabbinic texts, to a larger intellectual audience who worked with other data but who asked similar questions. Within this context, much of the criticism leveled against Neusner emanated from the seminary approach to these data. Zeitlin's criticisms, for example, are little more than "nitpicking," what Neusner would later classify under the genre of "catalogues of trivial errors."[65] One example should suffice:

> On p. 71 the author quotes M. Ket. 13, 3, "it is also recorded that Gamaliel I approved the decisions of Admon." The sage who approved the decision of Admon was Rabban Gamaliel II. Admon was a judge during the last years before the destruction of the Temple, while Gamaliel I died many years before. To the name Rabban Gamaliel I was always appended the term Elder.[66]

Later in the review, Zeitlin was concerned that the types of questions that Neusner asked might well confuse Christian readers who know very little about the Talmud. This is a silly criticism and works on the assumption that it is up to the scholar of Judaism to reproduce faithfully all that the sages of antiquity said in a way that does not confuse non-Jews. Zeitlin ended his review with the Latin phrase *Disce aut discede* (learn or leave)! The point, though, is not, as Zeitlin implies, that Neusner was not interested in learning Talmud, but that Neusner was not interested in learning Talmud or other works of rabbinic literature in a traditional system, the one in which the likes of Zeitlin were firmly embedded.

The dissertation would subsequently win the Abraham Berliner Prize at JTS. Neusner described the prize as recognition for "what is certainly the most conventional book I have ever written, one lacking all critical perspective."[67] The prize made the young Neusner believe that he was doing good and "critical" work. He would later realize that this was not the case at all because instead of asking critical questions of his sources, he simply accepted them at face value. In this, he followed in the footsteps of his predecessors, both in the yeshiva and in the university. There was a widespread unwillingness to admit that the sources might be wrong or corrupted.

Influenced by the critical methods that he learned in the academic study of religion, especially from those working in biblical studies, he sought to find ways of dealing with sources that did not simply describe them or take their allegations as truthful utterances. "My work," he admitted, "could have been done in 1200 or 1900, but it should not have been done in 1960. The world had learned lessons in criticism that had yet to reach my field."[68]

The National Council on Religion in Higher Education

From 1957 to 1960, which coincided with his entire time at Columbia, Neusner was a Kent Fellow at the National Council on Religion in Higher Education. This organization was originally founded as the

National Council of Schools of Religion in 1921 by Charles Foster Kent. Kent was the Woolsey Professor of Biblical Literature at Yale University, and the first president of NABI from 1910 to 1925. He was an advocate for the teaching of religion in American colleges and universities, believing that such instruction would prepare men and women for ethical practice in any profession. The goal of the Council was to create more and better trained scholars of religion who would go out and instruct the next generation of leaders and thinkers. In 1923 the organization changed its name to the National Council on Religion in Higher Education with the objective of furthering inquiry into values in higher education. Seeking to create a new generation of professors of religion, the organization also sought to promote a positive view of religion and ethical issues on campus. It was also eager to foster numerous religious points of view to address such issues. From the minutes of its 1934 Board of Directors' meeting, we read that the "Council has survived, has kept its morale, and dares to have plans for the future. . . . We have had to discover what our place is in the life of our times. . . . We are a fellowship that believes in the values of holding together, in a process of fruitful exchange of beliefs and convictions among persons of widely diverse viewpoints and backgrounds. . . . We attach great value to understanding and to mind meeting mind. . . . We are trying to develop and foster the growth of teachers who are intellectually and technically equipped and productive in their own fields, who have paid the price of hard work and discipline and who are expert in the guidance of youth."[69]

Kent Fellows attended annual meetings that were designed for sharing scholarly work and teaching ideas. These meetings brought together senior fellows, many of whom were prominent scholars in religious studies, with graduate students and new professors. They were academically rigorous but informal, with social events alongside scholarly debates. Neusner appreciated the meetings of the Fellows because, unlike his experiences at both JTS and Columbia, the Council was composed of individuals who took teaching seriously. It was also an organization that was characterized by diversity, not only of the religious variety, but also concerning commitment, viewpoint, and personality. It was this organization that enabled Neusner to see in a clear light what it meant to have a vocation as an academic.[70]

In terms of his own personal development, the Kent Fellowship had three major effects. First, Neusner encountered non-Jewish scholars who, like him, believed that the study of Judaism belonged in the academy, in departments of religious studies, and not in the ghetto of the yeshiva. That this sentiment coincided with his own came as a shock to Neusner at a formative moment in his career. Certainly the Protestant model of the academic study of religion might not be particularly amenable to the study of Jewish (or other) data, but that others—that is, non-Jews—recognized this oversight and still wanted to include Judaism within the curriculum pleased him greatly. It seems that the Kent Fellowships played a large role in trying to address various gaps in higher education in religion in the United States. For example, those in charge of the fellowship program noted that postbiblical Judaism was rarely, if ever, taught in departments of religion, so they tried to get young scholars, such as Jacob Neusner, into the program as a way to introduce Judaism into the curriculum in subsequent years.

Second, if Neusner had been mistrustful of gentiles, especially Christians, since his first personal encounter with the Holocaust while reading Reitlinger's book, *The Final Solution*, in Oxford, he now began to see non-Jews not only as colleagues, but as friends with whom he now felt at home. Indeed, much of Neusner's career would be spent making the texts of Judaism understandable to such individuals. Many of his works were read and celebrated in non-Jewish contexts, particularly in Europe, even as they were simultaneously often overlooked or criticized in more specifically Jewish contexts, such as in Israel or even at JTS.

Third, Neusner was now afforded a model of pedagogy and education that formed the polar opposite of what he had experienced at Harvard, Oxford, JTS, and Columbia. While all of these were great schools with tremendous reputations, their faculties were largely uninterested in pedagogy. Their reputation as scholars was assumed to be enough to transform them into first-rate teachers. Yet, as Neusner knew from personal experience, this was indeed far from the case. As the years passed, Neusner would also be critical of those teachers who claimed to be scholars despite the fact that they never published a word. In a letter to Leon Botstein, president of Bard College, where he worked later in his life, Neusner wrote,

> The notion that scholars can't teach and teachers can't do scholarship is not only self-serving for those that hold it (I know of no publishing scholar who concurs, and I know of no publishing scholars who do not value teaching as part of their professional commitment), but also wrong. Teachers who are not publishing scholars possess no passion (and probably teach outdated learning, and certainly uncriticized, stale learning), and scholars who can't teach are very few. I know of none at Bard. The non-publishing teachers, though, excel at substituting personality for intellectual power, winning students and (mediocre) colleagues to their cause, and set the stage for a life full of academic indolence and scholarly inactivity, ultimately yielding the dismantling of the College itself.[71]

Most of Neusner's early impressions about teaching came largely from his own endeavors, but the Kent Fellowship now permitted him to stand back from his auto-didacticism and reflect on pedagogy, the vocation of education. Education, for Neusner—and this is a topic on which he would write regularly and frequently over the coming years— was not simply about memorization and facts, but about the transformation of the individual in terms of both intellect and character. If Neusner now knew or believed that he knew what good education was, he was also aware of what bad education consisted of. For him, unfortunately, one of the primary culprits was the Jewish education system in America. He would become highly critical of this system, and, as we shall see, attention to the sorry state of Jewish education in America would, in addition to his masterful study of rabbinics, form one of the major foundations of his massive oeuvre.

The Fallout

It seems that while he held the Kent Fellowship, Neusner still did not know in what direction he wanted to go academically. As his dissertation was nearing completion, he asked his committee for advice. Abraham Joshua Heschel advised Neusner to learn Yiddish and begin the process of studying systematically the sources of Eastern Europe, many of whose inhabitants had been wiped out in the Second World War. Baron, the ostensible director of his dissertation committee, suggested that he continue with rabbinics, but redirect his focus by learning Pahlavi, the language of Iranian elites, and begin the process of examining the Babylonian Talmud within the larger context of Iranian civilization.

In 1960, as he prepared to graduate from the doctoral program at Columbia, John A. Hutchison—chair of the Department of Religion and someone whom Neusner had known from his time as a Kent Fellow—asked him to teach as an instructor at Columbia in the fall, with the understanding that the position would turn into a permanent one in the future. Indeed Neusner says that Hutchison was the first person to make him aware that there was an academic field known as religious studies. Hutchison, however, would soon depart for the West Coast, and this would make Neusner's position at Columbia increasingly tenuous. Shortly after Neusner was appointed at Columbia, Seymour Fox, the dean of the Teachers Institute of JTS, approached him with an offer to also teach part-time at the Seminary.

Given his experience at the Seminary as a student and the adversarial nature of the place, Neusner refused outright. Rather than say he would think about it, Neusner instead complained about the administration and informed them that he now wanted to devote his academic career to the study of Judaism in the secular university as opposed to the parochial world of the Seminary. As one of the first Americans to study rabbinic texts in a university rather than a religious setting, Neusner contended that he got under the skin of the European-born and yeshiva-trained faculty of JTS, the majority of whom knew both Yiddish and German, which they believed to be the languages of Jewishness and scholarship, respectively. Their Old World ways bothered Neusner, and this unease increased with time. The one exception, for him, was Abraham Joshua Heschel, who, as we have already witnessed, Neusner believed genuinely tried to make the world a better place and who wrote books that all could understand. The rest, he argued, produced dull publications with little or no system. As he would remark later, the majority of the faculty at JTS "were at best erudites, but at worst *idiots-savants*. Only in so small and parochial a subject as the study of Judaism could the empty illusion find credibility that not publishing marked authentic learning."[72]

His refusal to teach part-time at JTS, Neusner believed, cost him his job at Columbia. This was confirmed to him years later by his teacher at Columbia at the time and his later colleague, Jakob Taubes. Not long after he refused, John Krumm, the acting chair of the Religion Department at Columbia, informed him that his position would not be renewed the following year. This news, according to Neusner, "broke [his] heart." Furthermore, Columbia University Press, which had accepted his dissertation for publication, now rejected the book. On top of all this, his father passed away. As he mourned his father and rued what might have been at Columbia, Neusner now found himself on the job market and looking for a new publisher. Neusner, again with the vision of hindsight, believed that his fallout with the Seminary had to do with a generational shift in rabbinic studies. Whereas the long-standing faculty wanted to keep it under guard in the yeshiva where a select few could study it, he desired to bring the study of these texts into the mainstream, for all to read and study. If they were content to publish obscure monographs on technical issues, he was interested in big questions that he hoped others would be able to examine and test. This is certainly not to imply that after Neusner broke the mold all would follow in his path. However, once rabbinic texts made their way into mainstream departments of religion at secular universities, the paradigm had certainly shifted.[73]

What is new here, however, are the options that the young Neusner faced. In the 1960s it was rare for a young scholar of Judaica to earn a secular PhD and gain immediate employment in a secular university, while this is today the norm. Many in previous generations would have been content with pulpit work or part-time university employment while serving a synagogue, with the hope of eventually finding some sort of full-time academic appointment. The young Neusner, however, despite the fact that he was a rabbi, did not want rabbinic employment, even if only temporarily. Instead, he desired a full-time academic position.

* * *

As Neusner prepared to move from New York City to Milwaukee, Wisconsin, to take up a position at the University of Wisconsin–Milwaukee in the summer of 1961, he had little idea that he was moving from campus politics to community politics.

3

Community Tensions

For a young scholar of Judaica in the late 1950s and early 1960s, there were few career options. While certainly every rabbi did not have aspirations to secular teaching or scholarship, those who were interested in such extracurricular activities could, if the opportunity presented itself, teach the odd course at a local college or university. Campus administrators liked such an arrangement because local Jewish communities, rather than the universities, funded these positions to ensure that Jewish topics would be taught on campus. For many years, and even on some campuses today, the "scholar" of Judaism was or is the local rabbi, often with very little or no training in scholarly method. His or her job is to make Jewish students feel good about themselves and provide a nice account of the tradition for interested non-Jews. Another possible option for someone with seminary training who was interested in secular Jewish scholarship was to become involved with the growing Hillel Foundation, whether as campus rabbi or executive director. Founded in 1923 at the University of Illinois at Urbana-Champaign, by the mid-1960s Hillel had spread to over a hundred campuses. The goal of this organization, then as now, was to create a welcoming environment for Jewish students on campus, and to provide a space to create a positive Jewish identity. How secular and objective scholarship on Jews and Judaism fit into this mandate was not and indeed is still not clear.

The Jewish person teaching Jewish topics on campus had, and still does have, a tense relationship to both the campus and the local community. Colleagues tend to see him or her as a community appointment, and the local community often expects the scholar to have a positive Jewish identity. This, in turn, has led to all kinds of ambiguities. Were individuals hired because of academic promise or group membership?

Is the scholar's primary allegiance to the canons of scholarship or to the truth claims of Judaism? Or, if it was the local rabbi, someone without academic qualifications, teaching courses on Judaism, how would that person interact with nonreligious colleagues? If intellectual recognition was to accelerate social acceptance, what did it say that local communities had to pay for it themselves?

All of these issues have had the effect of making the teaching of Jewish topics parochial and have meant, at the least on Neusner's reading, that the study of Judaism has largely existed outside of the intellectual structures of the contemporary university. This lack of regard for engaging Jewish data from the perspective of those disciplines—such as history or sociology—firmly entrenched in the academy reinforced the long-held view of the singularity or uniqueness of Judaism, which could well function as a variation on the age-old theme of "chosenness." If Judaism is seen as unique, then what need is there for secular disciplines to illumine it? As Neusner was soon to recognize, the study of Judaism on American campuses risked manifesting itself as little more than an ethnic enclave, one whose primary business was special pleading for Jews and Jewish causes. This meant that there was always the danger that instructors of topics dealing with Jews or Judaism might well function more as rabbis than as professors. University courses risked being folded into communal expectations and encouraged to address issues of communal instability brought about by the rise of intermarriage, indifference, and decreasing standards in community-sponsored educational institutions, such as day schools or Sunday schools.[1]

Jewish Semitics: Three Portraits

Neusner's first real appointment was as a professor of Hebrew studies at the University of Wisconsin–Milwaukee. Stepping back to examine the larger context of the fields of Hebrew and Jewish Semitics in this country just prior to his appointment, we can see that at a time when Jewish community building was beginning in earnest, perceived access to numerous American cultural institutions, such as the university, was now within reach in ways not seen in Europe. Jewish Semitics, the precursor to Jewish studies, thus offered a potential path toward social, cultural, and political inclusion.[2]

University recognition of Jewish Semitics created a sense of social, religious, and intellectual acceptance on the part of many within the Jewish community. Although not as involved in the sectarian debates as it had been in Europe, Jewish scholarship tended to be supported primarily by Reform Jews, many of whom sought both to legitimate and to strengthen themselves in the face of more traditional denominations. Many of the latter were either not interested in or outwardly hostile to the higher criticism of university Semitics. By the end of the nineteenth century, Jewish Semitics in select institutions thrived, largely owing to what Ritterband and Wechsler call "American Jewish communal subventions."[3] Increasingly, however, such communal support began to diminish for a number of reasons. Some were certainly economic and sociological, but also important was the fact that numerous Jewish scholars of Jewish data no longer knew how to speak to communities, seeking instead professional as opposed to community recognition. Many scholars were more interested in receiving tenure, promotion, and professional fame based on highly technical studies, and they did not want to be seen simply as having community appointments.

Positions in Jewish Semitics appeared in universities that had significant Jewish communities, such as the University of California, Berkeley, the University of Chicago, Columbia, Harvard, Johns Hopkins, UCLA, and the University of Pennsylvania. All of these positions were largely funded by local communities. As early as the first decades of the twentieth century, university presidents hoped that successful Semitics programs would encourage the munificence of the local Jewish community for other projects. What is worth noting here is that Jewish studies entered the university not because university presidents thought that Jewish topics needed to be taught. Rather, the establishment of courses and chairs in Jewish topics was the result almost solely of community support. Although Neusner would eventually make his name as a scholar of rabbinic Judaism, rabbinic texts in the early years of Jewish Semitics were rarely taught due to their specialized nature. If comparative Semitics showed the relationship between Hebrew and cognate languages in the Ancient Near East, texts such as the Talmud showed Judaism at its most strange and legalistic, and thus had the potential to reinforce negative stereotypes. The avoidance of such texts also reflected the aesthetic sensibilities of Reform Jews, many of whom were the benefactors of these positions.

For example, Emil Gustav Hirsch was born in 1852 in Luxembourg before immigrating to America with his family in 1866. He studied at the University of Pennsylvania before returning to Berlin to receive his doctorate, after which he became a Reform rabbi in Chicago in 1880. "His universalism, visible commitment to Judaism, knowledge, and influence in the Jewish community," write Ritterband and Wechsler, "account for the University of Chicago's interest in him."[4] In 1892, he was appointed professor of rabbinical philosophy and literature at the university, in addition to maintaining his rabbinical duties at Chicago's Temple Sinai Congregation, where he was the highest paid clergyman in the United States. However, unlike his colleagues at the University of Chicago, Hirsh received no salary, nor did he engage in scholarship, except the odd contribution to the *Jewish Encyclopedia*. His appointment to the faculty of the University of Chicago seems to have been, wrote one of his colleagues, "secured through the contributions of the wealthy Jews of Chicago" whom, it was believed, he could tap for further donations to the university.[5] When Hirsch retired, Rabbi Louis Mann, his successor at Temple Sinai, replaced him on the Chicago faculty.

Another example is Richard Gottheil (1862–1936), the founder of the Semitics Department at Columbia University. Gottheil, whose father was the chief rabbi at Temple Emanu-El, the largest Reform synagogue in New York City, was trained at Columbia before earning his doctorate in Leipzig in 1886. Much of Gottheil's work was in comparative Semitic literature, including Arabic, Aramaic, Hebrew, and Syriac, for which he was an internationally known and respected scholar. However, Gottheil was also an ardent Zionist. He attended the second Zionist Congress in Basel in 1898, became friends with Theodor Herzl and Max Nordau, and from 1898 to 1904 he was president of the American Federation of Zionists. Like that of Hirsch, Gottheil's salary had been paid by external funds until Columbia decided to normalize the position. Gottheil was responsible for establishing a minor in comparative religion at Columbia that would eventually become the department in which Neusner would study. But if Gottheil could keep his communal and scholarly interests separate from one another, many of his colleagues in the faculty could not or refused to, accusing him of holding, in Ritterband and Wechsler's words, Columbia's "Zionist Chair."[6]

The final example is Neusner's senior thesis advisor at Harvard, Harry Austryn Wolfson. Harry Wolfson represents the middle point in the shift in the study of Judaism from Jewish Semitics to religious studies. Wolfson was born in modern-day Belarus, and attended Knesset Yisrael yeshiva of Slobodka, the same yeshiva that Saul Lieberman would attend, before immigrating to the United States with his family in 1903. He attended Rabbi Isaac Elchanan Theological Seminary in New York City, and then took up a position at a Hebrew day school in Scranton, Pennsylvania. He was encouraged to take the entrance exam for Harvard, which he passed. He received a scholarship and began his studies there in 1908. Wolfson was a strange match for Harvard. He did not play sports, lacked many of the social graces of the other students, and spoke with a heavy East European Jewish accent.[7] Although he contemplated a career in medicine, he decided to do his PhD in medieval Jewish philosophy, which was virtually unheard of in American universities at the time. He graduated and remained at Harvard for the rest of his career.

Wolfson's story is different from the previous two because, unlike them, he was less interested in philology and comparative linguistics in the Ancient Near East than he was in philosophy, especially with showing the intersections between medieval Islamic, Jewish, and Christian philosophers. Yet, despite the fact that Wolfson's interest was in philosophy, his interest in medieval *Jewish* philosophy meant that he had to undertake his work in the context of a Semitics department. And although he dreamed of an academic career, he was well aware that there were virtually no positions in universities for those interested in Jewish learning. Despite his pathbreaking research, Wolfson was always isolated at Harvard. He worked in the basement of Harvard's library, suffered from institutional anti-Semitism, and went from year to year not knowing whether or not he would retain his position. The money for his salary initially came from the community. He was offered positions at other institutions, such as Hebrew Union College in Cincinnati, but he wanted to remain at Harvard so that his work would not be seen as merely of parochial interest. Harvard did very little for Wolfson for close to twenty years, but he insisted on staying so that Judaism, in particular medieval Jewish philosophical texts, could garner recognition in non-Jewish contexts. Wolfson also maintained that the work being produced in seminaries was less critical and objective than that produced in university contexts. Finally in 1925, Lucius Littauer, a wealthy glove-making tycoon and congressman from upstate New York, agreed to pay Wolfson's salary of $6,000 for three years, at which point he would establish a $150,000 endowment. From that time forward, Wolfson was promoted to the rank of full professor and became the Nathan Littauer Chair in Jewish Literature and Philosophy. His position, the first endowed chair in Jewish studies at an American university, would be split between the Semitics and Philosophy departments. That it was split shows the gradual movement of Jewish learning outside of the context of Semitics departments to other disciplines within the university.[8]

These three portraits illustrate some of the career options open to a scholar of Judaica in the first half of the twentieth century. Every position was in some way the product of community largesse. No American university president or academic dean, in other words, thought that Jewish topics should be taught for their own sake. Donors were humored with the hope that they might make gifts to non-Jewish topics that presidents believed would be of more "universal" interest. As exemplified in the stories of the three scholars, if there was no community support, there quite literally would have been no such thing as the study of Judaism on academic campuses. Even so, filling such positions was a challenge. Consider the case of Harvie Branscomb, the chancellor at Vanderbilt University in Nashville between 1946 and 1963. Branscomb was charged with creating a chair in Jewish studies at Vanderbilt and, reflecting on it later, wrote,

> In the first place, we had to find someone willing to take the job, willing to work, that is, in a not unfriendly but nevertheless alien religious environment. He must be interested in the problem of communication across frontiers too often closed. He should be a person of outgoing temperament who would enjoy contact with Christian scholars and invite friendship in turn. Without question he must be a good scholar. And finally, he must be a loyal representative of his faith. This last was based on the belief that to correct inveterate misunderstandings and prejudices it was important to convey not only the literary and historical facts but also the ethos of the Jewish faith as well, its spiritual meaning to its adherents.[9]

Branscomb's comments here get to the heart of the problem. What is the role and function of the scholar of Judaism on college campuses? Is he—and I do not think he ever had a she in mind—to be a scholar like any other scholar on the faculty? Or must he be, to use Branscomb's words, "a loyal representative of his faith"? What happens if the scholar of Judaism is not interested in Judaism? Or, framed in today's terms, what happens if the person is not Jewish or is critical, say, of Israel? None of these questions are easy to answer, but they all reveal the tensions and paradoxes that exist within Jewish studies, then and now.

As we have seen, Jewish studies emerged from and was nourished by a quasi-ghetto mentality. Then, as now, it consisted of Jewish faculty teaching Jewish topics (language, literature, history) to Jews, an endeavor that was often heavily subsidized by the local Jewish community. The number of endowed chairs today in Jewish studies, for example, is certainly disproportionate to the number of such chairs in other fields or disciplines within the humanities. There was very little room for making the study of Jewish data intellectually or academically respectable. Someone like Wolfson, who did try to do this, was met with marginalization and anti-Semitism. This was the intellectual and social context that Neusner encountered as he graduated from Columbia in 1960. Even in the position that was taken away from him at Columbia, it was assumed that he would also teach part-time at JTS. The scholar of Judaism, it was assumed, would always have to scrape by, working several jobs and, if paid at all, receiving wages well below those of his non-Jewish colleagues. When Neusner declined the job at JTS and was, in his own words, "fired" from the position at Columbia, he had to go in search of one of those elusive positions in Jewish studies. Given his experiences at JTS, he was not interested in seminary work. Although he would eventually secure one of the very first non-endowed positions in Judaism when he was appointed to the faculty at Dartmouth College, he would first have to experience the contortions and tensions of what it meant to be a community appointment.

Leaving New York

Emerging from Columbia, Neusner found the nascent or fledgling field of Jewish studies very political, very ethnic, and stunted by the indifference of more established scholars. Although those like Harry Wolfson and Salo Wittmayer Baron—with Alexander Altmann arriving at Brandeis in 1959—were beginning to train students at this point, Neusner found little guidance or support from those he had worked with either at Columbia or JTS. The major scholarly guild for those few people working in Judaica at both the university and seminary worlds was the American Academy of Jewish Research (AAJR), with membership—then as now—by invitation only. The AAJR was, in Neusner's words, "a very restrictive organization that was not open to new ideas."[10] It was membership in this organization, and not a PhD from a recognized university, that decided who would and who would not be a "scholar of Judaism."[11] Whereas Neusner regarded anyone—Jew and, presumably in the future, Gentile—with a PhD in Jewish data to be a scholar of Judaism, the AAJR was much more restrictive. Neusner recalls an encounter with Abraham Halkin, whose own position at Columbia was subsidized by the Gustav Gottheil (a Reform rabbi and father of Richard Gottheil) Lectureship in Semitic Languages, who argued that the fellows of the AAJR and only they—not Neusner and a generation of younger scholars—would decide who was qualified to study Judaism academically and, by extension, what the academic study of Judaism would look like.[12]

It is difficult to know how exactly Neusner defined himself in these early years. Although he would later call himself a scholar of religion who worked with Jewish data, this conceptualization would emerge only when he got to Dartmouth. While he certainly regarded himself, even at this early stage in his career, as someone who used Jewish texts to illumine larger questions, the terminology is unclear. This is because he would have had no well-established paradigm with which to define himself. It seems that initially Neusner defined himself by what he was not, namely, he was beginning to imagine himself as the opposite of those scholars at places like JTS who took their sources at face value and assumed them to be historically unproblematic. This antagonism with JTS—both intellectual and personal—led him to new ways of defining himself, such as "religionist" or as someone engaged in the "social scientific study" of Judaism. Such definitions, however, would come about only in a piecemeal fashion as he encountered other scholars, primarily scholars of religions other than Judaism, and began to rethink the place of Judaism and Jewish studies in the secular academy. Certainly these competing ideas—the introverted world of the Seminary and the more extroverted one of the secular Department of Religion at Columbia—would have been on full, if inchoate, display while he was trying to complete, simultaneously, graduate and rabbinical school.

The world of the seminary in which data were self-evidently important simply because they were written by Jews and the world of the secular academy where one had to argue for why one's data were important in the first place were bound to come into conflict with one another. Indeed, Neusner—perhaps due to the fact that he had a foot in both of these worlds or, perhaps, because he realized that the seminary world was no longer the only option for studying Jewish data at this point or, perhaps, because of his own intellectual prowess, such that he felt that he did not need the identity politics of the yeshivah—seems to have been one of the first individuals in which these tensions fully manifested themselves. Was it the self-assuredness of his personality? In part yes, but his critical phase would come only later, when he was at Dartmouth and beginning at Brown. Was it his unwillingness to conform to existing conventions? Indeed, he would spend his life resisting conventional approaches—intellectually, pedagogically, religiously, and politically. Or was it his desire to make himself and what he studied legitimate in the eyes of the rest of the academy? It was likely a combination of all of these.[13]

University of Wisconsin–Milwaukee (1961–1962)

After losing his position at Columbia, Neusner landed a job at the University of Wisconsin–Milwaukee, and made his way from New York City, traveling from the center of the academic world to its margins. The inexperienced scholar, still scarred by his recent experiences at Columbia, arrived at an equally inexperienced institution, one with, at the time, little sense of what an institution of higher learning ought to either offer or expect. A conglomerate of various schools (Milwaukee Normal School, later renamed as the Wisconsin State College at Milwaukee), this institution joined the University of Wisconsin System in 1959 as the newly coined University of Wisconsin–Milwaukee. This university and Neusner, it turns out, would spend much of the academic year of 1961–1962 defining themselves in opposition to one another.

Neusner was hired to chair the newly created Department of Hebrew Studies at Milwaukee. The position was largely funded by the local Jewish community, in particular, by the Wisconsin Society for Jewish Learn-ing based in Madison, a group set up by a local Reform rabbi to sponsor Jewish education at University of Wisconsin campuses in Madison and Milwaukee. When the local community leaves the scholar alone to pur-sue his or her research, a modus vivendi is often reached; if, however, the community regards the scholar as little more than another employee of the local Jewish Federation, tensions inevitably emerge. Neusner soon found himself in the middle of such a situation. Since he had spent the past few years straightening out in his own mind what the academic study of Judaism was or should be, devoid of special interest groups or cheerleading, he was in for a surprise when he had to ask the local Jew-ish community in Wisconsin to sign off on lecturers he wanted to bring to campus, what courses he was teaching, his research expenses, and so on. If Neusner had been of another personality type, he might well have just accepted this way of doing things. However, his stubbornness and his insistence on doing things his own way would eventually exacerbate an already tense situation.

Neusner delivered his inaugural lecture to the Wisconsin Society for Jewish Learning on October 15, 1961. It is perhaps telling that he gave it there rather than to the university in front of his new colleagues. The lecture was titled "The Place of Judaism in the American University," and, in retrospect, it would prove to be important. Not only did it signal the high hopes Neusner had for the academic study of Judaism, hopes that made his funders uncomfortable, but it also represented one of the very first installments of what would amount to a lifetime of trying to reflect theoretically on where and how Judaism fit in the contemporary university. Indeed, these reflections—here and in other places—are as important to the endeavor of Jewish studies and the development of American Judaism as the contributions that he made to the academic study of rabbinic texts. This is because his sometimes technical work on rabbinic texts fed into his redefinition of the study of Judaism, which is on much clearer display in places such as this inaugural lecture. The texts of rabbinic Judaism, framed somewhat differently, form the point of departure for his second-order reflections on the study of Judaism and what this tradition means for the disciplines associated with the much larger conceptual field of the humanities.

Neusner began his lecture by remarking, "No one would ask himself why teach physics or philosophy, but one may quite legitimately, it seems to me, ask, why teach Hebrew, Jewish history, literature, or philosophy?"[14] From this question, Neusner went on to talk less about the uniqueness of Judaism and Jewish texts than about how such texts illumine larger civilizational questions:

> If the continuing theme of social science and humane letters is the nature of human experience, then Jewish studies represent the effort to recover and record experience in man's history which manifests few parallels and no precise duplicate. Judaism, viewed dispassionately and analytically, provides interesting examples of the continued interactions between ideas and men, religion and society, and history and culture, all of which interactions in varying forms deeply concern social scientists and humanists.[15]

For Neusner, Judaism represented a variation on the "classic paradigm of the tension between human freedom and creativity on the one hand, and cultural continuity and authority, represented by the inherited text on the other hand."[16] The tension between freedom and being bound by tradition leads to a creativity that informs human culture. Judaism, even the highly technical texts found in rabbinic literature, on Neusner's reading, needs to inform and be informed by much larger human questions. Whereas a previous generation of scholars had tried to downplay rabbinic literature due to either Reform or academic sensibilities, Neusner put such literature at the epicenter of human understanding.

In appreciating the tension between human freedom and inherited traditions, Neusner here proposed that we need to think not of an eternal and reified "Judaism," but of a set of overlapping, even antithetical, "Judaisms":

The pedagogical problem to be solved by Jewish scholars is, however, to reduce the complex disciplines of Jewish learning to a simple sequence and order. Jewish culture cannot be reduced to a geometry, of course, but it needs to be reduced to a history, or, more specifically, to a history-of-ideas. Approaching the history of Jewish civilization, one finds order and development only with great difficulty because there has never been such a thing as unitary and monolithic "Judaism," but rather "Judaisms," the Judaism of the prophets and the mystics, the Judaism of the rationalists, the Judaism of the lawyers, the Judaism of the moralists, the Judaism of the poets, the Judaism of the codifiers, the Judaism of the nationalists— and even the Judaism of the municipal authorities. All these constitute expressions of Jewish culture and all offer significant insight. The continuities of Judaism will emerge from study of their complexities; to reduce "Judaisms" to the "essentials of Judaism" yields something neither authentic nor even recognizable.[17]

This statement offers new ideas about understanding the complexity of Judaism—a set of overlapping Judaisms—that cannot be reduced to a basic narrative. The traditional way—the way that Neusner would have learned at JTS—to study Judaism was to focus on one specific text. This meant knowing it inside and out, producing, if necessary, a critical edition and translation, and then writing a commentary on it. It most certainly did not mean trying to contextualize texts within the broader currents of Western civilization. Neusner was here calling for a massive overhaul of how we think about and study Judaism, a way that was thematic, sequential, and interactive with the larger cultures in which Jews lived.

In this passage Neusner was among the first to speak of Judaism in the plural. This approach had the distinct advantage of permitting him to show that, although the texts of rabbinic Judaism looking from the hindsight of the present seemed to create a whole, when understood historically they often differed from one another on very significant points. Rather than speak of a unified and monolithic "rabbinic Judaism," Neusner here encouraged us to speak of "rabbinic Judaisms" that contested with one another. In addition to giving this lecture outlining his vision for the future of the study of Judaism, Neusner also created that same year a lecture series titled "Hebrew Studies and Western Civilization." The goal of the lecture series was twofold. First, he wanted to implement his vision by getting other scholars in the field on board. The second was to show his non-Jewish colleagues in the university that Judaism had a role to play in their respective disciplinary conversations. In his justification of the series, he wrote,

> While the Jews have lived in the West for two thousand years and have contributed considerably, both through the Scriptures and through their post-biblical literature and history, to the formation of that civilization, they have at the same time preserved another, quite different way of confronting reality. They have found a way to live within two civilizations. Their intellectual life has thus paralleled, shared in, and also diverged from the intellect and imagination of the West at different periods and in different aspects. They provide, therefore, an example of men whose millennial experience, like America's today, is one of continued cultural confrontation with other men and other viewpoints, of mediation between two civilizations in one world.[18]

Neusner sought to bring a number of well-known scholars to campus with the aim of showing his colleagues how and why Jewish data could fit within the contemporary university. Not only, he reasoned, would such a lecture series contribute to the intellectual program of the fledgling university, but it could also reveal how the study of Judaism would fit within the contemporary humanities. To this end, Neusner brought to Milwaukee in the spring semester of the academic year 1961–1962 several well-known scholars of Judaism. These were David Daube (Oxford), to speak on connections between Western and Jewish law, Arthur Cohen on philosophy, Ben Halperin (Brandeis) on social sciences, Arnold Band (UCLA) on literature, and Morton Smith (Columbia) on history.[19]

In order to fund the lecture series that he had already set up and for which he had already sent out invitations to the speakers, Neusner had to approach the president of the Wisconsin Society for Jewish Learning to secure a small grant to supplement what the university had allocated. The president consulted the Board of Trustees of the Society and reported back to Neusner that the lecture series could not proceed on the grounds that Neusner had not initially asked their permission to run it. The president of the Society also duly noted that the lecture titles did not sound particularly appealing. Most disturbing of all, at least to Neusner, was that the board was worried that if the Department of Hebrew Studies did too well, then non-Jews—both on- and off-campus—might get jealous. This was a variation on the age-old trope, "Would it (i.e., the lecture series) be good for the Jews?" The Society, in other words, was worried that Neusner was doing too much for Jewish studies; rather than try to integrate the study of Judaism successfully into the center of humanistic learning at the university, they wanted him to teach Hebrew as a service to the Jewish students on campus.[20]

Neusner ignored the Society, and instead secured funding for the series from the University of Wisconsin–Madison. The encounter with the Society encapsulated for him all that was wrong with "the Jewish Community" in America and what it considered Jewish studies to be. It also reflected the larger tensions endemic to the academic study of religion. The community wanted one thing, and the scholar whose position they financially supported at the university might want something different. That Neusner had ignored the warnings of the Society meant that he had now alienated himself from them, and they from him. Could they pull their money out from under his position?

Neusner believed that the local community saw his position as little more than a program assistant, assistant rabbi, and junior culture officer all rolled into one. He was to be another employee of the local Jewish Federation. This glorified Sunday school teacher, so common a description for those in both Jewish studies and religious studies more generally, was a role that Neusner sought to fight. Indeed, as we shall see in subsequent chapters, his relationship to local Jewish communities and their leadership would frequently be a source of irritation.

This dynamic so bothered Neusner that he decided to leave Milwaukee no matter what at the end of the academic year. This decision was solidified by the fact that the powers that be at the university did not take his scholarship seriously. The majority of his colleagues were people who had been around since the old Normal School days, who had little respect for publishing, and instead were happy with maintaining the status quo. That individuals could get ahead in the academy without engaging in scholarship would always prove to be a major frustration to Neusner. If his teachers at JTS formed one type of scholar that he would spend the rest of his career defining himself against, another type was the person who claimed to be a scholar based solely on his or her teaching record. Publishing scholars, according to Neusner, were always ostracized by their colleagues not only at places such as the University of Wisconsin–Milwaukee but also at Ivy League institutions such as Brown, where Neusner would eventually spend a good deal of his academic career.

When Neusner put in a request with the 1960s version of Inter Library Loan—a truck that ran weekly to the well-stocked Madison library—to bring back twenty-five to fifty volumes a week, he was refused. The reason that the director gave was that Neusner could not possibly read so many books in a week. The local synagogue, which did have a relatively large collection of Judaica including manuscripts, permitted him to take one book out a week for one week.[21] Neusner needed the books because, at the time, he was working on his multivolume *History of the Jews of Babylonia*, which aimed to situate the Jewish community of Babylonia at the time of the codification of the Babylonian Talmud in its immediate historical, linguistic, intellectual, and religious context. It was a daring project and, once again, reflects the topic of his inaugural lecture—if Judaism is to be properly understood in the context of the modern university, then it must be studied the way one would study any other topic therein.

Had Neusner remained in Milwaukee, who knows what would have happened. He certainly would not have had, despite his later complaints, the opportunities that were later afforded to him at research-intensive universities. During his job hunt after his position was not renewed at Columbia, he had also been offered a two-year postdoctoral appointment at the Lown Institute for Advanced Jewish Studies at Brandeis University. He had turned it down because he had secured the permanent position in Milwaukee; however, he now wrote to the head of the Lown Institute, Alexander Altmann, and asked if he could be re-offered the position. He received the offer and prepared to move back to the Cambridge area of Massachusetts at the end of the spring semester.

Ever the Reporter

While Neusner was engaged in the project of trying to redefine the academic study of Judaism in the American academy, he continued to write, and write profusely, not only in the *Ledger*, but also in other Jewish media. These included his publishing of reviews of pretty much every book that came out dealing with Jewish topics. In one such review, of Daniel J. Silver's *Maimonidean Criticism and the Maimonidean Controversy, 1180–1240* (1965), he wrote presciently, "[T]hat Rabbi Silver's book had to be published abroad indicates that there is as of yet no satisfactory domestic publisher, or audience, for serious Jewish scholarship. But that too will come."[22] And come it would when Neusner helped to create Scholars Press years later to make Jewish scholarship both available and affordable to American readers.

Neusner also continued to write numerous articles on the state of American Jewry. In an opinion piece titled "How Do You Make Good Jews?" that was syndicated as far away as the *Israelite Press* in Winnipeg, Canada, he wrote,

> How do you "manufacture" good Jews? There is only one way. It is not the
> way of ghettoization, of assuring that they will play basketball and swim

with other Jews only. No one wants to take that road. All of America is open before us. If we choose the Jewish path, it will not be because others are not available. It will be voluntarily, freely, because we find in Judaism a source of truth, of meaningful values, a guide to life's conduct, a way of preserving and adding to our patrimony.[23]

Similarly, in the following op-ed, titled "Meeting the Crisis of Today," he criticized, as he would frequently in the coming years, the lethargy of American Jewish leadership, who continued to respond to issues that the community had faced decades ago. "We spend millions," he wrote,

> every year on so-called "defense" activities, fighting a kind of anti-Semitism that no longer exists. We spend millions every year on institutions designed to Americanize us while most of us are so deeply engaged by American culture and society that we do not know how to preserve even a corner of our lives for Judaism and Jewish culture. We spend millions every year on a refuge for homeless Jews, and yet we have not found a home for the Jewish spirit. We spend millions every year on institutions of social welfare, and yet are the most affluent group in America.[24]

Rather than respond to the past, Neusner urged Jewish leaders to focus on the present and on how to connect a generation of college-educated and increasingly alienated young Jews with Judaism as a living religion as opposed to just, what he called appreciating their "Jewishness," that is, their ethnicity. These op-eds and reviews were always concise and well thought-out. Neusner was a master of taking larger issues and framing them in simple terms for all to understand. These pieces also established Neusner as an important public intellectual in the national Jewish media. He would spend the rest of his life writing for newspapers and magazines because, having worked as a journalist since he was an adolescent, he realized how to get his points across, not just in the academy, but also among the general reading public.

4

Finding His Way

Brandeis (1962–1964)

After the time in Milwaukee, occupying a position for which Neusner acknowledged in retrospect he was ill suited, Brandeis appeared heavenly. It was not so much the Lown Center for Advanced Jewish Studies that stimulated Neusner, but living again in Cambridge, just a short walk from Harvard Yard, where he was able to access the wonderful collection at Harvard's Widener Library and engage in pure research for two years without having to worry about either teaching or administrative duties. He had barely had access to a library in Milwaukee, and his arrival back to one of the major research libraries in America enabled him to take advantage of its rich Persian collection to complete his work on the Jews of Babylonia. The terms of his postdoctoral fellowship required only that Neusner meet with Alexander Altmann, a German-trained intellectual historian and the recently appointed director of the Lown Institute, once a year, and that he attend various lectures that the Institute sponsored. Neusner later described Altmann—one of the foremost scholars of Jewish thought and philosophy—as aloof, most likely due to the subject matter that Neusner was pursuing at the time.

In Cambridge, Neusner encountered three role models for what he considered to be a true scholar. The first was Richard N. Frye (1920–2014), the famed scholar of Persian and Central Asian studies. Neusner studied weekly with Frye, learning Farsi, Pahlavi, and Armenian. These languages were instrumental for his multivolume *A History of the Jews of Babylonia* (1965–1970). Whereas many scholars at the time were content to study works such as the Babylonian Talmud in a bubble, isolated from their immediate cultural milieus, Neusner pioneered a new way to understand these texts by connecting them to their immediate social, historical, and intellectual contexts. One could not be intellectually responsible, Neusner argued, by studying Jews as if they were a people apart, existing in isolation from non-Jews.

This approach, of course, had significant repercussions. If Neusner argued that we had to study the Jews of Iran within their immediate Persian environment, how could one possibly study, say, Maimonides—the great medieval thinker—without knowing Arabic and fully understanding the Islamic philosophical, theological, and religious environment in which he lived? At the heart of Neusner's new approach to understanding the larger contexts in which the Babylonian Talmud was produced is what it means to study Judaism. Neusner refused to make the Jews special or chosen. To him they represented but one social group trying to make sense of their immediate situation in light of a host of ideas and textual strategies developed in relation to other social groups. This intellectual framework clashed, however, with the traditional theological notion of Jewish "chosenness," which still makes its way into academic discussions. If Jews are the so-called chosen people and inherently unique, then they should be studied on their own terms rather than situating them within the larger civilizational currents in which they found themselves. Neusner, needless to say, had very little time for such arguments.

Frye's personality appealed to the still young and impressionable Neusner. Neusner found him refreshingly unpretentious and vigorously committed to his ideas, both of which were virtues that Neusner believed enabled him to create single-handedly the field of Iranian studies in America by establishing the first program devoted to Persian research at Harvard. Neusner appreciated Frye's large intellectual vision, his imagination, and his willingness to take risks in creating a new field of study. It was at this point that Neusner realized that he hoped to do something similar in the field of rabbinic studies, which would form the cornerstone of his rethinking of Jewish studies.[1] This new field needed to be rebuilt from the bottom up and ought not be beholden to the past, but based on new intellectual and curricular paradigms that drew from other disciplines in the humanities and social sciences. So impressed was Neusner by Frye that he dedicated the first volume of his *History of the Jews of Babylonia* to him, along with Morton Smith.[2]

The second person who left a mark on the impressionable Neusner was Erwin Ramsdell Goodenough (1893–1965), who had moved to Cambridge after his retirement from Yale in order to be closer to the Widener Library. Goodenough, a non-Jew, was a New Testament scholar by training, but was especially interested in Philo of Alexandria (d. 50 CE) and Hellenistic Judaism.[3] He taught at Yale from 1923 through 1962, and is primarily remembered for his massive thirteen-volume *Jewish Symbols in the Greco-Roman Period* (1953–1968). Therein, Goodenough collected what he considered to be all of the iconographic remains from the ancient and early late antique world, the so-called Greco-Roman period, with the aim of showing that, contrary to contemporaneous rabbinic accounts, popular Judaism was primarily interested in mysticism and salvation, two themes that were very common in the various mystery cults and religions of the period, including, of course, Christianity.

For Goodenough, the religious forms—texts, symbols, art—produced by Jews in the late antique period could be understood only within the context of the larger cultures in which Jews happened to find themselves. This was an argument, as we have just seen, that Neusner was starting to develop regarding the Jews of Iran. One of Goodenough's major theses was that popular Judaism in these early centuries largely rejected the authority of the "official" Judaism produced by the rabbis. Other scholars roundly attacked Goodenough for his reliance on Jungian interpretation of the artistic symbols in question and for his desire to remove the rabbis from "Greco-Roman" influence. Nevertheless, Goodenough's argument that scholars of the period had to take into consideration both text and context, in addition to the methodological problems of reconstructing these early periods, would prove both important and influential.[4]

It seems that Goodenough's approach—his ability to speak to other religionists working with other data sets from cognate religious traditions—for all its theoretical and hermeneutical shortcomings, was instrumental in subsequent efforts to get the study of Judaism taught in departments of religious studies in the 1960s and 1970s, a period that would see Neusner become one of the first appointees in such a department. Perhaps it was no coincidence that as Goodenough's vision of Jewish symbols, tied as they were to the then in-vogue Jungian archetypes, reached a large audience, Jewish studies began to draw new life in religious studies departments.

In their regular conversations Goodenough reinforced Neusner's claim, which he had begun to raise while at Milwaukee, that we should not simply assume that there existed a single and monolithic Judaism in the late antique period. Neusner increasingly began to speak of a plurality of mutually exclusive Judaisms. Neusner also appreciated the intellectual curiosity that drove Goodenough's work and the subsequent lucid presentation of his results.[5] Neusner remained friends with Goodenough from their first encounter in 1962 until the latter's death in 1965. They became so close that Goodenough even asked Neusner to be his literary executor. Although Neusner would later say that he disagreed with Goodenough's interpretive enterprise, he admitted that Goodenough's examination of the iconic sources represents his enduring legacy.[6] Days before he died, Goodenough asked Neusner to come visit him in the hospital, and thanked him for all that he had done, before saying good-bye. Only much later did Neusner learn that Goodenough had committed suicide rather than face a final battle with his cancer. After Goodenough's death, Neusner edited a Festschrift in his honor titled *Religions in Antiquity: Essays in Memory of Erwin Ramsdell Goodenough*.[7]

The third person with whom Neusner became close during these two years in Cambridge was Harry A. Wolfson, his former undergraduate advisor at Harvard. Neusner's relationship to Wolfson was more complex than his relationships to either Frye or Goodenough. Although they spoke regularly when Neusner was in Cambridge on the fellowship,

Neusner had several disagreements with Wolfson. Indeed it seems that when Neusner later left Cambridge for Dartmouth, Wolfson was not speaking to him because Neusner had not bothered to send him a copy of an article that he had written in which he disagreed with his former advisor. They subsequently reconciled, and Neusner would later drive to Cambridge from Dartmouth, and later Providence, every couple of months to spend time with both Wolfson and Frye. Neusner's relationship to Isaac Twersky, Wolfson's successor at Harvard in the Littauer Chair, was not nearly as productive. Neusner recalled that when, after finishing his dissertation at Columbia, he asked Twersky what he should do next, Twersky's main reply was that Neusner should begin studying Torah. He thought that Neusner, who was studying the Persian framework of the Bavli at the time, was wasting his time.[8]

Suzanne Richter

At the time that Neusner was finishing up his postdoc in Cambridge, he became reacquainted with Suzanne Richter, the daughter of Max Richter, a successful businessman from Paterson, New Jersey, and Mildred Rabinowitz Richter. Neusner had first met Suzanne, who was eight years his junior, at Camp Ramah—then located in Connecticut before its move to Palmer, Massachusetts, in the mid-1960s. As a young rabbinical student at JTS, Neusner went to Camp Ramah in the summer of 1955 to improve his Hebrew, work as a librarian, and teach a class on the biblical book of Jeremiah. Suzanne decided to buck the trend among her camp mates and take a class with Neusner instead of a class on Amos that all her friends were taking, taught by a young Yosef Hayim Yerushalmi, later a historian at Columbia.[9]

One of three students in Neusner's class, Suzanne thought Neusner a wonderful teacher, especially when compared to those who had taught her at home in Paterson. Proclaiming him the first good teacher she had ever had, she related how they were expected to memorize a lot of material and required to write a lot, preparing compositions, in both English and Hebrew, for each class. Neusner remarked that he was "enchanted" by the young student. Several years later, around 1960, "when the law no longer prohibited it" to use his words, they would spend time with one another. He was interested in getting married, but Suzanne at the time wanted to receive an education and continue with her art training. They went their separate ways, and after she received her education and traveled to Paris and Jerusalem,[10] she returned to Paterson to teach art in a local school. At this point her father, having read something that Neusner had published in a Jewish newspaper, telephoned him to ask if he was married yet. He replied that he was not, so Max Richter gave him Suzanne's phone number and said that she would very much like to hear from him.[11]

Neusner telephoned her that night. Two months later they were engaged, with their engagement announced in the Saturday, January 11, edition of the *New York Times*.[12] Neusner would commute every weekend from the Boston area to visit Suzanne in Paterson. They were married on March 15, 1964, and that summer moved to Norwich, Vermont, just across the river from Hanover, New Hampshire, where he would begin teaching at Dartmouth in the fall. They would go on to have four children: Samuel (in 1965), Eli (in 1967), Noam (in 1969), and Margalit (in 1973). Later came nine grandchildren (seven granddaughters and two grandsons). Neusner would go on to write several books with Noam, who subsequently became a speechwriter for President George W. Bush.[13]

Suzanne became the rock of the Neusner household. Neusner claimed that he never had any interest in cooking, cleaning, or shopping—indeed, when he was a bachelor, he would get by on cold cereal and, on special occasions, would make himself a hard-boiled egg—and frequently claimed that "Suzanne does it all." She was also an artist who would display and sell her work at various art fairs in the New England area and in Westchester County, New York. Much of her art—in a variety of media—employs traditional Jewish motifs.[14] Several reproductions graced the covers of Neusner's books.

Suzanne's family helped to support the young Neusners as they began their life together and started a family. By way of thanks, Jacob set up, in 1969, the Max Richter Foundation as a birthday present to his father-in-law. He funded it out of royalties from his books and meant it as a "way of returning to the field of Judaic studies income derived from colleagues," that is, those colleagues who bought his books. Neusner's aim was to help subsidize new books in ancient Judaism. When Max Richter died in 1973, he bequeathed a hundred thousand dollars to the Foundation, which would annually be supplemented by Neusner's royalties that he continued to reinvest into it. Neusner used the monies associated with the Foundation to offset the costs of his vision for re-creating a field of study. In a 1980 memo to the Foundation's Board, for example, Neusner, as its president, offered insight into how he used its by now quite sizeable resources:

> [G]rants have gone for the following purposes: publication of scholarly books, funds to support students in study in the State of Israel in preparation for study at Brown, funds to support Brown undergraduates in travel and study abroad and for other purposes; supplementary support for lectures and research projects in Judaic Studies at Brown and elsewhere (for example: a grant to help Dr. Norman Lamm prepare an English translation of his dissertation); supplementary support for graduate students at Brown and elsewhere; the Max Richter Publication Fund at Brown University; support for Brown Judaic Studies; the endowment of the Charles Berlin Fund at Harvard College Library; annual grants to help enlarge the *Journal of Jewish Studies* and occasional grants in support of other scholarly journals; support for publications in Studies in Judaism in Late Antiquity, Studies in Judaism in Modern Times, and similar projects. There is a regular and systematic grant program in projects in industrial medicine and public health in the State of Israel, including medical education and research in the field of public health at Hadassah Medical School of the Hebrew University. In 1981

the Foundation will support a conference on "Jewish Studies and the humanities" at Brandeis University, and in 1982 on "the concept of tradition in religions" at the University of Rochester. In 1982 the Foundation will provide $15,000 for the publication of the Yigael Yadin Festschrift as the 1982 volume of the *Journal of Jewish Studies*. There also have been regular, and sizable, grants to local religious and philanthropic activities of the Jewish community of Jerusalem, and grants have gone to certain Israeli projects of the same character.[15]

Funds associated with the Max Richter Foundation enabled Neusner to accomplish a lot. Most importantly they provided him the financial freedom to proceed as he saw fit and without having to worry about colleagues who disagreed with him. Though he subsequently fell out with many in the field, he was always able to do what he wanted, when he wanted, and for whom he wanted. For example, he hosted annual workshops at Brown (e.g., "The Max Richter Conversation on Ancient Judaism"), and at other universities, such as Brandeis, he organized conferences with titles such as "Judaic Studies and the University."[16] The Foundation also permitted him to fund his students and send them for language training in Israel, and to create almost single-handedly the European Association for Jewish Studies (EAJS), to this day the largest organization in Europe devoted to the academic study of Judaism. It also helped him to contribute to the creation of Scholars Press, which he would use as an important venue to disseminate his and his students' work. The Max Richter Foundation, in sum, enabled Neusner to have a much larger impact than he would otherwise have had simply as a publishing scholar. As time went on, the Foundation would be regularly supplemented by funds from wealthy benefactors who believed in Neusner's vision and from book royalties that were reinvested. Neusner closed the Max Richter Foundation in 2008, giving the remaining funds to the Institute for Advanced Theology at Bard College, where he later moved, to support programming and other projects in Judaism.[17]

The Discipline of Writing

As we have seen, Neusner wrote copiously. His CV lists over one thousand books yet includes neither articles nor book chapters, nor lists the countless newspaper articles and op-eds that he composed over the years. His productivity is staggering. I once asked him point-blank, "Did you ever think you wrote too much?" His response: "I do not understand your question."[18] He was always criticized for writing too much, however. How, one might ask, did Neusner do it?[19] As we have seen, Neusner spent his life, starting at a very young age at his father's paper, with words. He could express himself effortlessly in written prose. He knew how to type, and type quickly. But this tells only part of the story. Just as important was his work ethic and tremendous sense of discipline. "Graduate students are working people," he once remarked in an interview. "I am a working man like any other working man. I get paid to do my work. I don't ask my students to do anything I don't do. The first thing you learn as an adult is that you do your job before anything else."[20] He wrote every day for a set amount of time. As someone who wrote so much, not just academically but also journalistically, Neusner worked nonstop. In what seems like an impromptu letter sent to "Mrs. Neusner," the late Cairo Geniza scholar, Shlomo Dov Goitein, wrote, "Restrain this overflow of energy. We have seen too many of our younger friends doing this in their late thirties and they break down in their fifties and even forties. Jack has already done a lifetime's work. Do not permit him to waste away that wonderful creative élan."[21]

In a letter to Ithamar Gruenwald, Neusner explained his daily routine:

> I get up around 4:30–5 a.m. and am at my desk a half hour later, I find the morning hours the best for composing new thoughts; later in the day I can read or write essays or whatever, but my most original and taxing & rigorous thought takes place before sunrise. I generally fall asleep by 9 p.m., without really trying; I just drift off, so getting up early is easy enough; if something is on my mind toward bedtime, if I'm thinking

about some problem, it will occupy my sleep and by the hour before I wake up, I will be meditating on that; when I get up the paragraph or chapter is then pretty much written out and I have only to transcribe it.[22]

As his former graduate students note, though, they could not call him except at a fixed time. He worked from five to eight o'clock in the morning, and he accepted calls at eight precisely, not seven forty-five or eight twenty, and would budget fifteen minutes for phone calls. He would teach only in the afternoons because that was when he was tired, though he never worried about falling asleep during a lecture. Although as Alan Avery-Peck, a former grad student, remembers, Neusner would call him at seven o'clock every morning because he was worried that Avery-Peck was not getting up early enough to work. Neusner once remarked that "you don't do a lot in any one day. But if you work 365 days a year you get an awful lot done."[23]

Writing years later to a colleague at the University of South Florida who had called an impromptu department meeting, Neusner explained that he could not attend because

my work is planned over time and has its own rhythm, through seven day weeks. If I lose a day of work, it takes me two days to get back into the discipline; it involves long-term repetitions of the same analytical mode, yielding results only when the same thing is done again and again. If I work everyday I keep up the pace. When the pace breaks, I have to start thinking over every little thing.[24]

In an interview with William Novak for *New Traditions*, Neusner claimed that what also made him such a prolific writer was his ability to compose in his mind. "I write in my head before putting it on paper," he said, comparing himself to Mozart. "I'll work on an essay for months in my head. When I go to write it, I just put it down on paper as fast as I can type."[25]

Yet, even when Neusner was at the height of his publication activities, according to Suzanne, he was not a "workaholic." That said, a quotation from the preface to Part 20 of his massive *A History of the Mishnaic Law of Purities*, written on July 28, 1976, on the occasion of his forty-fourth birthday, gives us some sense of how he worked and conceived of his task:

> The work imposed its own rhythm. There have been no Sabbaths or festivals, no days or nights. Once a tractate came into view, I could not allow it to pass from mind, since breaking the train of thought would enter all possibility of entering into the problematic and logic of the law. By the end I knew, because I had to know, the whole tractate by heart. I did not undertake the center of the conceptual inquiry into the problematic of a tractate, "the weaving of the law," until I could recite each pericope of Mishnah from memory. At no point have I conceived that I have penetrated to the ultimate depths of a pericope, let alone of a chapter or a tractate. At each I did what I could, and, as I said, for the particular purpose defined at the very beginning.[26]

Suzanne claimed that Neusner worked very hard, but always knew how to relax a little each day. He worked in his own study, swam, took a nap, and often stopped work after dinner. One of his keys to success, and this is verified by his students, was the fact that he was a phenomenally accurate and very fast typist. Alan Avery-Peck, the former graduate student, remarked that when he needed a letter of recommendation, Neusner would tell him to come to his office two minutes before their graduate seminar; he would then put a piece of paper into the typewriter and within a minute produce a cogent letter free of any errors. One of the main ways in which Neusner relaxed was through exercise, particularly swimming, before lunch. He would then go to the office on teaching days, lead the class, and then work a few more hours before returning home. After dinner, he might do a little more work before stopping and then would watch television with his family before falling asleep around nine o'clock.[27]

Writing to Larry Tisch many years later, Neusner remarked, "I was so puzzled by your surprise at my writing a chapter a day (which always seemed to me rather routine) that I decided to see for myself; so I wrote the enclosed chapter of my new book in one day; when that was done, I rewrote it twice; I also then outlined the whole book, and at the end of the day ran it by my editor at Doubleday, who loved the result. So, yes, it really is routine."[28]

Fellowship in Judaism (1963)

Neusner always had an uncanny ability to write works unconnected to rabbinic Judaism, his main area of study and research. Within this context, he composed a small book in 1963 titled *Fellowship in Judaism: The First Century and Today*. The book's goal was, as he makes clear in its foreword, to examine the "Pharisaic emphasis on the study of Torah," and the "implications of first-century Jewish religious fellowship for contemporary Judaism." While we need not delve into his detailed analysis of fellowship among the Pharisees, a sectarian movement in the Second Temple period and the predecessors to what would emerge as rabbis, it is worth pointing out that his analysis of Jewish fellowship in the modern period was one of the earliest calls for what would emerge only in the late 1960s as the "havurah movement." This movement witnessed rabbis, academics, and political activists create grassroots groups for prayer and study to combat what they considered to be an over-institutionalized and unspiritual Jewish establishment. Given the realities of secularism and the bureaucratic nature of the modern synagogue with its cold and impersonal services, Neusner wrote that it "is no wonder, then, that the Jewish community seems desiccated and colorless by contrast to that of earlier centuries."[29] Such remarks, again, reflected his major criticism of contemporary American Jews: they have very little to cling to except outmoded concepts such as an identity based on another time (the Holocaust) and another place (Israel). Neusner's response to this dilemma—here and in so many of his other writings—was to create a renaissance of Jewish life in America by getting Jews to learn and study the texts of Judaism instead of holding on to sophomoric stories. Neusner blamed the institutionalization and subsequent dissemination of such stories—chosenness, treating myths as history, anti-Semitism—on the Jewish establishment, with whom he clashed almost as regularly as he did with his colleagues in Jewish studies.

In the place of community, Neusner continued, we have a loose collection of communities that define themselves by, alternatively, ethnicity, country club or resort membership, or synagogue attendance. But in all of these "communities," there is no sense of belonging, no real connections to the types of piety that had sustained Judaism over its lengthy and rich history. Instead what we have is the modern synagogue that, Neusner claimed, failed to create an organic sense of community on fundamental levels. Neusner went on to ask some basic questions of the American iteration of this ancient institution:

> What place, in truth, does the synagogue have in the social life of its members? For some few, it is the place where they sometimes go to pray; for some others, it is the instrument for the transmission of the rudiments of Judaism to the young (and that not very effectively); for others it may provide the framework for certain recreational activities. In synagogues of more than a few dozen families, it is even possible for all members not to know one another, and in larger places, it is even possible for the rabbi not to know each member of his "flock." Whatever the synagogue ought to be, it is very rarely a community or a religious fellowship. The various lodges and chapters and posts (their name is legion) usually consist of a small number of activists, and a long mailing list.[30]

The question before the organized Jewish community, Neusner argued, is how to create meaningful community and avoid the reality of so much modern institutional life where strangers meet strangers, and still remain strangers to one another. Neusner suggested that one of the ways to energize contemporary American Jewish life was to look back to the first century of the Common Era, which saw the establishment of the havurah. This is not to be confused with simple friendship, but rather is a fellowship involving two or more people and an ideal held in common. Gathering in fellowship, Neusner concluded, was intended to "meet very humble problems of social and personal conduct by directing the attention of perplexed men to higher purposes that they may achieve together."[31]

Neusner was truly revolutionary here, and his thinking was really at the forefront of what would emerge, by the end of the decade, as a movement within Judaism to create or re-create this type of fellowship. Most *havurot* in America had their origins in the North American countercultural trends of the late 1960s and early 1970s. During this period, groups of young rabbis, academics, and political activists founded experimental *havurot* to find meaning over and above or distinct from mainstream synagogue life. Like Neusner, such activists turned to the pietistic fellowship practiced by the likes of the Pharisees. Neusner's short *Fellowship in Judaism*, then, needs to be seen as having a not insignificant influence on the rise of the havurah movement, an impetus that would gradually flow into Jewish Renewal in the contemporary period.[32]

This is not to claim that Neusner was the architect behind the havurah movement in America of the 1960s. But his work on this topic anticipated a need that many American Jews felt at the time. Here, it is worth underscoring that it was his work as a journalist that really enabled him to gain a firm grasp of the needs, wishes, and shortcomings of American Jews. Books like *Fellowship in Judaism* afford a sense of how his two careers—scholar and journalist—overlapped and cross-pollinated. Also worth noting is that, as far as I am aware, Neusner was never part of a havurah, unless of course we characterize his graduate seminars at Brown as one.

History of the Jews of Babylonia (1965–1970)

During his postdoc at Brandeis, Neusner continued to work on his five-volume *A History of the Jews of Babylonia*. In the first volume, he set forth the aim of the project: to "begin the task of writing a history of the Jews in Babylonia under the Arsacid and Sasanid empires."[33] This was an ambitious project because so much work on formative Judaism—that is, the period that witnessed, among other things, the codification of the Babylonian Talmud, or Bavli—until this time had been insular, all but ignoring the larger cultural and intellectual contexts of its production. Yet, for Neusner, this project nevertheless remained a part of his "pre-critical" phase, when he was using, by his own reckoning, traditional models of historical research that assumed he could use sources to re-create accurately the time period in question. As he wrote in the preface to volume 2, dedicated to his new wife Suzanne, and devoted to the early Sasanian period (third to fifth centuries CE), his focus was on Rav and Samuel, and his "effort is to provide more than a joint biography of these two important men, but rather, through a study of their sayings and those of their adult contemporaries, to recover some clear, sequential, and well-organized ideas about the history of Babylonian Jewry and Judaism in this age."[34] Although he acknowledged that many of his sources were edited much later (as many as two and a half centuries later), he nonetheless proceeded as if the words of these later recensions accurately reflected the views of those purported to have said them.

Despite his own later reservations, Neusner succeeded in this five-volume work in opening up the study of late antique Babylonian Jewry and, especially, its most important document, the Babylonian Talmud. Rather than just look at internal evidence, Neusner also surveyed Iranian and Christian sources in addition to archaeological evidence. Furthermore, Neusner also moved Talmudic history forward in time. Traditional histories stopped around 500 CE, when it was assumed that the Babylonian Talmud had been completed. By linking the Babylonian Jewish community to Iranian history, Neusner succeeded in connecting parochial Jewish concerns to much larger historical and sociological trends.

The second printing of the first volume also saw him thank his critics of the first volume for pointing out inaccuracies, and assure his readers that he had taken account of critical reviews. Indeed, this would be a trait of virtually all of his publications: redoing them or printing second (or even third and fourth) editions of works in light of criticism. "I take my critics more seriously," he once told me, "than they take themselves."[35] It is in the prefaces to his various books, especially later in his career, where he could be the most scathing and uncensored in dealing with those whose criticism he disagreed with, or with various institutions of which he was critical. When he had left Brown, for example, he would often expatiate in these prefaces about how bad his working conditions were (even though in his prefaces from earlier publications he would say how good they were) and that his new conditions at South Florida were the best that he had ever enjoyed.

Dartmouth (1964–1968)

As Neusner's postdoc wound down, he had to seek employment. Luckily in the early autumn of 1963, he received a call from Fred Berthold, the chair of the Department of Religion at Dartmouth College. He went to Hanover to discuss a possible appointment and at the same time received an offer for a one-year appointment at Brown University in Providence, Rhode Island. Although the position at Brown offered more money, it was unclear what would happen after the academic year had ended. So Neusner chose to take the offer at Dartmouth. This would turn out to be a very significant move for the future of his intellectual development. At Dartmouth at that time were Hans Penner and Jonathan Z. Smith, two individuals who were trying to create new, more naturalistic and analytical, paradigms for the academic study of religion that would replace the more theological discourses so prevalent at the time.

Hans Penner was a student of the then doyen of religious studies in America, Mircea Eliade (1907–1986). A Rumanian émigré, Eliade taught in the Divinity School at the University of Chicago and was responsible for training a generation of religionists in this country and beyond. Whereas Eliade stressed the experiential dimension of religion and the fact that numerous religious events in different cultures were structurally or morphologically similar, Penner challenged this by arguing that Eliade used an essentialist framework. Neusner's relationship with Penner was, as it was with most people, contentious or, for lack of a better term, on-again and off-again. Neusner recalled that Penner was uncomfortable with him when he first came to Dartmouth because Neusner had already published a lot and Penner hardly at all. At a departmental colloquium in his first year that included, among others, Smith in addition to the New Testament scholar Wayne Meeks, Neusner presented a paper on his current work. Penner asked him in front of the others why he was in a religion department, and accused him of being a historian rather than a religionist. Offended by the comments, Neusner nevertheless took the challenge very seriously. Although he suspected that professional jealousy precipitated the harshness of the challenge, it is at this point that we can begin to notice a shift in his own intellectual efforts. Whereas previous to this public critique his work tended to be rather traditional and descriptive, afterward we encounter a much more analytic and interpretive method. Neusner referred to this event as the "turning point" in his career, marking the beginning of his "critical" phase of scholarship. He later referred to that which went before this shift, as we have seen, as his "pre-critical" phase. Much of the rest of his career was a response to Penner's challenge by showing not only why, but also how, the study of Jewish data could simultaneously illumine and be illumined by the categories supplied by the academic study of religion.[36] It is only at this point in his career that we can begin to define Neusner as a scholar of religion.

Another important colleague was Jonathan Z. Smith, today one of the most influential names in the academic study of religion. Even back then Neusner said of Smith, "he was able to teach us things we didn't know possible in the field of religion." Smith was, like Penner, also critical of Eliade, and instead of positing a structure based on the morphology of the sacred, he stressed the cultural aspect of religion. Rather than look for an essence that underscores all religions, Smith advocated looking for difference. For Smith, scholarship is always an act of choice, selection, and focus rather than an exercise in interpreting timeless meanings in texts or symbols that are assumed to exist in a vacuum.[37]

Neusner first met Smith in the summer of 1958 when the latter was attending summer school at Columbia. Someone in the Religion Department introduced them, thinking they would have much in common with one another. Indeed, they would both go on to work on similar data sets, religion in antiquity—Smith working on Christian origins and Neusner on rabbinics. Smith's first job was at Dartmouth when, in the year 1965–1966, he served as an instructor for a faculty member on leave. This position enabled Smith to renew his friendship with Neusner, in addition to meeting Hans Penner for the first time. This time, according to Smith, was magical: "our association was the first opportunity I had to talk about the field with an individual rather than with a book. And talk we did . . . for hours each day. Whatever growing sense of security I felt as a neophyte in the history of religions I owe to these conversations."[38]

Neusner and Smith would become exceedingly close over the years, and the types of questions that both asked were remarkably similar to one another.[39] Like Smith, Neusner was not a grand theoretician of religion. Both were interested in difference and incongruity, and how these two features enabled various social groups—in Neusner's case, the ancient sages or rabbis—to make sense of the social worlds that they inhabited. Neusner would subsequently focus on the social construction of religion without making appeals to divine causation or some essence that various religious expressions are believed to manifest. In this respect, he was interested not in the origins of religion or even the origins of Judaism, but in how the chaotic social situation created by the destruction of the Second Temple in 70 CE led to a series of conditions that ultimately produced a set of documents that tried to make sense of life in the absence of that Temple. Neusner was not a comparative religionist interested in making a set of superficial comparisons between religions that he did not know particularly well. He was, however, interested in how certain questions generated by other scholars of religion illumined

Jewish data and how his Jewish data, when understood in a particular way, could expand our understanding of these larger questions. Neusner, then, knew one tradition very well, and all of his generalizations about religion came out of a very specific body of literature.

Like any good religionist, Neusner was intent to show how his data exemplified larger questions. If we were to encapsulate Neusner's theory of religion, it would be to show how rabbinic Judaism provides us with an example of human ingenuity and creativity in the midst of social change. It is within this context that Neusner demonstrated how rabbinic Judaism was able to create a social world that sought stability in the past as it simultaneously faced an uncertain future. In making Judaism exemplary of larger issues, Neusner transformed this religious tradition into part of the mainstream of religious studies in this country. He created connections between the academic study of Judaism and that of other religions and, in the process, showed how Judaism could shed light on intellectual and analytical problems raised within the academic study of religion. Neusner's main contribution was his focus on religions as "systems." This meant that analysis between religions, or even within a religion, could not take place on the level of ad hoc comparisons. Such comparisons lead to analyses where "x" in one religion is like "y" in another. Instead, Neusner argued that work on religion—and, by extension, comparisons between religions—had to be comprehensive, taking into consideration the interrelationships between worldview, way of life, and the view of the social order. The study of religion is accordingly a secular and this-worldly study. It is about understanding the social worlds that communities create for themselves and attempting to explain the relationship between such worlds and the ideas that they hold. Much of this conceptualization Neusner articulated in conversation with Smith at a formative moment in his career and then continuously throughout that career.

Although Smith and Neusner would remain close over the years, they would eventually have a falling out when Smith, at least from Neusner's perspective, refused to come to his defense when, in 1984, graduate students at the University of Chicago invited Neusner to give a series of lectures there, but then did not follow through with the planning, with the result that his visit was cancelled. Neusner was so inflamed by the incident that he even wrote to the then president of the university, Hanna Holborn Gray, threatening to give back his honorary doctorate unless he was reimbursed for his expenses. Neusner, for some reason, thought that Smith would come to his defense, even though Smith had very little to do with the Divinity School at that time, having largely moved his position to the Undergraduate College.[40] The tension in their relationship was perhaps exacerbated by the fact that Smith, unlike Neusner, was not an avid letter writer. Neusner would also fault Smith for being an essayist as opposed to writing full-length manuscripts. Writing to Smith in 1991, after the imbroglio at Chicago had been settled, Neusner tried to criticize constructively Smith's recently published *Drudgery Divine*:

> I think what you need to do is write one sustained, well unpacked and carefully expressed statement on this problem of comparison and its logic, which has long interested you; that will be an important contribution to the work of many others. Right now your ideas are scattered in many essays, and my sense is, you have yet to hold it all together. It can be your enduring statement.[41]

Smith, in turn, was critical of Neusner for writing too much and not reading enough. Smith was invited to take part in a panel that was organized at the 2012 annual meeting of the American Academy of Religion in Chicago to celebrate and assess Neusner's lengthy career in Judaica. Smith, however, failed to appear. Although it seems that he was ill, no word of apology or excuse was forthcoming. Neusner later admitted to me that he was tremendously disappointed.[42]

Another important colleague at Dartmouth was Wayne Meeks, a well-known scholar of the New Testament and Christian origins, who subsequently moved to Yale University. Meeks's work in Christian origins, in addition to the work of Brevard Childs in the Old Testament, introduced Neusner to the historical and formal criticism of ancient texts, an approach that he would soon adopt and adapt to the study of rabbinic texts. Neusner first encountered Childs when the latter had come to the JTS summer program in 1958 and 1959, when he was an assistant professor at Yale Divinity School. It was he who asked Neusner, after the appearance of *Life of Yohanan ben Zakkai*, "Is it possible that you are doing history too soon, and might you be asking the wrong questions?"[43]

Another person whom Neusner would meet at Dartmouth was the young undergraduate student William Scott Green. Green would subsequently follow Neusner to Brown, where he would be among his first graduate students. He would go on to hold the Phillip S. Bernstein Chair at the University of Rochester, in addition to becoming the dean of the college and then eventually moving to the University of Miami to become the senior vice provost and dean of undergraduate education. Green would become a principal collaborator with Neusner on numerous publications, and an editor of Neusner's Brown Judaic Studies and later South Florida Studies on the History of Judaism, in addition to becoming a lifelong friend and confidant, often speaking to Neusner daily on the phone.[44]

The Turn: Yohanan ben Zakkai Revisited

The period at Dartmouth is perhaps best summarized by Penner's challenge and the resultant change in Neusner's scholarly profile. Perhaps this new approach is most clearly on display in the second, revised edition to his *Life of Yohanan Ben Zakkai*. In this new edition Neusner repudiated the approach and conclusions taken in the original work as "merely conjectural, subjective, and . . . probably in the main anachronistic."[45] This repudiation, of course, also functioned as a repudiation of those he worked with at JTS. In the new edition, for example, he dropped the thank-you to Saul Lieberman in the preface. He did, however, keep the very favorable acknowledgment to his teacher, Morton Smith.[46]

In addition to the second edition of his first book, Neusner also published another work on Yohanan ben Zakkai, titled *Development of a Legend: Studies on the Traditions Concerning Yohanan ben Zakkai*, published in 1970, the same year as the second revised version of the biography appeared. Although these works came out when he was at Brown, he completed both while still at Dartmouth. This new work further signaled a change in his scholarly focus, from recounting the supposed "actual" life of ben Zakkai, something that could be done only based on much later sources, to now being critical of these sources in the first place. Neusner, in other words, began to realize that the sources he had taken as reliable in his first books were anything but. Instead, he now regarded them as the product of later times and places, and, thus, as extremely problematic in terms of any type of accurate reconstruction. This stance not only reflected the repudiation of his earlier scholarly endeavors, but was tantamount to criticism of the entire discipline as practiced up until this point. His new approach to rabbinic sources now put him at odds with the dominant paradigm of scholarship at both JTS and in Israel.

If *A Life of Yohanan ben Zakkai* claimed to describe the content of Yohanan ben Zakkai's life, the *Development of a Legend* sought to examine the various traditions that made the formation of this life possible in the first place. In the preface, Neusner wrote that

> I do not suppose we can come to a final and positive assessment of the historicity of various stories and sayings. We surely cannot declare a narrative to be historically reliable simply because it contains no improbabilities or merely because some details are accurate. We must not confuse verisimilitude with authenticity. At best we may reach a comprehensive and critical estimate of what we know about Yohanan ben Zakkai than was available earlier.[47]

Neusner had in mind the form and redaction criticism found in New Testament scholarship, especially the ways in which such criticism reveals how biographical materials are shaped by the process of subsequent traditions. That is, a particular individual might not actually have said what later tradition ascribes to him. So the question must become, why and how was such a phrase put in the mouth of, for example, Yohanan ben Zakkai? In a later volume titled *Rabbinic Judaism: Structure and System*, Neusner makes clear to the reader, in his typical pugnacious manner, what he thought was new in his oeuvre beginning with *Development of a Legend*:

> And what if, further, we no longer assume the inerrancy of the oral Torah's writings? In Jerusalem they say we are required to accept as historical fact whatever the stories say, unless we have reason to reject it. In Tel Aviv they maintain that attributions are sacrosanct, arguing, "If it were not true, why should the sages have assigned a saying to a given authority?" In Ramat Gan, at Bar Ilan University, professors have been known to argue with a perfectly straight face, "Do you really think our holy rabbis would lie?" So the proposed premise set forth in [my] rubric should be regarded as revolutionary, even though in all other fields of humanistic learning it has lost all novelty.[48]

Leaving Dartmouth

Neusner's experiences at Dartmouth were very positive. He would always look back at his time there fondly, especially when compared to his experiences at Brown. It is safe to say that Dartmouth ingrained in him the difference between religious studies scholarship and that which passed for scholarship in the quasi-seminary model of Jewish studies. The individuals he encountered at Dartmouth—Hans Penner, Jonathan Z. Smith, Wayne Meeks, and Fred Berthold—were veritable powerhouses in the field. From Penner, he took the challenge to make his work more amenable to the types of questions asked by students of religion; from Smith, he learned the theoretical language of religious studies; from Meeks, he learned the type of critical scholarship being carried out in New Testament scholarship; and from Berthold, he gained a style of teaching that was much more dynamic and Socratic than what he himself had experienced as either an undergraduate or graduate student.

Although he certainly was aware of the academic study of religion from his days as a graduate student in the Department of Religion at Columbia, there was really no one at that institution interested in the types of questions being posed by the likes of Penner and Smith at Dartmouth. While Meeks certainly asked some of the questions that Morton Smith had, he did so in a much different way.

Neusner's primary impetus for leaving Dartmouth had nothing to do with the intellectual climate, but everything to do with personal reasons. The greater Hanover area offered very little in the way of Jewish education or Jewish life for a young Jewish family. There was, for example, neither a synagogue nor a Jewish day school. The Neusners were living in Norwich, Vermont, just over the river from Hanover and with very few prospects for bringing their children up with any positive Jewish identity. Neusner did not want his kids to grow up like him, where Judaism was something private and internal that could easily be subsumed when encountering the larger non-Jewish world. In typical fashion, Neusner did what he always did—he wrote about it. In an opinion article titled "The Scandal of the Jewish College Student," for example, he wrote,

> The scandal of the Jewish college student is that he is not perceptibly different from his gentile friends and colleagues. As Rabbi Arthur Hertzberg pointed out (in *The Jewish Frontier*), American Jewry has en masse decided that being Jewish will not be a very different experience for the Jew from what being a Methodist is for the Methodist. The result is that the Jewish student studies as little, drinks as much, and finds no easier the sexuality and personality adjustment required of him than his non-Jewish classmates.[49]

Neusner blamed the Jewish establishment for ignoring what happens to Jews when they go away to college. Rather than give money to the

Hebrew University of Jerusalem or the Technion in Israel, Neusner argued that American Jews ought to support the establishment of Jewish studies in American universities. The way to do this, he suggests in the above article, is to provide the funds for "professorships of Jewish studies in colleges and universities, for providing adequate Judaica libraries, for the support of Jewish scholarly research and publication." While today this kind of philanthropy is largely taken for granted, in the early 1960s it was certainly novel. In drawing attention to this paradox at such an early period in the development of the study of Judaism in this country, Neusner saw clearly what was necessary.

Note that Neusner was not calling for an ethnic enclave or ghetto where Jewish studies was designed to make Jewish students (and their non-Jewish friends) feel good about themselves, their Jewishness, or the State of Israel. Nor was he calling for a revamped Jewish Semitics taught by local rabbis. Rather, he was calling for an academically rigorous study of Jewish texts using the larger questions supplied by the academic study of religion. Writing years later to his colleagues at Brown in a memo, he wrote,

> This emphasis upon ethnic studies, characteristic of the larger part of Jewish studies in this country, which we have avoided at Brown in our department, cheapens and diminishes the human achievement of the Jewish people. . . . Now in doing things the way we have—in insisting that the study of Judaism is part of the disciplinary framework of discourse, in insisting that "non-Jews" as much as Jews have much to perceive, therefore to learn and to teach, in insisting that teaching and scholarship be based not on sentiment but on demonstrated learning—we have fought a difficult battle.[50]

Neusner took his role as critic very seriously. He was always critical, for example, of the lack of education found among Jewish students he encountered at Dartmouth, and then at Brown. "Their Jewish education is abominable," he wrote in an op-ed in the *Ledger*, their "Jewish experiences, if any, are generally shallow and irrelevant to their real interests and needs. Their Jewish social experiences have done little if anything to raise their sights or ennoble their minds."[51] Constantly, in the pages of the *Ledger* and in other Jewish media, he wrote on the ignorance of American Jews, the ostrich-like quality of American Jewish leaders, the abysmal state of Jewish education, the problems besetting JTS, and so on. In another op-ed in the *Ledger*, titled "Criticism and the Community," Neusner offered insight into his rationale for such a sustained critique:

> The best way to insure that we shall stagnate, and inevitably decline, as a Jewish community is to ignore criticism and to attack the critic. . . . Yet that is mostly what we do today. When honest and informed criticism is offered of Jewish communal practices, the most common reaction of the leadership of the Jewish communities is to ignore the criticism but to pounce upon the critic. . . . But if criticism is taken seriously, whether wrong or right, it may prove to be an occasion for serious reflection on what we do and why, and for the discovery of new and perhaps better ways to pursue communal affairs.[52]

* * *

In March 1967, Neusner accepted a position as associate professor at Brown University, in Providence, Rhode Island, a community that had a significantly larger Jewish population than Norwich.[53] Brown would not only enable him to create a new vision for what Jewish studies should represent to the larger academy, but also give him the institutional wherewithal for putting this vision into place.

5

Institutional Acceptance

At the same time that Neusner was preparing to leave Dartmouth for Brown, Jewish studies was slowly beginning to emerge on college campuses. The debate now was less over whether or not postbiblical Judaism should be taught on campus, but how and where it should be taught. Jewish studies programs would soon proliferate in public and private universities, again largely with the support of Jewish donors. This growth seems to have mirrored the increasing economic prosperity of American Jews and their swelling ethnic pride, something that was certainly boosted by Israel's swift victory in the 1967 Six-Day War. The funding of Jewish studies professorships and programs, it was hoped by donors, would create a positive space on campus where young Jews could come to learn about themselves and their history. The risk, as Neusner realized very early, was that such programs could quickly become a forum for little more than ethnic appreciation. This rise of Jewish studies was certainly enhanced by the emergence of "area studies" in American higher education. Such programs offered a new interdisciplinary way of organizing accumulated knowledge outside of the traditional disciplines, and focused specifically on the cultures and viewpoints of ethnic minorities that had been previously excluded or marginalized. Other such programs that came into existence at around the same time included black studies and women's studies.

In the aftermath of the *School District of Abington Township, Pennsylvania v. Schempp* Supreme Court case, which saw the lifting of First Amendment restrictions concerning teaching about religion in public institutions, religious studies departments quickly became established in public universities.[1] Such departments offered a comparative study of world religions, in places where the teaching of religion was previously forbidden. Although this model certainly exhibited a Protestant bias, there was nevertheless a desire to study and present other religions of the globe to American undergraduates.[2] Judaism now became an important part of this curriculum, where it would largely be conceptualized and taught, as it continues to be in the present.[3] Whereas some relished the thought of studying and comparing Judaism to other religions, others instead argued that Judaism needed to be studied on its own terms and using its own frames of reference based on internal criteria. What, in other words, is the best way to study Judaism in the secular university? If the issue before had been whether or not Judaism even belonged in the university, it now shifted to how it should be studied in this new context.

Many newly created Jewish studies programs often functioned less as a place of objective scholarship and learning, and more as definers of positive identity for Jewish students on campus. The result is that it was, and indeed still often is, difficult to know where Hillel ends and where Jewish studies begins. Jewish studies, in hands other than Neusner's, could quickly become a place that celebrates Jewish contributions to Western civilization as opposed to being a scholarly unit that undertakes critical investigations of Jewish data. If many of his previous years had witnessed him try to make the study of Judaism acceptable in the eyes of non-Jews (e.g., students, administrators, colleagues), Neusner now feared that it risked becoming an ethnic enclave entrenched in identity politics.[4]

Neusner always wanted the study of Judaism to take place within the parameters of religious studies. He was opposed to the program model even though, paradoxically, Jewish studies would end up as a program at Brown. This, however, had more to do with Neusner's personality and many interpersonal conflicts he had there than with anything intellectual. In a series of popular articles published in the *Jewish Advocate* of Boston in the winter of 1968, titled "Reflections on Jewish Studies in Universities," Neusner reflected on the place of Jewish studies in higher education as he was preparing to take up his new position at Brown.

He begins by noting that the university is "the most recent, and at present important, setting for the enterprise of the Jewish intellect."[5] He is particularly attracted to how the study of Judaism can inform and be informed by the academic study of religion. He expatiates on this for his general readership:

> For example, taken in isolation, the rabbinical academy may be studied from antiquity to the present day, but without a significant awareness of what it really was, or what gave it its particular shape or method at a given time or place. When, however, one asks how the rabbinical school compared to the Hellenistic academy or to the Christian monastery, how it functioned in society and in the faith, contrasted to the equivalent structures in Manichaeism, Buddhism, or Islam, much new insight may result. And it was the rabbinical academy which was the apparently unique leadership-training institution of Judaism. How much other central institutions, structures of belief, or ritual or myth, and the like may be illumined by contrast or comparison with those of other religious traditions, we may only guess.[6]

In these popular articles, Neusner not only stresses the importance of studying Judaism in comparative perspective, but also underscores for his predominantly Jewish reading audience that being Jewish ought not be the prerequisite for specializing in Judaism in a university setting. Neusner is particularly critical of the Jewish community and their attempts to hijack Jewish studies on campus:

> The development of Jewish studies in universities must not be shaped to meet the parochial interests of the Jewish community, the synagogue or Judaism. Jewish community groups in recent times have discovered that "the future of the community" is being decided on the campus, they have therefore chosen to strengthen programs aimed at influencing the Jewish college student to come to an alternative decision upon basic issues of Jewish identity and commitment.[7]

While Neusner does not object to the funding of Jewish chaplains or Hillel on campus, he subsequently argues that the scholar of Judaism, as a scholar, must be nonpartisan:

> It is, however, quite natural for Jewish community groups to look upon professors in the field of Jewish learning in general, and of the history of Judaism in particular, as allies in the "struggle." They are widely expected to continue in the classroom the advocacy of Judaism which begins in the synagogue schools and continues in the pulpit. . . . However, neither such studies nor those responsible for pursuing them must be used for propagandist purposes of any kind. It is not the responsibility of the historian of Judaism, or of Hebrew, to interest himself in the state of the soul of his students, whether Jewish or gentile. It will render his true task impossible if he does so, except as he sees himself and his students as themselves constituting data for the study of the history of Judaism.[8]

The scholar of Judaism, Neusner maintained, is by definition a critic, a role that necessarily removed him or her from the community. Were this not the case, he warned throughout his life, Jewish studies would cease to be intellectually rigorous or responsible, and would be little more than the extension of local Jewish organizations.

Association for Jewish Studies (AJS)

Given Neusner's warning of the potential for the ghettoization of the study of Judaism, it should come as no surprise that he would have a complicated relationship to those national scholarly organizations devoted to the topic.[9] When pretty much every other person engaged in the study of Jewish texts was focused solely on their particular text or set of texts, Neusner was singular because he insisted on looking at the big picture of what it meant—intellectually, pedagogically, scientifically—to study Judaism. Since he had published regularly on the place of Judaism within American higher education, he was an important voice. Until the 1960s the only scholarly association devoted to Judaica was the American Academy of Jewish Research (AAJR), which had been founded in 1919. The major goals of the AAJR were "the organization of periodic meetings for the presentation of learned papers; the publication of scholarly work in Judaica; and the promotion of fellowship and cooperation between scholars and learned societies in America and other countries."[10] By the mid-1960s, as Association for Jewish Studies historian Kristen Loveland well notes, "younger scholars saw the AAJR as an exclusive organization dominated by elder statesmen unable to meet the transforming field's need."[11] One had to be elected into the AAJR, and many younger scholars felt, certainly not without merit, that this organization did very little to take their needs as young professionals teaching Judaica on American campuses, especially outside of the traditional schools such as Columbia, Brandeis, and Penn, into account.[12]

Writing in 1966, Arnold Band, then a young professor of Hebrew literature at UCLA, noted "a spread of Jewish studies as an accepted academic discipline in the American liberal-arts colleges and universities."[13] Reflecting the growth of positions across American campuses, there arose a new generation of young scholars who sought to communicate with one another on an academic level. In response, Leon Jick decided to organize a colloquium at his home institution, Brandeis University, from September 7 to September 10, 1969. With financial support from the Boston philanthropist Philip W. Lown, Jick convened a group of forty-seven scholars with the intention of discussing their work and addressing problems in the new field of Jewish studies.[14] Shortly thereafter, the Association for Jewish Studies (AJS), to this day the major organization for scholars of Judaica, was founded. This new organization, unlike the AAJR, was open to all working in the field of Jewish studies who paid membership dues.[15]

In his contribution to the proceedings, Joseph L. Blau wrote that the task of this newly formed, if rather inchoate, field of Jewish studies was to create "a place in American higher education for studies in the life, thought, and culture of Jews, past and present, not only as a means of stimulating the enrichment of educational content now, and as a factor in Jewish survival in time to come, but also because we are convinced that these studies have an intrinsic value that is like and yet unlike comparable studies of other ethnic groups."[16] This idea that the study of Jews and Judaism is both "like and yet unlike" the study of other ethnic groups returns us to the heart of the academic study of Judaism. What does it mean to be both "like and unlike" other groups, religions, or cultures? If Jews and Judaism are like other groups, they can presumably be understood using the same methods used to analyze those other groups. If, however, they are "unlike" them, Jews are somehow sui generis and accordingly must be understood on their own terms, something that amounts to little more than a quasi-religious or theological claim. Also significant is Blau's comment that the academic study of Judaism should be concerned with "Jewish survival." Again, then, we witness the intersection of the scholarly study of Judaism and how it is intimately bound up with the fate of Jewish communities. It is perhaps worth noting that at this initial meeting of scholars of Jewish studies, only Jewish practitioners of Jewish studies were invited to discuss the future of the field, a decision that one participant acknowledged served as "recognition that more is at stake in Jewish Studies than increasing research and teaching efforts in the field."[17] The fact that non-Jewish scholars of Jewish studies were not invited might not be as odd as it first appears when it is remembered that, at the time, there were very few non-Jewish scholars of Jewish studies. Moreover, because there were very few places where scholars of Judaica could be trained in these early years outside of Columbia (where Salo Wittmayer Baron taught), Harvard (Harry A. Wolfson), and Brandeis (Alexander Altmann), the majority of scholars arrived at Jewish studies through rabbinical training. Many of these senior scholars, all members of the AAJR, were not that interested in the more democratic AJS.

The most immediate outcome of the Brandeis colloquium was the emergence of a scholarly and professional organization for the field of

Jewish studies. While Neusner would play a role in the formation of this new organization, he would, for a variety of ideological and personal reasons, eventually repudiate it as an ethnic enclave that never justified their data other than with the claim that "if a Jew wrote it, it must be important." Among the earliest debates that Neusner was involved in was whether the term "Judaic studies" or "Jewish studies" should be used. Neusner, as we know, preferred the former, but the other members outvoted him. In the words of Michael A Meyer, the fledgling organization opted for "the living, if more problematic designation" of "Jewish studies" to avoid an "implied narrowing of [the] field which does it injustice."[18]

Neusner, never shy to offer a contrary position to the status quo, also objected in an early memo that the leaders of the organization were making the AJS too close to the Jewish community. He was particularly critical of the wishes of the AJS's leadership to approach large Jewish agencies with the aim of raising money. He asks, "Why did we found the AJS? Was it to serve 'the Jewish community'?" Neusner wanted the AJS to be a scholarly organization, not an ethnic club beholden to the interests of the Jewish community. "The 'Jewish community' is not our business," he writes in the same memo, "and even if it were, nothing worthwhile is likely to come from it, through it, or with it."[19]

The AJS also sought to spread knowledge of the field through publications. Writing as the interim editor of the new *Association for Jewish Studies Newsletter*, Neusner made the case for the creation of a new journal, one that would be substantially different from already existing journals, such as the *Jewish Quarterly Review*. His criteria were as follows:

> Its contents should reflect the judgment of a collegium of qualified scholars, not merely the prejudices of a single editor. It must be a collective enterprise, with support from, and responsible participation by, scholars in more than a single institution or in more than one field of study. In other words, such a journal must represent a mature and healthy field, one whose standards transcend pretention and private animosity, one

open to new methods and new opinions, above all, one with sufficient self-respect to foster self-criticism and with appropriate regard for the learning and rationality of those who hold unorthodox opinions.[20]

The new organization's journal, the *AJS Review*, would eventually appear a few years later, in 1976. Perhaps indicative of the fact that the overwhelming majority of Jewish studies scholars were Jewish, the earliest AJS conferences distributed benchers (small prayer books) with the AJS logo, courtesy of Ktav Publishing House. In addition, the *birkhat hamazon* (Grace after Meals) was recited at communal dinners. Although some AJS members expressed discomfort with the appearance of public religiosity at an academic conference, many argued for the continuation of the communal ritual.[21]

The need for scholarly legitimation, on the one hand, and the acknowledgment of the uniqueness of the Jewish tradition, on the other, is one of the tensions that runs throughout the academic study of Judaism. Neusner played a fairly large role in these early organizational meetings of the AJS. He agreed to take on the office of the membership secretary at a very important moment in the organization's genesis. It seems, however, that his involvement in the AJS gradually began to make clear to him all that was wrong with Jewish studies. It was too ethnic, and too parochial. Rather than open the study of Jewish texts up to the larger academy, it threatened to close it off. In this regard, the AJS had the potential to absorb all the bad qualities that he had associated with JTS and ignore all of the positive dimensions that defined his conversations with people like Jonathan Z. Smith and Hans Penner at Dartmouth. Indeed, he would later refer to the AJS as a "halfway house" for those trying to leave the yeshiva world and engage in a modicum of intellectual scholarship.[22]

Writing again as the interim editor of the *Bulletin of the AJS*, he takes note—after a four page, multiple-columned Hebrew article by Isadore Twersky—of the difference between the professor of Jewish studies and the Jewish educator:

University professors give lectures, while Jewish seminary professors are apt to read a text, but not to attempt to compose a complete lecture. The advantages [of the former] are obvious. One gains a grasp of a much larger amount of material, and perceives insight into the context and meaning, the value-structure, of a whole civilization. He gets perspective, self-conscious understanding, a truly historical, contextually accurate picture of the holy books. On the other hand, the disadvantages should not be ignored. University studies may produce superficiality, glibness, unfounded or meaningless generalizations, an effort to compare things which are not really comparable and to make use of false or misleading analogies.[23]

The discrepancy between these two models—then and now—is not always clear to discern. Neusner's lifework would be an attempt to separate them irreparably so that what went on in the university setting was not the same thing as what went on in the seminary. Indeed the AJS— again, both then and now—could not decide on what model it wanted: even though it claimed to engage in university-type research activity, it often bled over into a more seminary-type model of dealing with Jewish texts.

Neusner said years later that the AJS always struck him as ethnic and very closed. Writing at least as early 1983, he was critical of the "formless and inchoate" nature of the AJS. Of its annual meeting, he said, "It has room for every topic, but makes progress in none. It allows for masses of trivialities and makes provisions for few important statements. Everyone has a place, but the more distinguished names in learning are always absent. Non-Jews scarcely show their faces."[24] It is safe to say that not much has changed with the organization since his initial assessment. It is still largely an ethnic enclave where non-Jews rarely attend, and the endemic tension between scholarship and identity is often on full display.

Indeed, his own work was moving in a much different direction because he was increasingly connecting his data to the themes and questions supplied by the also recently formed American Academy of

Religion (AAR), of which he would become president in 1968. He would be the first president of the organization whose work dealt explicitly with the topic of Jewish studies outside of the more narrow confines of the Bible. According to others, his vision of what Jewish studies—in his terminology, Judaic studies—should become was diametrically opposed to that of the AJS leadership based in Brandeis. Although he told me that he never attended an AJS gathering, according to records he attended at least some of the early meetings. Neusner indicated that this was the case because the founders of the AJS, many of whom set out with the earnest goal of redefining the study of Judaism in America—could never transcend their ethnic parameters. The AJS, for Neusner, amounted to "a society of Jews who tell self-evidently-interesting Jewish things to others Jews, without regard to issues of method or discipline."[25]

It does seem that Neusner still remained, albeit on the sidelines, in the AJS for its first decade. At one point, in 1979, Michael Meyer tried to get Neusner to play a more active role in the AJS by nominating him to the Board of Directors. It did not, however, go well. "You ploughed ahead," Neusner wrote, "clearly without having done the homework of checking in advance to see whether you had the votes; or to see whether you might face opposition. As a result, you produced a situation in which I was publicly attacked, and in part vilified; and in any event held up for public judgment. *I was on trial—and you put me there*."[26] Neusner was so bothered by the whole affair that he wrote, in the same letter, that "I am totally and permanently unavailable to the AJS. That is, I shall not agree to give any more plenary lectures; I shall never again print an article in the *AJS Review* . . . . I don't need to go where I am not wanted. That is the secret of survival in Golah."[27] This seems to have been Neusner's final break with the AJS. Neusner even encouraged his students "as a gesture of sheer dignity and self-respect" not to attend the 1980 meeting.[28] Neusner proposed to his students that they build up the Study of Judaism section at the AAR. In addition, Neusner used the funds associated with the Max Richter Foundation to sponsor an annual conference at Brown from 1972 to 1982.

American Academy of Religion Presidency

In 1964, as we have seen, the AAR rose from the ashes of the National Association of Bible Instructors (NABI). This event, intimately connected to the *School District of Abington Township, Pennsylvania v. Schempp* Supreme Court decision, would prove to be a momentous one for the transformation of the study of Judaism on college and university campuses in the United States. The study of Judaism would now see a dramatic shift from Semitics departments to newly created religious studies departments. This shift is reflected in Neusner's own story. From the time he graduated until he arrived at Dartmouth, he really considered himself to be a historian, and he saw his major professional affiliation to be the American Oriental Society (AOS).[29] Yet as the NABI/AAR began to shed its traditional narrow and largely Protestant focus to include those who worked in all different religions, Neusner gradually took note of this new organization. This was probably also facilitated by Hans Penner and Jonathan Z. Smith, his colleagues at Dartmouth and two early players in the AAR. Since he increasingly began to connect his own data to the questions and categories supplied by the academic study of religion, it was only natural that he would begin to become involved with the recently formed organization. If he had found the AJS to be too ethnic and narrow, the AAR provided him with willing conversation partners.

In a 2002 interview with Barbara DeConcini, executive director of the AAR from 1991 to 2006, Neusner relates how one day in 1967, out of the blue, Claude Welch (1922–2009), professor of religious thought at the University of Pennsylvania and later president of the AAR in 1970, phoned Neusner and asked him if he wanted to become vice president and program chair of the AAR. Not only had Neusner never been to a meeting of the organization, he was not even a member. He nevertheless agreed. So he joined the AAR and was responsible for organizing the 1968 meeting held in Dallas at the Statler Hotel between October 17 and 20.[30]

Neusner claims to be the one who organized the AAR into sections (e.g., Judaism, Islam, China-Japan, Religion and Social Science), which to this day continues to structure, with some modification, the annual meetings. According to the program book, those involved in Jewish studies at the AAR in those early years were Michael Meyer (HUC-JIR), Joseph Gutmann (HUC-JIR), William Braude (pulpit rabbi, Providence, RI), Irving Greenberg (Yeshiva University), Frank Talmage (Toronto), David Winston (GTU), Amos Funkenstein (UCLA), Alfred Gottschalk (HUC-JIR), Manfred Vogel (Northwestern), and Lou Silberman (Vanderbilt).[31] It is worth noting that, with the exception of Neusner and Vogel, none of these scholars had appointments in religious studies, but rather worked either in seminaries or in departments of history.

By virtue of his being vice president, Neusner was next in line to be president of the organization the following year. As president of the AAR he created permanent "chairs" of each section to structure and shape the program by soliciting and accepting papers—Henry A. Fischel (Indiana) was appointed the chair of the Study of Judaism section.[32] Prior to Neusner's action, plenary speakers would deliver lectures and that would be the extent of the annual meeting. Neusner's goal as president was to make the national meetings into research meetings, using the model supplied by the AOS, even though he notes that some members objected to this.[33] Another feature that he introduced in his presidency was to propose a general topic and then invite scholars working in different religious traditions to present papers on it. One such question he encouraged was on the topic comparative messianisms.[34] His presidential address in 1969 was titled "Graduate Studies in Judaica: Problems and Prospects."[35]

If Neusner had always had a problem with the quasi-seminary feel and methodological approach of the AJS, he was able to use the AAR, an organization that he helped structure, to further his own research ends and to collaborate with scholars from different areas. This was in keeping with Neusner's own understanding of the study of Judaism. For him, the secular study of religion had to take into account both social order and cultural systems. The aim, according to Neusner, was to explain the relationship between the religious ideas that people hold and the social world that they create for themselves. In this, Judaism was not special or unique, but provided one example that could be brought to bear on a much larger and cross-cultural problem. This approach would make him a relatively marginal player at the AJS, but colleagues in the AAR warmly endorsed it. A quick look at his numerous awards and honorary degrees backs this up. Many came from European universities where there was no semblance of Jewish studies, but often healthy traditions of religious studies. Compared to the AJS, he called the AAR "a breath of fresh air."[36]

After serving as president of the AAR, he became the coordinator for the Study of Judaism section, which Neusner had helped to form while vice president and president. Writing to the newly appointed board of the Study of Judaism section in 1978, Neusner outlines how he conceived of Judaism's place within the AAR's mission:

> I wish to propose, as the basic purpose of the section during our joint tenure, the principle that we wish to make the study of Judaism exemplary of problems of the study of religions. Success for our board's tenure, I suggest, is measured by the attendance of a fair number of specialists in other areas, responding to raising questions, within the study of Judaism, relevant to work in other areas.[37]

This proposal, as modest as it is revolutionary, does nothing less than make Jewish texts relevant to others working in the study of religion. What Neusner is doing here is diametrically opposed to the mandate of the AJS. To the latter, there is no need to make Judaism or Jewish texts exemplary of larger issues because they are important by virtue of the fact that Jews wrote them. At the AAR, however, at least under Neusner's watch, such an unstated methodology could not hold. The scholar of Judaism now had to justify why he or she studied the material that he or she did. It was not enough, in other words, that the text be written by a

Jew, nor was it enough simply to describe the contents of a text as if this alone were a question of interest. The ideal scholar of Judaism, according to Neusner, had to work with a problem, and then show how his or her data either supported or contradicted it. In this regard, the scholar of Judaism was no different from a scholar of Hinduism, Islam, Buddhism, and so on.[38]

It is also important to note that in creating the sections at the AAR, Neusner also created the space for traditionally marginal topics in Jewish studies, such as Jewish philosophy, to find a home. Norbert Samuelson once told me that Neusner, as chair of the Study of Judaism section, asked him how many sections he needed for Jewish philosophy. This helped to integrate the study of Jewish philosophy into the mainstream curriculum of the contemporary American university. It also put the study of Jewish philosophy in conversation with the philosophical traditions from other religious traditions, in addition to the more general philosophy of religion. Prior to this there was very little if any secular space to engage in the topic of Jewish philosophy in the American academy.[39]

Another novelty of Neusner's vision, although perhaps not apparent at the time, was that it made room for anyone to study Judaism and Jewish texts. Prior to this all scholars of Judaism were themselves Jews. There were, with very few exceptions (e.g., Erwin Goodenough, George Foot Moore), no non-Jews who studied Judaism. In putting the emphasis on data as opposed to ethnicity, problems as opposed to synagogue attendance, Neusner opened up the field to anyone who was willing to take Judaism seriously. Entry was based on advanced training at the doctoral level as opposed to in the seminary. This, of course, might bother some. Recall Jick's comments at the initial meeting that would soon thereafter be the AJS. For Jick, as for many others, the study of Judaism should be interested, at least in part, in "Jewish survival" as opposed to scholarship pure and simple. Neusner disagreed.

In May 1998, almost thirty years after his presidency, Neusner finally resigned his membership in the AAR because its journal, the *Journal of the American Academy of Religion*, had rejected one of his articles for publication.[40]

Arriving at Brown

Returning to the summer of 1968, Neusner arrived at Brown from Dartmouth with distinct ideas of what religious studies was, and how Jewish data ought to contribute to its disciplinary questions. He arrived in 1968 as a full professor of religious studies, and was appointed university professor and Ungerleider Distinguished Scholar of Judaic Studies in 1975. Neusner's time at Brown was certainly mixed, to say the least. As we have seen, the main reason he went there was to give his children a Jewish education, which was not possible at Dartmouth. He stayed, even after he had alienated himself from so many colleagues there, because Brown paid the equivalent of its tuition for children of its faculty members at any other university in the country.[41] Neusner, after the fact, recalled that he "was never really happy at Brown," primarily because he "wasn't with a very good group of people."[42] His tenure at Brown began full of promise, but for a variety of reasons—some his fault, some the administration's fault, and some his colleagues' fault—matters quickly deteriorated.

He arrived at Brown as the soon-to-be president of the AAR, as a founding member of the AJS, as a scholar publishing at great speed and, in the process, changing an entire field of study. By the time he claimed early retirement in 1990, however, he was all but isolated at Brown, ostracized by former friends and colleagues, unwilling to train any more graduate students, and contemplating a life beyond the academy. When I spent time with him in the summer of 2013, he did not want to rehash these events, saying merely, "I don't think it is important" or "what is important in my career is not the controversies I had to deal with."[43] Yet, many of these issues and controversies were not marginal but intimately connected to his life in scholarship. They drove him forward and precipitated new ideas. His academic success, in other words, cannot be neatly removed or separated from his pugnacious personality. It seems that rather early on Neusner received the reputation of someone who published too much and who was controversial. In a letter to Donald Hornig, president of Brown from 1970 to 1976, Neusner articulated his position:

> In reference to the layman's question about "publishing too/or so much." I think the only appropriate answer is that I work hard. The question would be more appropriately asked of those who do not work hard. In reference to the layman's question about "being controversial." I think to any person enjoying the privileges of tenure in a university the question should be asked about *not* "being controversial." The facts speak for themselves. I bear my scars and wounds of various controversies as marks of honor and dignity: they show I have done my duty. Had I not attempted a revolution in the central problem of my field, had I not utilized the security and freedom afforded by tenure to take public positions in favor of rationality (as I grasped the dictates of reason), then I should have served poorly indeed the values of the academy. These are not, after all, rhetoric or empty. If we are academicians, we identify ourselves with the very specific philosophy of Greek rationalism, do we not? My hero is Socrates: ask him why he was controversial, and his answer will explain all one needs to know about his followers for millennia, of whom I am last. These are things which should not require explanation; dignity and academic courtesy, however, make necessary giving the answer, even in the academy.[44]

Neusner would complain a great deal about Brown, even many years following his departure, as a quick look at the prefaces to his many works that appeared throughout the 1990s indicates. Since the political cannot be neatly separated from the particular, the story of Neusner's life cannot be told without at least some sort of examination of the trials and tribulations brought on during his career at Brown. Without wading into all the gossip, accusations, and counteraccusations, abundant as they were, we can uncover an accurate presentation of some of the debates that fueled his ego, his personality, and his career. In the preface to his 1998 *How Adin Steinsaltz Misrepresents the Talmud*, for example, we read,

> The research epitomized here was carried on at the University of South Florida and Bard College, in the years from my appointment in 1990 at USF and in 1994 at Bard College. Both centers of higher learning provide generous research grants, and, more important, through the professorships that I hold, on-going support, so that I am able to do this work. Since 1990 I have taken up problems of a far more demanding and weighty character than I was able to consider in the twenty-one years prior in a less fortunate, because slothful and intellectually inert, academic setting. I am inclined to credit my colleagues at USF and Bard for the shift. Their rigorous challenge, their sustained interest in the response to their questions, and their cordial collegiality have made a huge difference in my life, all to the good.[45]

Before discussing the falling out, however, it is important to examine some of the benefits of Brown. Almost immediately he was granted an institutional structure that would allow him to pave the way for the creation of a coherent program in Jewish studies along the model that previously he had conceived of only along theoretical lines. This model, as we shall see, would be in stark opposition to the type of curriculum that he had been exposed to at JTS, and was distinct from what was presented at the AJS, which was about to institutionalize the field along ethnic lines. Brown also offered immediate access to graduate students, since Dartmouth had only an undergraduate program. This would have important repercussions as Neusner would be able to train a generation of young scholars using his newly developed methods. Many would have academic careers in newly created departments of religious studies, thereby disseminating Neusner's model of both rabbinics and the academic study of Judaism.

These two features, in addition to the fact that he would again be working in a department of religious studies, greatly appealed to

Neusner. As at Milwaukee, Neusner again made sure that he kept Jewish studies front and center by running lectures and seminars and engaging others with the subject matter. Rather than keep the study of Judaism as an ethnic enclave, and thus interesting only fellow scholars of Judaism and the local Jewish community, Neusner fostered his object of study in such a way to be relevant to other humanists and social scientists.[46]

As an Undergraduate Teacher

In his 1984 *How to Grade Your Professors*, Neusner gives us his observations on what it means to be a good teacher:

> A good teacher is someone who can enter into the mind of another person and bring to life the mind of that other person. A good teacher does the work by arguing, pressing, asking questions, challenging answers, and asking more questions. The life of the good teacher is expressed in giving life to ideas, imparting meaning to what appears to lie entirely beyond intellect, making the obvious into a problem, turning the world of settled truths into an adventure. A good teacher is argumentative, disorderly, prepared for confrontation everywhere, all the time, with everyone, on everything—all for the sake of the vital mind, the freely inquiring spirit.[47]

A perusal of any one of Neusner's class syllabi bears this out. He makes it clear to the students that his classes are not about making them good Jews or, especially when he was teaching at the University of South Florida, about why Jews do not believe in Jesus. Instead, his stated goal is to understand religion by generalizing about Judaism. Each class

> is conducted mainly through questions and answers. [Students] will have to pay close attention to not only what I say, but also what other students say and how I respond to them. Every class should yield one main point and the educational process consists in how that main point is reached, examined, and expounded. Ideally, a class session should involve one

question and one answer; the process of thought and analysis of shared data, aimed at the discovery and elucidation of proposition of general intelligibility, defines education in this course. . . . Under these conditions, it goes without saying, you cannot come late; cannot engage in private conversations; cannot take notes (when needed, these will be provided); and cannot tune in and out.[48]

Not everyone agreed, however. In *The Brown Daily Herald*, the student newspaper, an article appeared with the title "When Profs Go Too Far." One of the faculty members discussed in this article was Neusner, whose style was described as "over-aggressive and intimidating to the point of being counter-productive." The article then went on to print comments from unnamed former students who said he would call them "schmucks" for a wrong answer, or engage in other ad hominem attacks for their writing style, or lack thereof. One other, unnamed student remarked that "he cares about the students, but does it in a way that can be very hurtful."[49]

It is difficult to know what to do with such comments. All professors receive negative reactions about their teaching style. I think it safe, and fair, to say, however, that Neusner's pedagogical style undoubtedly rubbed certain students the wrong way. He cared about his students, as his lifelong relationships with people like Thomas Tisch and William Scott Green clearly reveal. When at Brown he would invite several different students, male and female, over for Shabbat each week. He frequently wrote in the Brown student journal, including articles that discussed teaching, in addition to more general articles and letters attacking the administration and critical of other scholars on campus.

Noam Neusner, Neusner's son, once told me that his father's greatest sense of pride was his students. He began his career, as so many professors do, writing out lectures and then standing awkwardly in front of a classroom and reading. Such a model may be designed to impress students with vast knowledge, but it often has the opposite effect of putting them to sleep. Neusner said he realized this when he watched the different ways students reacted to a course he cotaught at Dartmouth with his colleague Fred Berthold. Whereas Neusner read technical lectures to the students, Berthold interacted with them and instructed in a more Socratic manner. The young Neusner changed his style of teaching almost immediately.

Reflecting on his life as a teacher in the academy, Neusner wrote *How to Grade Your Professors: And Other Unexpected Advice*, aimed at families about to send a child off to college. In it, Neusner explains, among other things, the role of the good teacher, who, he firmly believes and as we saw above, is charged with "making the obvious into a problem, [and] turning the world of settled truths into an adventure."[50] In order to make this possible, Neusner continues by stating that "a good teacher is argumentative . . . [and] prepared for confrontation everywhere."[51] This meant that a Neusner classroom had the potential to be an intellectual battleground, one wherein he cajoled, argued with, and pressed students to formulate their ideas in a coherent fashion.

Needless to say, some students loved this, others hated it. Neusner was not interested in the latter, those who either dropped his classes or complained bitterly about his teaching style. He was demanding in the classroom—a quick thinker and just as quick a critic, he set a high standard not just for work but for behavior and personal character. His goal was to force students to listen and to respond, to think actively and not for the sake of regurgitation or repetition's sake, but for themselves. As a result, he resisted the conventions of the formal lecture, and instead asked questions. He sought argument and not stenography. Those who came to class unprepared were doomed to fail, and those who rose to the challenge were rewarded.

Neusner hated two things more than any other when it came to the teaching profession in university settings. First, he loathed colleagues who watered down standards in order to be popular. Such professors, he thought, were primarily involved in a popularity contest and sought influence by currying student favor. He accused his nemesis at Brown, political scientist Edward Beiser, of being such an individual. Beiser was a celebrated teacher and administrator, but had very few publications to his name.[52] Such accusations, of course, did not endear him to his colleagues, and only served to exacerbate his relations with the university administration. Former students have told me that both Beiser and Neusner would regularly have Shabbat dinners for students and so the two colleagues also competed in this regard.[53] Neusner maintained that those who did not publish did not deserve to be called scholars and made a mockery out of the profession, despite the fact that they often accused publishing scholars as too busy to devote time to teaching.

The second problem that Neusner had with teaching was perhaps peculiar to Jewish studies—when the classroom environment became transformed into that of a summer camp, where nostalgia and ethnic pride filled the air. The majority of students who enroll in such courses, at least in the Northeast, tend to be Jews who believe that their genetic disposition will predispose them to good grades, and that university courses on Jewish topics will simply be a continuation of their Sunday school studies. This is why Neusner, as any good scholar must, always tried to maintain a healthy distance between the academic study of Judaism and Hillel, the Jewish student association, despite the fact that many Hillel rabbis were always more than willing to paper over the difference. "The case of Judaism," as he writes in the introduction to his *The Way of Torah*, an introductory textbook devoted to the analysis of Judaism, "represents one important example of what religion is and does."[54]

Despite the fact that Neusner is one of the most important American Jewish thinkers of the twentieth century, he was always able to draw a line between academic work in Judaism and being a Jewish public intellectual. The two must never blur into one another because, if they did, Jewish studies would be an ethnic enclave and, thus, of only parochial importance. This meant that while he would threaten to sue departments that did not hire his non-Jewish students for Jewish studies positions, he was opposed when JTS, a Jewish seminary, was on the verge of offering a position to a non-Jew, Peter Schaefer.[55] In like manner, he opposed intermarriage and refused to attend the wedding of his niece when she married a non-Jew. Unlike other scholars of Judaism, especially those he rebelled against at JTS, for Neusner the task of Jewish studies was not, as Saul Lieberman defined it, "to teach Torah to the children of Israel."[56] Although there were certainly many students who took his courses expecting one on Jewishness, what they received instead was an entry into a world of thinking. Neusner sought to teach Judaism as an example of an intellectual system to students interested in the study of religion without regard to personal religious commitment. Judaism, for him, was not an ethnic or cultural affiliation, but a thinking person's religion. "This is not a course in why Jews should practice Judaism (or otherwise, 'be Jewish'), nor one in ethnic celebration," he would write on his course syllabi, "students looking for either the why or how of being Jewish or practicing Judaism will not find answers here."[57] If Judaism was simply about ethnic pride, like Irishness or Scottishness, Neusner always argued that it would never survive as a vibrant tradition of intellectual activity. Judaism was not about Israel nor about the Holocaust; rather, it was about the life of Torah and of thinking.

In his course syllabi, Neusner was always quick to note that Judaism represented the data and that it would be used to study larger and more universal issues. In the syllabus for a course titled "Classics of Judaism," which he offered at Bard College in the fall of 1995, for example, he begins by stating that the classic texts of Judaism will demonstrate "how writing serves as a medium for preserving and handing on a religious experience in the life of an on-going religious community."[58] In the same syllabus, he tells students that he sets "high expectations for [them], and errs by asking too much, rather than too little." Although Bard was a private liberal arts college with, as Neusner admitted, the best students he ever taught, he also taught at a large state university, the University of South Florida. For his "Introduction to Judaism" course there, his syllabus explains how his goals are universal: "Introducing an ancient and complex religious tradition, this course asks and answers a simple question: how do we define a religion? That means, what is a religion? . . . what makes a religion definable at all? And what does a religion do?"[59] And, again, he makes explicit to his students what he will *not* be teaching:

> This is not a course in whether or not what Judaism teaches is true, let alone in why someone born to a Jewish mother should choose to be Jewish or marry a person of the Jewish religion; it is also not a course in religious disputations. E.g., "why didn't, or don't, the Jews believe in Jesus Christ?" Theological questions are entirely legitimate in the practice of religion, and they also form data for the study of religion, but they have no place in the descriptive, analytical, and interpretive program of an academic course.[60]

In another "Introduction to Judaism" syllabus, also from the University of South Florida, he tells his students what he is like as a teacher:

> I do not give formal lectures (of more than 10 minutes at a time), and I do not believe people learn much when you merely tell them things. For me an ideal class is one in which I just sit there and enjoy the students' cogent and interesting analysis of a problem as they learn, out of the data they have mastered, to solve problems for themselves. . . . I am not famed for suffering fools gladly. Students with weak egos or requiring lots of encouragement and praise (except as earned) will not like me. The few teachers in my life whom I respected and from whom I learned important and memorable lessons, which I could use, were those who listened with respect but criticized in a serious way—but also showed me how to do things in the way they thought right. . . . Publishing scholars are different from other professors, because they are used to criticism of their own work, indeed each book or major project conducts a severe critique of the prior one; publishing scholars are problem-solvers; they value learning and expect to learn from others; and they think argument and disagreement (conducted with a bit of courtesy) form the centerpiece of a happy life, and they do also like to joke a great deal. Be warned.[61]

Graduate Studies

As we have seen, Brown immediately gave Neusner a place to train graduate students, which would amount to a venue to produce the next generation of scholars, many of whom would be sympathetic to his approach to the material. Neusner, however, had a fixed idea about what graduate education should look like. Writing in the *Chronicle of Higher Education*, he proclaimed that graduate students were like apprentices who ought to be taught as much by deed as by word. "Disciples succeed," he writes, "when they know what the master knows." This meant that Neusner envisaged his graduate students—and he produced twenty-one of them over the years—as individuals who must be formed in such a manner that he (or she) would be able to do what the master does.[62]

At the time that Neusner set up his graduate program at Brown, there were really only two other places to engage in graduate work in rabbinics, at Harvard with Isadore Twersky and at Columbia where Morton Smith was still teaching. He certainly succeeded in differentiating his program from theirs. The primary difference was that he saw himself as training scholars of religion, or "religionists," with a specialty in rabbinic texts as opposed to, say, scholars of Mishnah or Talmud. For Neusner, unlike someone like Twersky, there was no practical significance in the texts that he taught. He expected his students not to become better Jews because of their work, but to become better scholars of religion. For this reason he had no problems admitting non-Jewish students into the program, so long as they were willing to learn Hebrew and do the work that he required.[63]

Before his fallout with the Religious Studies Department at Brown, Jewish studies represented one track (History of Religions: Judaism) within the graduate program. His ideal student was someone with a general liberal arts background, and with some knowledge of Hebrew. He would look for students, recalls Alan Avery-Peck, who could do critical work and who had enough language skills. All students came into his program already knowing how to work with rabbinic texts. He did not have the patience to teach them how to read the Talmud. While some came out of a religious background (for example, Baruch Boxser and Gary Porton), others (such as Martin Jaffee and Alan Avery-Peck) did not. He sent those who knew little Hebrew to Israel to learn the language, but warned them not to let the Israelis teach them anything about history. Many of the professors at the Hebrew University (e.g., Abraham Goldberg, a Mishnah scholar) were reluctant to work with the American students when they found out that they were returning to the United States to work with Neusner.[64]

Neusner funded these students through fellowships provided by the Max Richter Foundation, even before they were enrolled at Brown, so that they could, if they needed, go to Israel for a year or two of language study. When they returned and registered as graduate students, Neusner always told them exactly what they had to do. This is where his paradigm of the master and apprentice fully shows itself. It is probably also worth noting in this context that many graduate students are often in doubt and struggle tremendously when it comes to choosing and finishing a dissertation topic. Unlike such students, Neusner's were never in any doubt. If he accepted you, several of his students told me, you were not going to fail. With only a couple of exceptions, all of his students finished and secured employment. Those who failed did so because they were not intellectually or constitutionally up to such an intense program. He treated them roughly, according to his former students, but those who made it knew that it came from a good place.[65]

From the beginning of their graduate careers, Neusner brought his students into his vision of Jewish studies. Several called him "controlling, but in a positive sense." Whereas most doctoral programs consist of three years of coursework before the inchoate years of writing the dissertation, in "Neusner's program"—and this is the way that his students referred to it—they were given their dissertation topics, and were actively working on their doctoral projects, in their first week or two on campus. Neusner pretty much told them what they would work on, which, in turn, was based on what he was working on at the time. Many of his colleagues at Brown did not necessarily like this idea.[66]

Neusner made all his students take a graduate seminar with him. In this seminar, his students would work out the material for their dissertations, which often were translations and critical commentaries on texts that revolved around some issue that Neusner was himself working on. They were expected to come into each weekly seminar with twenty pages of translation and commentary. Often it would be torn to shreds, and they would be expected to do better the next week (or if it was particularly bad, the next day). Some confided it was a humiliating experience, but they noted that it was humiliation for the sake of getting better, never for the sake of humiliation. Unlike most university seminars, however, this seminar met all year, for twelve months, in the summer and in the winter. He gave his students four years maximum to finish. "No one could be so lazy," he said to me, "as to make the degree too many years."[67]

In addition to the doctoral seminar, Neusner also made his students take a course with him where they read his work in detail. This introduced the student to Neusner's methodology and helped to set the foundation for the coming year's work. Neusner did not forbid his students from reading the work of his critics, but in fact actively encouraged it. He also made all of his students, whether Jewish or Gentile, attend an Orthodox Jewish service every week for at least a year to hear the entire Torah chanted. His reason for doing this was that if the student did not hear the Torah chanted, he or she would not be able to see the text as a living presence and, thus, would miss what it meant to be a scholar of the religion.[68]

His students were expected to take not only courses on rabbinic Judaism with him, but also critical discourses in the study of religion, and on the Hebrew Bible, which he describes as "the foundation of everything." Finally, Neusner also made his students take courses in another religious tradition (for example, Islam or Christianity) so that they could work on the problem of comparison. Without comparison, he reasoned, they would not deserve to be in possession of a religious studies degree. Most of his students, however, with the exception of Judith Wegner, who worked on the topic of Judaism and Islam, did not actually go on to work on anything comparative.[69]

Neusner took an interest in virtually all aspects of his students' lives. This involved everything from how they dressed for class to giving them wake-up calls every morning so that he knew that they were up and working. He, thus, became a father figure, for better or worse, to his students. This closeness worked in one of two ways. For some—most notably William Scott Green and Alan Avery-Peck—it meant lifelong relationships of commitment and friendship, including almost daily phone calls and collaboration on projects. Others, however, wanted very little more to do with him after they had graduated. Regardless, he helped all of his students write their first books, helped them find jobs, and told them what jobs they should take (or not take). When Avery-Peck was offered a temporary position at Emory before he had finished his dissertation, Neusner demanded that he decline the job, which would not have allowed him to finish his dissertation or finish it well.[70]

When it came out during an interview that another one of his students, Paul Flesher, was not Jewish and, probably because of this, did not receive jobs at either Emory or the University of Nebraska, Neusner threatened to sue the university and handed the matter over to a solicitor. Both Neusner and Flesher learned from the chair at Nebraska that the position could not be offered to a non-Jew; because the local Jewish Federation was funding the position, they expected the professor to teach courses for and in the community. This called into question not only the academic integrity of the position, but also, according to Neusner, the entire academic study of Judaism. It was also in clear violation of state university policy. In a letter to the solicitor, Stuart Eizenstat, Neusner puts the matter in the following terms:

> I also take the view that public policy is not well served when any academic field is limited to a particular class of persons, e.g., Jews for Judaic

studies, blacks for Afro-American studies, women for Women's Studies, Italo-Americans for Italian, Hispanic-Americans for Spanish, Roman Catholics for Roman Catholic or medieval studies, Protestants for the study of the Reformations (or Roman Catholics for the study of the Catholic Reformation), Muslims for Islam, Buddhists for Buddhism, and the like. Once Judaic studies is the preserve of only Jews, moreover, we shall find universities making decisions as to what type of Jews, e.g., only Orthodox Jews can get jobs at Harvard in Judaic Studies (as is now the case), and so on. I do not think that it is in the public interest for universities to enter into such sectarian matters, which are not relevant to the academic enterprise and which can destroy the possibility of learning as we know it. . . . I have a strong and long-standing commitment, as do all of my colleagues, in favor of Judaic, Afro-American, and Women's Studies, which I believe to be important and critical components of learning today. For the academic integrity of those and similar fields, which focus upon the human experience and record of particular groups, we have to prepare the principle that at stake is learning, and that all qualified persons are welcome to participate.[71]

Neusner, for the same reasons, was also highly critical of Hillel rabbis who insisted on sponsoring symposia or other events on campus that had the veneer of scholarship. When the Brown Hillel sponsored a symposium on "Jewish Culture," Neusner wrote a scathing letter to its executive director showing that organizers had confused the academic study of religion with the needs of faith-based groups on campus. He believed that Hillel certainly had a role to play in the university, but that it should not interfere with the academic study of Judaism, which was open to all regardless of birth or ethnicity. This, it seems, was one of his major problems with the AJS.[72]

This could also work both ways. When one of his students, Howard Eilberg-Schwartz, had an article rejected by the journal *Prooftexts*, he pleaded with Neusner not to make a scene about what the latter referred to as "the ethnics" at the journal: "please consider not publishing a column about this incident or going to Johns Hopkins University Press about it. What occurred is an issue between myself and the editors of *Prooftexts*. I prefer dealing with them directly about this issue."[73]

Neusner also read critically every book his students wrote before it was printed. He did not want his students to be criticized for making silly mistakes, which would, in turn, reflect badly on him. Most importantly, though, he trained his students for careers in religious studies as opposed to Jewish studies. This meant that he provided them with the intellectual and conceptual wherewithal to talk to other scholars of religion. He provided them with a language that would make them employable in departments of religious studies. Rather than use the rabbinic term *sugya*, for example, he would make them use the more familiar "pericope." In so doing, Neusner trained a generation of scholars who were religionists. Without this model, religious studies becomes little more than a canopy, under which scholars of diverse religions cannot dialogue. Under Neusner's model, however, a religious studies department would consist of numerous scholars working with different data who could nonetheless converse. In so doing, Neusner contributed to his lifelong goal of making the study of Judaism intellectually respectable, rather than an extension of the local community.[74]

Rabbinic Studies: Literature

If many of Neusner's scholarly interests had been in examining the historical issues and problems surrounding rabbinic texts, his work now began to gravitate to a more literary analysis of these texts. This involved, first and foremost, the translation of all of Judaism's canonical books into an American English idiom. These included the Mishnah, Tosefta, Talmud of the Land of Israel, Talmud of Babylonia, and all of the many compilations of scriptural exegesis—often given the blanket name Midrashim—that came into existence and closure by the time of the advent of Islam in the seventh century CE. Not only did he translate all of these works, he also developed a reference system—equivalent to chapter and verse—that would make form analysis possible. Finally, this period also saw him apply the documentary hypothesis to these texts. This approach, developed by biblical scholars as early as the late eighteenth century, tried to show that what we regard today as a text, say the Hebrew Bible, was derived from originally independent narratives, which were subsequently combined into their current form by a series of later redactors. Although this hypothesis was fairly standard in the world of biblical studies, it had never really made its way into rabbinic texts. For Neusner, this also meant that he would have to examine each document of rabbinic Judaism as an individual unit that revealed its own coherent statement of what it perceived to be Israel's social order. He referred to each such statement as a "system." Each text, then, was to be read not as forming part of a whole, that is, as part of a grandiose and monolithic rabbinic Judaism, but as a discrete unit with its own unique system and set of concerns.[75]

Each document of rabbinic Judaism—the Mishnah, the *Sifra*, the two *Sifres*, Genesis Rabbah, Leviticus Rabbah, the Babylonian Talmud, the Yerushalmi Talmud, and so forth—clearly differentiates itself, both stylistically and topically, from the others. Although certain passages may well exist in different documents, they should not necessarily be conflated. Each document must be seen as the product of a particular group and, as such, as reflecting that group's distinctive culture and society. In order to understand something as mammoth and convoluted as "rabbinic Judaism," Neusner argues that it is first necessary to understand each text as an *autonomous* unit, as possessing its "own framework, exhibiting its own distinctive traits of rhetoric, topic, and logic, as a complete book with a beginning, middle, and end, in preserving that book, the canon presents us with a document on its own and not solely as part of a larger composition or construct."[76]

One of his earliest attempts at translation and form critical analysis may be found in his twenty-two-volume *A History of the Mishnaic Law of Purities* (1974–1977). In this work, Neusner translates, analyzes, and provides a methodological framework to examine the last of the

Six Orders of the Mishnah. His goal in translation evolved as he progressed with his project, but the defining element was accuracy, giving a word-for-word translation, in order to make the text accessible to a non-Hebrew readership. In this, his translation was meant to supersede that of Herbert Danby, an Oxford-trained Anglican minister, who first translated the entire Mishnah into English in 1933. Neusner claimed that Danby did not offer a good pathway into the Hebrew text, but provided only a paraphrastic as opposed to literal rendition of the original. In contrast, Neusner offered his translation to the reader who wanted to find out what exactly the document contained.[77]

Writing in the *Journal of the American Academy of Religion*, the major outlet of the AAR, Samson H. Levey of Hebrew Union College called *A History of the Mishnaic Law of Purities* "a profound, methodical, and meticulous study" that "establishes him beyond any reservation as one of the foremost Jewish scholars of our day, and as the pioneer *par excellence* in the form-critical analysis of Rabbinic literature."[78] It is worth noting here, however, that he conflated a "Jewish scholar" with a scholar of Judaism. Levey concludes the essay with the bold claim that "Neusner has established himself among the towering personalities of the Rabbinic Tradition and among the critical rabbinic scholars of all time."[79] Writing in the *Association for Jewish Studies Newsletter* in 1981, Marvin Fox, Neusner's friend and colleague at Brandeis, reviewing the later five-volume *A History of the Mishnaic Law of Women*, said of the translation that "it does not strive for elegance in English, but strives rather to reproduce the Hebrew in all respects as faithfully as possible" and that "while determinations of meanings are matters about which there may well be legitimate differences among scholars, no one can have any doubt that Neusner has given us a fresh and most interesting reading of the ancient text."[80] Most important, Fox, like Levey, is keenly aware of the novelty of Neusner's larger project, namely, to read the text on its own terms without all the later commentary tradition. His assessment is worth quoting at length:

This way of reading runs counter to the patterns to which we have become accustomed and which we have inherited from the work of many centuries. Just as it never occurred to most of us, particularly those with a traditional education that it was possible to read scripture without commentaries, so did it not occur to us that we could read Mishnah without commentaries. . . . Neusner is attempting to show us, similarly, that there is much to be learned by reading Mishnah as a fully integrated systematic work with its own meaning and its own history. The effort requires great self-discipline, since it forces us to cast off, as we read, the accumulated baggage of commentary and exegesis which has formed our conventional approach to Mishnah. It demands a direct confrontation with the text, a reading which allows the text to speak to us on its own terms, a structuring which deals not only with the organization of a particular segment of the text, but which ultimately tries to understand the whole from the perspective of its parts. There is a kind of intellectual daring and risk-taking here which evoke admiration. More important, there is a detailed implementation of the program which shows us how one scholar does this pioneering work.[81]

In addition to all of his pioneering work on the Mishnah, Neusner was also engaged in a similar project with the two Talmuds, that of the Land of Israel and of Babylonia. His method in these works was virtually identical to that which he produced in his multivolume works on the Mishnah. He does admit, though, that some of his translative work on the Talmud, especially the Babylonian Talmud (the Bavli), was paraphrastic. Since the latter's use of language was much too complicated, he could not translate the weight of its contents accurately into English. This is in addition to providing translations and analyses of Tosefta, *Sifra*, and *Sifre*.[82]

Although those like Levey and Fox praised Neusner for his risk taking and the novelty and freshness of his approach, others—more traditionally inclined—were not nearly so charitable. Many questioned his knowledge of Hebrew and his ability to use the manuscripts associated with these texts. These negative reactions to Neusner's translative work would perhaps best be summarized by the scathing review produced by Saul Lieberman on his deathbed.

European Association for Jewish Studies (EAJS)

Neusner, as we have seen many times already, was an indefatigable organizer, especially if he believed in the project. It is within this context that he single-handedly organized and funded—through the Max Richter Foundation—the European Association of Jewish Studies (EAJS), today one of the largest academic organizations devoted to the study of Judaism in the world and certainly the largest in Europe. In the late 1970s and early 1980s, Neusner had given several lectures in both Britain and Continental Europe. He noticed a tremendous interest in scholarship on Jewish topics, which impressed him, especially since Jewish studies had all but been destroyed in Europe during the Second World War. In the summer of 1980, he sent out what he called a Proposal for a European Consultative Conference on Judaic Studies. In the letter he wrote, "My recent trip to lecture at a number of universities in Germany, France, The Netherlands, and Britain, left the impression that Judaic studies in Europe are now poised for an important step of stabilization and consolidation. The purpose of this letter is briefly to describe the situation as I see it and to propose a modest but concrete act to improve that situation." Neusner then invited twenty-five European scholars of Jewish studies to attend an organizational meeting at the Oriental Institute in Oxford from May 11 to May 13, 1981. Geza Vermes chaired the meeting and also served as the local organizer and planner. At the meeting Neusner gave the Sacks Lecture, and the committee agreed to have periodic conferences, inventories of research, a newsletter, and a journal. A conference was announced for July of the following year at Hertford College, Oxford.[83]

Neusner single-handedly birthed this organization. He wrote hundreds of letters to scholars throughout Europe, encouraging them to attend. He subsidized the annual conference for several years before it could support itself. Although Neusner was extremely critical of the AJS, he seems to have had no qualms supporting, literally out of his own pocket, the formation of the EAJS. Perhaps this is because the latter was outside of America and he did not have the same personality conflicts that he had with members of the AJS, in addition to the fact that the EAJS did not have the same ethnic framework as the AJS. He could set up the EAJS, in other words, as he saw fit.

Brown Judaic Studies

Neusner not only created a curriculum at Brown, but also established a new book series, Brown Judaic Studies, published by Scholars Press, which would revolutionize the academic study of Judaism. As early as his first book reviews in the *Jewish Ledger*, Neusner had called for the creation of an American press to disseminate Judaica in this country. Yet Neusner credits the idea to Thomas Tisch, his former student. Neusner had wanted Tisch to do graduate work, but he instead entered the family business (Loews Corporation). Despite this, Tisch and Neusner remained close, with the former helping fund many of Neusner's initiatives, including Brown Judaic Studies. Indeed, in one letter Neusner calls Tisch "the silent partner in the work of giving a hearing to scholarship on the history of Judaism." Neusner also funded the project by not paying authors royalties; profits were instead rolled back into the series.[84]

Neusner's initial goal behind creating the series was to provide an outlet for his doctoral students' dissertations. Since his main publisher at the time, Brill of the Netherlands, could not keep up with his writings, he also published many of his own books in the series. In the process, however, he succeeded in creating a publishing venue for Jewish studies at a time when there were very few publishing opportunities for the field's scholars. In this, again, Neusner single-handedly created space for the various subfields in Jewish studies, just as he had done at the AAR. He was the general editor of the entire project and appointed project editors to collect monographs in their own series. These included David J. Blumenthal soliciting proposals in "Approaches to Medieval Judaism," William Brinner in "Studies in Islam and Judaism," William Scott Green in "Approaches to Ancient Judaism," Norbert Samuelson in "Jewish Philosophy," and Jonathan Z. Smith in "Studia Philonica." Even though Brown appeared in the title of the series, the university contributed nothing to its production. It was Neusner who organized and funded the series and thus had near total control over the entire series; yet he did not blacklist authors with whom he disagreed. In fact, he published several volumes of which he was critical. He thought such authors deserved a hearing and responded to them in print. He never censored the series, in other words, even if he disagreed with the topic or the methodology to be published.[85]

The arrangement with Scholars Press was that Neusner, with the support of Tisch, paid the up-front costs of production and the press managed printing and publication, with Neusner receiving 50 percent of the net proceeds from sales. Because of Tisch's support, which was often as much as fifty thousand dollars annually, the series never ran a deficit. The return on the sale of the backlist was reinvested in the production and publication of new volumes. Neusner reckons that through the combined support of Tisch and the income generated from sales, Brown Judaic Studies from 1979 to 1990 (and then South Florida Studies from 1990 to 2000) published roughly one book per week.[86]

The books were peer-reviewed. This usually meant a reading by Neusner and, if he deemed it necessary, one other person. For his own work, he seems to have used Brown Judaic Studies to publish his detailed volumes that dealt with case studies, but would then publish more synthetic volumes with reputable university presses, such as the University of Chicago Press. Under Neusner's reign Brown Judaic Studies published well over 250 volumes in Judaica. When Neusner left Brown, the university retained the series and gave it to his successor there, Shaye J. D. Cohen. Neusner was furious and resigned his emeritus status from Brown in protest. In response, Neusner founded a new series, again with the help of Thomas Tisch, titled University of South Florida Studies in the History of Judaism. Both series exist today, with Brown Judaic Studies now published through the Society of Biblical Literature (SBL), South Florida Studies through the University Press of America.[87]

Judaism: The Evidence of the Mishnah

After he had finished the translation and commentary to the Mishnah, Neusner began to experiment with how one could rewrite the history of Judaism, what he called the natural next step from the translation and commentary.[88] One of his earliest attempts may be found in *Judaism: The Evidence of the Mishnah*, a work that he and others consider to be among his most important. As he states in the preface to the second edition,

> The reason that I chose the Mishnah for the present exercise is that in earlier works of mine I have made possible the critical historical reconstruction which is undertaken here. . . . My task is to reconstruct evidence which I have already translated, analyzed in its component parts, and laid out chronologically. My hope is to tell what that evidence allows us to report about the state of mind of people who flourished at diverse moments in the accumulation and agglutination of the document, the Mishnah, which has now been dissected and forced into decomposition. So from exegesis and analysis, I turn to reconstruction and interpretation.[89]

In his reader report for the University of Chicago Press, Jonathan Z. Smith, his former colleague at Dartmouth, noted that this was Neusner's most exciting manuscript, and that it offered a "Copernican Revolution" in rabbinic studies. Smith noted that the work "promises to be one of the most important and exciting books in the field of religious studies in decades. . . . Note that I have written 'in the field of religious studies,' for it would be a mistake to treat this work as one confined to Judaica." As is fitting with Neusner's embrace of the field of religious studies, and that field's embrace of him, Smith continues that the manuscript "presents a set of issues, a method, a thesis that transcends its particular subject matter."[90] This statement sums up succinctly all that Neusner was trying to achieve. He was a scholar of religion whose data happened to be Jewish.

The book originally appeared in 1982, just after he had completed his massive study, translation, and interpretation of the Mishnah and the Tosefta. The book simultaneously summarizes his previous research and breaks new methodological ground. Neusner defined his approach in the work as "radical nominalism," which he later characterized with the slogan "what we cannot show we do not know." In the work, as even critics would note, is the articulation of a fresh vision and a new set of questions applied to the Mishnah and related works. Therein, Neusner set out to discuss the formation and social meaning of the Mishnah, codified in 200 CE, a work that would eventually form the backbone of subsequent articulations of rabbinic Judaism.[91]

Neusner was among the first students of the Mishnah to refuse to regard it as normative in a religious sense of the term. Moreover, he was also original in his unwillingness to go to later rabbinic interpretations of the Mishnah—in, say, the Talmud or midrashic collection—to shed light on it. He dismissed as later reactions all subsequent interpretations and claimed that they, in coming later, have no bearing whatsoever on our ability to understand the Mishnah "on its own terms." This formed the bedrock of Neusner's methodological foundation, which he characterized as the "documentary hypothesis." He was quick to argue that we need to understand the Mishnah not as it was articulated through a later prism, but as a single work that constituted but one version of what its framers thought Judaism should be. If we do not do this, we risk confusing distinct systems. This means that the Mishnah represents *a* type of Judaism in the first century CE, and that we ought to be aware that other types of Judaisms—other types of religious and/or philosophical systems—existed concurrently with it.[92]

Each one of these Judaisms thought itself to be and described itself as the authentic veritable Judaism. Neusner writes,

> The testimonies to these other kinds of Judaism are contained not only in parts of the New Testament—for example, Matthew—produced in the later first century. They also persist in those massive and important compilations under the names of Baruch and Ezra. Like the Mishnah, they were prepared in the aftermath of the destruction of the Second Temple and in response to the crisis of the later Israelite spirit precipitated by it.[93]

The ideas contained within the Mishnah, then, reflect only the worldview of one group among many, which only later would coalesce into a singular Judaism that would go by the name "rabbinic" (what he had earlier called "continuity" or "matrix"). The relationship of these multiple Judaisms to "rabbinic Judaism" is not always easy to ascertain on account of the paucity of evidence available, just as it is difficult to trace how exactly the framers of the Mishnah would form what would later emerge as normative Judaism. Here Neusner was critical of his predecessors— most notably George Foot Moore and Ephraim E. Urbach—who, he argued, used later normative sources to describe what Judaism (note the singular) would have looked like in the first century. Of Moore's work, Neusner was particularly critical, claiming that it is primarily a theological work, all of whose categories derive from theology as opposed to history, and that it "describes many kinds of Judaism as if they formed a single, fully symmetrical construct."[94] Moore's analysis, in other words, lacked the tripartite schema that Neusner had championed in his use of the documentary approach.[95]

The Mishnah attributes sayings to authorities who are believed to have lived before the work's ultimate redaction in 200 CE, indeed who lived centuries before this time. Rather than take all these sayings at face value, as Moore and so many others had, indeed as Neusner had at the beginning of his career, he developed an elaborate way of subjecting to verification or falsification, or as excluding as not subject to verification or falsification, the attribution of these sayings. He bases his theory on the anteriority and posteriority of sayings and the names in which they appear. To use Neusner's own words,

> Authorities A, B, C, and D always occurred in juxtaposition with sayings of one another, but rarely, if ever, occurred in juxtaposition with sayings in the names of W, X, Y, and Z. Further, as I shall explain, evidence internal to the Mishnah itself, not adduced from other documents, showed that authorities A, B, C, and D generally said things which in logic stood prior to what was placed in the mouths of W, X, Y, and Z. It seemed to me to follow that what I found in the names of authorities A, B, C, and D should tell me conceptions or principles or problems worked out prior to what I found in the names of authorities W, X, Y, and Z. The correlation between priority in the period in which an authority lived and anteriority in the logic of what was said by that authority forms the foundation for my claim that the Mishnah tells us something about the world before the period of its own closure, that is, the second half of the second century.[96]

In a period of chaos ushered in by the wars with Rome, the framers of the Mishnah—unlike the followers of Jesus, and unlike the authors of more apocalyptic works such as 2 Baruch or 4 Ezra—sought ahistorical stasis grounded in the cult, Neusner argues, even if the cult no longer existed. Most of the rest of the book is devoted to a detailed analysis of the contents of the Mishnah before, during, and after the wars that culminated in the destruction of the Second Temple and the Bar Kokhba Revolt. If before and during the wars we encounter "the formation of bits and pieces of the parts" of the Mishnah, by the time the Mishnah has been codified, we need to examine it as a whole, "and not merely as the agglutination of an infinite number of all-too-clearly-differentiated parts."[97]

For Neusner, the framers of the Mishnah were philosophers who created a treatise that, when read whole and not just as the sum of its parts, reflected intellectually on life after the destruction of the Temple. When these individuals turned their attention to the law, they were most interested in its "gray areas," that is, those that fell between contrasting legal principles. Influenced by Mary Douglas's pathbreaking *Purity and Danger: An Analysis of Concepts of Pollution and Taboo* (1966), Neusner contends that these philosophers sought to posit two principles, juxtapose them, and determine the limits of each. This is why, he argues, they were so interested in food mixtures (priestly offerings in unholy food, kosher food in unkosher food, mixed plantings), and entities that fall between conflicting principles, such as women, minors, and hermaphrodites.[98]

It is on the level of the whole that Neusner moves from description to analysis. Whereas previously he had examined the redactional histories of the various tractates, Neusner now turned to the complete divisions and orders of which they form component parts. Here his interest shifted to the ways in which ideas are organized, in addition to how, and in what order, the Mishnah's topics are treated. In Neusner's deft hands, the rationality and philosophical acumen of the Mishnah's framers are on clear display. He concluded the book with the following statement that is worth quoting:

> The Mishnah's Judaism is a system built to celebrate that power of man to form intention, willfully to make the world with full deliberation, in entire awareness, through decision and articulated intent. So does the Mishnah assess the condition of Israel, defeated and helpless, yet in its Land: without power, yet holy; lacking all focus, in no particular place, certainly without Jerusalem, yet separate from the nations. This message of the Mishnah clashes with a reality itself cacophonous, full of dissonance and disorder. The evidence of the Mishnah points to a Judaism defiant of the human condition of Israel, triumphant over the circumstance of subjugation and humiliation, thus surpassing all reality. All of this is to be through the act of Israel's own mind and heart.[99]

Any work that seeks to break with the status quo is bound to engender criticism of the first order. Because Neusner went against the major academic trends in rabbinic Judaism—moving it from theological studies to religious studies—it is perhaps not surprising that his approach met with considerable negative reaction. Charges ranging from "sloppiness" and "wild theorizing" to a "disgraceful" bibliography and "torturous" prose abound in the responses not only to *Judaism: The Evidence of the Mishnah*, but to his corpus as a whole. It should come as little surprise to learn that Neusner's attempt to overturn traditional approaches to the Mishnah in particular and rabbinics in general would meet with such vociferous criticism. It is a testament to Neusner that he took all the criticisms against his work seriously and both responded to them in print and worked the more positive aspects into later iterations of his works.[100]

However, even those who were highly critical of *Judaism: The Evidence of the Mishnah* were quick to acknowledge the innovative nature of his methodology. Despite his negative assessment of the work as a whole, Shaye J. D. Cohen, then of JTS and subsequently Neusner's successor at Brown before moving onto Harvard, for example, called it "a brilliant failure," "a noble failure," and concluded his review with the remark that "this is a brilliant and imaginative book of the first rank, an important and stimulating contribution to the modern study of rabbinics."[101] Hyam Maccoby, an English scholar, remarked on, though ultimately he would disagree with, the "Copernican revolution" of Neusner and his students.[102] And Yaakov Elman of Yeshiva University commented that Neusner's "arduous labor deserves sober consideration by the scholarly world of the Academe . . . for more than anyone else in the last 150 years, [Neusner] has made a case for the *development* of the [Mishnah] in the first centuries of the Common Era."[103]

Many, needless to say, were critical of his documentary approach. Even those favorably disposed to the book, such as Elman, were nevertheless exceedingly critical in their reviews. Shaye Cohen, in his aforementioned review, criticized Neusner's approach with the comments that "synoptic texts must always be studied synoptically, even if one text is 'later' than another." Maccoby argued that Neusner is on shaky ground when he "proceeds on the assumption that the Judaism of the Mishnah authors can be fully described on the evidence of the Mishnah alone."[104]

One of the biggest critics of the work was E. P. Sanders of Duke University, who took Neusner to task for calling the Mishnah a work of "philosophy."[105] This is untenable for Sanders because Neusner works on the assumption that, although the Mishnah is a work of philosophy, those who framed it actually coded it—and thus imagined it—in another genre altogether, that of a legal code. This confusion of genres created fundamental problems, meaning that "Neusner wants the Mishnah to be more profound than it is."[106] Furthermore,

> The mistake about the Mishnah's genre, then, has several aspects. Thinking that its authors intended to express an entire world view, Neusner assumes that they denied whatever they did not include. Then he offers a positive account of their world view, and in doing this he misrepresents some of the Mishnah's stylistic features, such as the present tense and repeated formulas. These are characteristic of its true genre—legal discussion—but he tries to derive metaphysics from them. The result is the remarkable proposal that the Rabbis wrote in code: they wrote about everyday matters, but intended to convey a philosophical message about Timelessness. The mistake about genre leads Neusner further astray: not only does he fail to say what the Mishnah is, he bases his positive description on stylistic elements which should be explained in another way, and finally he offers a fantastic solution to the dilemma in which he has put himself.[107]

Because of this, according to Sanders, Neusner violated his own guiding and cardinal methodological principle that "what we cannot show we do not know." "The truth is," writes Sanders, "Neusner, like everyone else, attempts to glean from a text information which is not there in so many words. The only curiosity is that he claims not to do this."[108]

Several others critics also accused Neusner's work of being distorted by bias. Maccoby, for example, claimed that Neusner's analysis is composed of a mixture of "dry-as-dust fact gathering and wild theorizing" supplied by structuralism. Not in firm control of the complex material of rabbinical and biblical literature, Neusner "frequently blunders painfully."[109] Maccoby concludes that Neusner

> [d]eclares that we must not import into the Mishnah any ideas from outside sources, even from the liturgy, and we must allow the Mishnah to generate its own theology arising from its own chief preoccupations. Steadfastly closing his eyes to everything outside it, he has developed from the Mishnah alone a weird theology based on ritual purity, a theology that was in fact entirely unknown to the rabbis and is not expressed in the liturgy in which they articulated their deepest religious feelings. It is, to be blunt, the invention of Jacob Neusner, with some help from fashionable structuralist formulations.[110]

Shaye Cohen assented, in part, to this assessment. However, his comments are, perhaps, a tad more charitable. He writes,

> Neusner himself reads the Mishnah in the light of his own interests, which, being seventeen hundred years and several thousand miles further removed from the Mishnah than were the interests of the Tosefta and Tannaim, cannot be defended by chronological or geographical proximity. Neusner's interests, in fact, are not those of the second century but those of the twentieth. His Palestinian Jews are archetypes from contemporary American Jews, his "catastrophes" of 70 and 135 are archetypes for the Holocaust, and his Mishnaic theology is an archetype for theology after Auschwitz. Neusner has not read the Mishnah "on its own terms."[111]

Whether or not these are fair assessments is, of course, difficult to ascertain. Neusner certainly was aware of the fact that his methodological concerns did not operate in a vacuum. Moreover, his own desire to get a new generation of American Jews (and non-Jews) interested in the literature of early Judaism can be neither blamed nor discounted. Whether this amounts to a set of concerns when he approaches rabbinic texts that are hidden from view is a problematic charge.

Neusner responded to his critics. And responded. And responded. In the second, augmented edition of *Judaism: The Evidence of the Mishnah* he included several appendices in which he confronted, what he calls, their "cheap shots" and "feeble" attempts to discredit him by listing his book's misprints or trivial errors.[112] Neusner claims, and I think quite rightly, that behind such cheap shots and erroneous criticisms reside other, much more weighty matters, namely, a challenge to the status quo. He writes,

> So when paradigms shift, as they have, and the social foundations of learning change, as they have, we return to the original arena of Judaic discourse, the Mishnah. Scholarly debates today take the place of theological ones in medieval times; at issue in a misprint or a mistranslation is not correcting secular error but demonstrating sin and heresy.[113]

Neusner here argues that much of the criticism directed at him stems from his institutional setting. Rather than be based in a denominationally affiliated seminary, he worked within a secular and nonaffiliated university. In addition, Neusner is extremely critical of the Israeli university system, which he lumps in with the affiliated seminaries of the United States. Despite Neusner's willingness to engage his critics in the appendices of his *Judaism: The Evidence of the Mishnah*, nothing was resolved. He and his students remained committed to the documentary hypothesis, whereas critics such as Sanders, Maccoby, and Cohen were convinced that his exegesis amounted to a form of eisegesis. And, it is clear that Neusner believed that his approach to rabbinics has carried the day, as the title of one of his 1995 books clearly reveals: *The Documentary Foundation of Rabbinic Culture: Mopping Up after Debates with Gerald L. Bruns, S. J. D. Cohen, Arnold Maria Goldberg, Susan Handelman, Christine Hayes, James Kugel, Peter Schaefer, Eliezer Segal, E. P. Sanders, and Lawrence H. Schiffman.*[114]

Commentator on Judaism in America: *Stranger at Home* (1981)

Neusner was also proving himself to be an astute commentator of the experiences of American Jews. Since his days as a student in Oxford, when he first encountered Gerald Reitlinger's *The Final Solution*, he had been preoccupied not only with the Holocaust, but with the fate of Jews, especially in America. Many of these topics would come to the fore in his *Stranger at Home: "The Holocaust," Zionism, and American Judaism*. Here, Neusner concerns himself, unlike other scholars, not with how Jews can come to terms with the Holocaust, but with whether or not Judaism can survive without anti-Semitism. He writes that "the real test of Judaism has yet, therefore, to be faced: it is whether Judaism can flourish when unnatural conditions of persecution and oppression do *not* prevail, but when freedom does. Is Judaism a frail flower that can live only when protected in a hothouse, or is it hardy enough to grace perennially the garden of humanity."[115]

Neusner is particularly critical of the American Jewish community that, he believed, lacked any sense of its own history, and thus of its identity or purpose. As a result, it clings to the Holocaust and Zionism to give it meaning. These two phenomena, Neusner argued, are far removed from American Jews' everyday experience, yet nevertheless form the myth by which American Jews define themselves. This is what informs them what it means for them to "be Jewish." Since most American Jews, especially today, neither witnessed the Holocaust nor are particularly interested in living in, let alone visiting, the modern State of Israel, the question must be asked, why be Jewish? In the essays in this book, Neusner explores the ideological and the theological problems associated with the rather strange choices that American Jews make in order to identify as "Jewish" over against their otherwise normal American identities. Neusner states the paradox in the following terms: "why American Jews sustain the contradictory position of deeming the State of Israel to be critical to their own existence as a distinctive, self-sustaining group in American society, and also insisting that they and their future find a permanent place within American society" is by no means clear and needs to be worked out.[116]

For Neusner, the myth of destruction (the Holocaust) and rebirth (the formation of the State of Israel) becomes the prism through which American Jews experience and understand their own reality. This myth, however, entered into American Jewish discourse only in 1967 when Israel's existence was threatened amid the world's indifference, and its rapid victory over its enemies. This myth now provides the rationale for Jewish existence in America, especially among nonreligious Jews, who have nothing left to cling to. Neusner explains the ramifications of this myth on American Jews as follows:

> So if you want to know why be Jewish, you have to remember that (1) the gentiles wiped out the Jews of Europe, so are not to be trusted, let alone joined; (2) if there had been "Israel," meaning the State of Israel, there would have been no "holocaust"; and so (3) for the sake of your personal safety, you have to "support Israel." Though you do not have to go live there, it is a mark of piety to feel guilty for not living there.[117]

The result, for Neusner, is that American Judaism lives behind a veil that separates it from its own realities. It has constructed itself around myths and symbols that invoke other times and places. This means that American Judaism is adrift, largely ignorant of its own set of unique concerns. Bondage and anti-Semitism seem to be much easier than freedom for Jews for maintaining an identity. Such an identity, however, will always prove to be negative and simplistic. Neusner encourages American Jews to demand more. If American Jews do not, all that will remain is an ethnic identity bereft of any religious content. This ethnicization of Judaism means that, for most Jews, "the chief Jewish issue is phrased in wholly ethnic terms: whether children marry Jews is more important than whether they build Jewish homes, whether people live in Jewish neighborhoods matters more than whether the neighborhoods in which they do live are places of dignity and commonplace justice."[118]

These are bold claims, indeed as bold as anything that he wrote concerning the formation of rabbinic Judaism in the late antique period. His solution was as daring as it was universal. American Jews must, on his reading, remove both the Holocaust and the State of Israel from the center of existence and allow for religion to replace ethnicity. The result should be a renewed Judaism that contributes positively to American civilization. The myth of destruction and redemption, in other words, prevents American Jews from creating their own theological understanding of themselves.

* * *

The president of Brown once told Neusner that if he wanted another appointment in Jewish studies, he would need to raise a two-million-dollar endowment and create a list of potential donors. Neusner's response: Are Catholics expected to pay for medieval history? Or do local Protestants fund positions in the Reformation? Neusner rightly saw two potential paths for Jewish studies. One, which he chose to take, involved studying Jewish data as any other data set, not because the data were somehow intrinsically special, and doing so in an objective and nonjudgmental fashion. The other path, the one not taken by him but often taken by others, was that of an ethnic ghetto, one entrenched with identity politics.[119] His was a path, however, upon which he would increasingly walk alone.

6

"Orwell's 1984—and Mine"

The 1970s and 1980s witnessed Neusner's increasing disillusionment with and alienation from Brown. In his 1995 *apologia pro vita sua, The Price of Excellence*, he blames this on the diminution of academic standards at the university in particular and in American higher education in general. This decrease in standards, Neusner argued, was brought about by affirmative action, the politicization of the classroom that occurred during the Cold War, and the growing separation between research and teaching in the professoriate. He blamed the Brown administration for watering down the curriculum and encouraging mediocrity among both students and faculty.[1] He also faulted the so-called New Curriculum that was instated at Brown the year after African American students walked out in protest in 1968. This curriculum was predicated on the notion that students should be actively responsible for their education, which meant that they should be able to develop independent concentrations with a faculty adviser rather than having to major in traditional subjects.[2] Neusner became so critical of affirmative action that it, more than anything, seems to have precipitated his switch from the Democratic Party to the Republicans.[3]

This, of course, was Neusner's take on things. Like most academics, he often elevated the debates he had with colleagues into ideological battles. He was not afraid of being—and indeed he seemed to derive energy from being—a contrarian voice. It was probably no coincidence that his critique of the liberalization on American college campuses at the time of Vietnam occurred when he was becoming an increasingly active Republican. He frequently wrote in the Brown student newspaper, the *Daily Herald*, about how bad the administration was, and how students no longer met, what he perceived to be, the high standards of the late 1950s and early 1960s. This "golden age," not surprisingly, coincided with the time when he himself was a student at Harvard, at Oxford, and then at JTS and Columbia—though he complained bitterly throughout his life about all four institutions. Although he thought that all of these issues should be a matter of public debate, his Brown colleagues disagreed. While he saw a meritocracy of the mediocre, his colleagues undoubtedly saw an increasingly disgruntled and problematic colleague.

It is safe to say that Neusner alienated himself from his colleagues, from Brown, and, increasingly, from the field of Jewish studies. He was very critical of the latter, as we have seen, on account of how the field was structured along predominantly ethnic lines. In terms of rabbinics, this alienation was perhaps inevitable since he thought that because he was right, everyone who did not agree with him had to be wrong. And he had to show publicly how and why his critics were wrong and he was right. In the 1990s, we begin to see the publication of numerous books with highly polemical titles such as *Are the Talmuds Interchangeable? Christine Hayes's Blunder.* Furthermore, he never curtailed the urge to air publicly his grievances with deans, provosts, and presidents of his university, in addition to writing harsh book reviews on pretty much everything that came out in the field of Jewish studies that did not agree with him. He also continued to be a vociferous critic of American Jewish leadership and other mainstream Jewish organizations, and frequently took them to task in the Jewish press. He was critical of JTS, for example, for offering an endowed chair to a non-Jew, and wrote a disparaging article about the lack of academic credentials of the new president of Hebrew Union College.[4]

If the home front grew increasingly problematic, however, Neusner's career was in full blossom, and this saw him feted in other circles. In 1988, for example, he received the Dottore ad Honorem in Scienze Politiche (indirizzo storico-politico) from the University of Bologna, which was conferred during the celebration of the nine hundredth anniversary of the university. In addition, he would go on to receive eighteen academic medals and honorary degrees. Despite this, he increasingly became isolated and alienated at Brown. It is unfortunate that when Neusner is remembered, it is primarily because of his notoriously difficult personality, and not necessarily on account of his massively important contributions to the study of rabbinics and religious studies. The year 1984 was key for Neusner, and he frequently framed the time in Orwellian terms. It was a year in which he faced growing criticism not only at Brown, but also in the field. It was a year, writing to Zev Garber, about which he said, "Orwell himself would not have been surprised."[5] Neusner wrote a lengthy piece documenting his trials and tribulations, to which he gave the name "Orwell's 1984—and Mine," in which he wrote,

> When George Orwell wrote "1984," he was not thinking of the state of Jewish scholarship. But in 1984 I found out how much Orwell knew about the political world of Judaic studies. The thought police, the resort to newspeak, above all, the memory hole—we've got them all. I know—I nearly slid down the memory hole or, at least, people tried to shove me in. . . . Orwell's great insight is that the best way to destroy your enemy is to pretend he never existed. Having been a non-person in circles of Jewish scholars, particularly in Jerusalem and at Jewish seminaries in the USA, for more than a quarter of a century, a non-person whose work may not be reviewed, quoted, or even cited in bibliographies, I know whereof he speaks.[6]

A Commencement Speech You'll Never Hear (1981)

A sign of things to come with both his colleagues and the administration at Brown occurred as early as May 1981. Neusner—frustrated with the administration, his colleagues, and the students on campus—wrote an infamous article in the campus newspaper, the *Daily Herald*, that focused on what he considered to be the dilution of academic standards at Brown, something that had bothered him ever since the implementation of the New Curriculum in 1969. To coincide with the end of the academic year, Neusner composed a mock commencement speech that he claimed students would never hear because they were too busy being praised by their professors, the very same professors who, in their desire to be appreciated by the students, had lowered academic standards in the first place. The piece caused such a furor that it is worth quoting in its entirety:

A Commencement Speech You'll Never Hear

We the faculty take no pride in our educational achievements with you. We have prepared you for a world that does not exist, indeed that cannot exist. You have spent four years supposing that failure leaves no record. You have learned at Brown that when your work goes poorly, the painless solution is to drop out. But starting now, in the world to which you go, failure marks you. Confronting difficulty by quitting leaves you changed. Outside Brown, quitters are no heroes.

With us you could argue about why your errors were not errors, why mediocre work really was excellent, why you could take pride in routine and slipshod presentation. Most of you, after all, can look back on honor grades for most of what you have done. So here grades can have meant little in distinguishing the excellent from the ordinary. But tomorrow, in the world to which you go, you had best not defend errors but learn from them. You will be ill-advised to demand praise for what does not deserve it, and to abuse those who do not give it.

For four years we created an altogether forgiving world, in which-ever slight effort you gave was all that was demanded. When you did not keep appointments, we made new ones. When you were late to class, we ignored it. When your work came in beyond the deadline, we pre-tended not to care. Worse still, when you were boring, we acted as if you were saying something important. When you were garrulous and talked to hear yourself talk, we listened as if it mattered. When you tossed on our desks writing upon which you had not labored, we read it and even responded, as though you earned a response. When you were dull, we pretended you were smart. When you were predictable, unimaginative, and routine, we listened as if to new and wonderful things. When you demanded free lunch, we served it. And all this why? Despite your fantasies, it was not to be bothered, and the easy way out was the pretense: smiles and easy B's.

It is conventional to quote in addresses such as these. Let me quote someone you've never heard of, Professor Carter A. Daniel, Rutgers University, in the *Chronicle of Higher Education*:

> College has spoiled you by reading papers that don't deserve to be read, listening to comments that don't deserve a hearing, paying attention to the lazy, ill-informed, and rude. We had to do it, for the sake of education. But nobody will ever do it again. College has deprived you of adequate preparation for the next fifty years. It has failed you by being easy, free, forgiving, attentive, comfortable, interesting, challenging, fun. Good luck tomorrow.

That is why, on this commencement day, we have nothing in which to take much pride.

Oh, yes, there is one more thing. Try not to act toward your coworkers and bosses as you have acted toward us. I mean, when they give you what you want but have not earned, don't abuse them, insult them, act out with them your parlous relationships with your parents. This too we have tolerated. It was, as I said, not to be liked. Few professors actually care whether or not they are liked by peer-paralyzed adolescents, fools so shallow as to imagine professors care not about education but about popularity. It was, again, to be rid of you. So go, unlearn the lies we taught you. To Life![7]

The fallout was massive. In a few hundred words, Neusner attacked his students, his colleagues, and the administration of the university that employed him. Many took him to be calling students lazy, claiming his colleagues to be involved in a popularity contest as opposed to education, and excoriating the administration for allowing this to happen. Although Neusner subsequently said that his goal was to attack not the students but a professoriate that had become too lax and permissive, students seem to have taken the most affront, hearing in Neusner's words that their degrees were essentially worthless. Seniors, just weeks from graduation, wrote hundreds of letters to the paper and, personally, to Neusner at his home. The response was so bad he had to get a new, unlisted telephone number. In a little over six hundred words, he had effectively alienated himself from the entire campus. As if this was not enough, the faux commencement speech was picked up by the national media, reprinted in daily newspapers throughout the nation and even overseas, and he was invited on the *Today Show* and *Phil Donahue* to talk about the brewing maelstrom.[8] Jacob Neusner had become a household name.

Both the administration and the faculty maintained a position of official silence on the matter. Neusner, however, claimed that this was the beginning of the end for him on campus. The faculty began to ostracize him and the administration began to treat him with contempt. He believes that had he not been tenured he would have been fired. Neusner maintained that faculty who wanted to be popular, at Brown or any other campus in the country, had made students lose their capacity for working hard and for taking responsibility for their actions and had deprived them of the ability to learn from their mistakes. As a growing conservative, Neusner argued that the dumbing down on college campuses witnessed in the 1980s was the direct result of the permissiveness of the 1960s, especially its liberal and antiestablishment biases.[9]

Departure from Religious Studies at Brown

In the aftermath of the faux commencement speech, relations between Neusner and the Department of Religious Studies, his academic home since his arrival at Brown in 1968, began to crumble. While Neusner blamed this souring relationship on the commencement speech, his colleagues at the time, Giles Milhaven and Sumner B. Twiss, blamed it on various long-standing conflicts between Neusner and the department. These conflicts, for them, could be reduced to his treatment of students and his difficult personality.[10]

In the midst of the fallout from the mock commencement speech, Neusner accused his departmental colleagues of making appointments without his input, of refusing to authorize new courses that he wanted to teach, of not allowing him to teach at the times that he wanted, and of calling departmental meetings behind his back. In a memo to Twiss, then chair of the Department of Religious Studies, Neusner wrote, "The freedom to teach the subject one wishes to teach, in the way one wishes to teach it, is so fundamental that any claim on the part of a chairman to infringe upon that freedom or to have the right to abrogate it—as indicated in your memo to me—must be regarded as a danger and a threat to the very integrity of the academic work of this University."[11] He also took particular exception when the department co-appointed (with Comparative Literature) Elinor Grumet, a specialist in American Jewish literature, as a visiting assistant professor without consulting him or others who specialized in Judaism in the department.[12]

In order to end the growing impasse between Neusner and his colleagues in the department, Maurice Glicksman, the provost, began an initiative to separate them from one another. The best way to accomplish this, he thought, was by creating a distinct Program in Judaic Studies that would be housed in a different location. To this end, the Center for the Study of Judaism came into existence in the fall of 1982. This new arrangement gave Neusner the intellectual freedom to continue his revolution in Jewish studies, even though, of course, he had always been critical of the potential for "ghettoization" that programs devoted solely to Judaism faced.[13] After the new program had been formed, Neusner wrote to Twiss, "There is no reason to pursue any discussion with you. You are beneath contempt. It is now clear and fully exposed for all to see that you devised and pursued a program aimed at attacking me and a policy aimed at removing me from the life of the Department of Religious Studies. . . . I shall accept no further memos from you; I shall toss into the waste basket, unread, any further writings from you, and will not only not reply, but will not even take the trouble to return to you what I do not read."[14] Around the same time Neusner was nominated for the presidency of Brandeis University, but seems to have withdrawn after an initial interview.[15]

Writing to his former colleagues in religious studies, Neusner attached an anonymous poem clipped from the pages of the *National Review*, a magazine to which he was a regular contributor. He reproduced it because "it has sustained me for the hell of the past year and a half, and I leave it as my gift to you." It reads,

> We asked for strength that we might achieve;
> God made us weak that we might obey.
> We asked for health that we might do great things;
> He gave us infirmity that we might do better things.
> We asked for riches that we might be happy;
> We were given poverty that we might be wise.
> We asked for power that we might have the praise of men;
> We were given weakness that we might feel the need of God.
> We asked for all things that we might enjoy life;
> We were given life that we might enjoy all things.
> We received nothing that we asked for: all that we hoped for.
> And our prayers were answered.
> We were most blessed.[16]

Despite the fact that Neusner had spent his life trying to integrate the academic study of Judaism into the discipline of religious studies, his experiences in that department at Brown ended in failure and mutual recriminations. After he left, the department refused to cross-list any of the courses on Judaism taught in the new program. In a memo dating to November 22, 1983, Neusner subsequently refused to have any of his courses listed in the Religious Studies graduate brochure. Fortunately for both fields, he did not universalize his negative experiences with his department and Brown, and would continue the task of integration at both the national and international levels. This is to say that although he now found himself within a Jewish Studies Program at Brown, he sought to do in that program that which he could not do in the Department of Religious Studies. The new program afforded him the freedom to continue the revolution in the study of Judaism that he had launched decades earlier. He and Ernest Frerichs began to bring in other humanists, social scientists, and historians who enabled the program to become a cosmopolitan research center, one of the foremost centers in the country. In the summer of 1983, Neusner had threatened to resign as codirector of the program because a program "is a lesser academic unit than a department," and he felt that there was little option beyond dissolution. In response, Provost Glicksman informed Neusner and Frerichs that a visiting committee would come to Brown in the fall to evaluate the program's research, undergraduate and graduate programs, and external funding with an eye toward applying for departmental status.[17]

Neusner's Jewish Studies Program, unlike pretty much every other Jewish studies program or department in the country, was staffed primarily by non-Jews. Frerichs, for example, was a Methodist minister, and another colleague, Wendell S. Dietrich, the specialist in modern Jewish thought, was also a Presbyterian minister.[18] In 1983 they hired a young historian, David Sorkin (now at Yale University), who had just completed his doctoral dissertation at the University of California, Berkeley. Sorkin worked on modern European Jewish history, especially in Germany, a focus that would complement Neusner's primary area of expertise in the late antique period and Frerichs's work in the biblical period. Things did not go well, however. I assume it would have been difficult for a young scholar to keep up with the publication rate and personality of someone like Neusner. Although Neusner would be a wonderful mentor to his own students, it is not always clear how much of a mentor he was with younger colleagues who graduated from other programs and who then came to work with him as a colleague.[19]

At a May 31, 1985, meeting—which included Neusner, Frerichs, and Sorkin, essentially the Jewish studies faculty at Brown—Neusner informed Sorkin that he did not intend to recommend his appointment for renewal. Neusner was critical of Sorkin's teaching and his research portfolio, since he had yet to produce a monograph. Because the program formed such a small faculty, Neusner reasoned at that meeting that they did not want to have any "deadwood" within it. Sorkin appealed the decision, citing that Neusner's criteria for reappointment were more stringent than those of the university as a whole.[20] Sorkin was, in 1987, offered a position at Oxford University, before going on to distinguish himself as a well-respected historian of European Judaism at the University of Wisconsin–Madison, City University in New York City, and now Yale.[21]

Despite the negative assessment of Neusner, Brown's Committee on Faculty Reappointment and Tenure (CONFRAT) unanimously overruled the decision. They instead appointed Sorkin to the History Department. Neusner reacted poorly, accusing the administration of trying to undermine his own professional stature while simultaneously trying to dismantle the Program in Judaic Studies as an effective academic unit within the university. Neusner immediately resigned as co-director when he found out about CONFRAT's decision on November 5, 1985. In a letter to President Swearer and Provost Glicksman, he also resigned as a member of the Graduate Committee, which meant that he would refuse to admit any further graduate students (agreeing to see through those already in the program), in addition to refusing to engage in all programs and activities at the university, including the project of working toward departmental status for the Program in Judaic Studies. "You can compose your own list," he writes to both of them, "it is all abolished. Henceforth I teach my courses and do my research: nothing more, like everyone else." He also accused the administration of being opportunistic: "It is not possible to build something of excellence in this University under your administration, because my standards are high, demanding good writing, clear conceptualization, well composed books and articles, teaching theoretical and disciplinary character, and yours are accommodating and political and adventitious and merely opportunistic."[22]

The following month, on December 16, 1985, Neusner heard that the university had denied departmental status to the Program in Judaic

Studies, which he took as a further slap in the face from the administration. This was despite the fact that an external review committee, chaired by the president of Emory University, James Laney, had recommended the upgrade to full department, which would have meant an increase in the university's financial commitment to Jewish studies. The external committee, however, did note that there was a potential problem of having a department that was so dominated by the personality of one person. If such a person should leave, they reasoned, the department might find itself on unsolid footing. One of the reasons mentioned was that the program needed more time to show that it could attract sufficient students and create "a nurturing environment for junior faculty." The latter seemed to refer not just to Sorkin, but also to other young faculty members who had left the Program in Judaic Studies over the years, such as Robert Fleck, Leo Weinstock, and Robert Fradkin. Neusner responded that this was incorrect and he had done all that he could to nourish his young faculty, and instead accused President Swearer's administration of "intemperate deeds."[23]

To top it all off, Neusner had a rogue graduate student, Richard E. Cohen, at this time. Cohen had come to Brown from Harvard Divinity School to work with Neusner in the fall of 1985, at the height of the impasse between Neusner and Brown. Cohen was accepted, the first student since 1982, on the condition that he spend a year in Israel doing preparatory language work. By 1987, Cohen and Neusner were at odds with one another. Cohen accused Neusner of taking his fellowship check out of his mailbox and withholding it, of inappropriate grading procedures, of blocking the publication of an article that he was preparing for one of Neusner's books, and of engaging in a campaign of defamation. Neusner, who it is worth noting had never had such a negative relationship with a graduate student, replied that Cohen was unstable and that he was innocent of the accusations. Cohen filed an official complaint against Neusner, and compiled a sixty-three-page dossier documenting his complaint.[24] Cohen also seems to have filed a formal complaint against Neusner and Brown with the Department of Education.[25]

The Faculty Executive Committee (FEC) heard the complaint and held a two-day hearing on the matter on June 14 and 15, 1988. Neusner refused to attend and, by this point, was communicating with the university about the incident only through his lawyer. The FEC ruled that the Program in Judaic Studies should grant Cohen a master's degree for work having been completed, and that the president should reprimand Neusner in writing for "harassment of a graduate student."[26]

Neusner, needless to say, interpreted the whole Cohen affair in light of the Sorkin incident and the refusal to grant the Program in Judaic Studies department status, indeed in light of his whole career at Brown since he wrote "A Commencement Speech You'll Never Hear." He saw the committee as a "lynching party" out to get him. Summing up Neusner's behavior from the side of his faculty colleagues, George Landow, professor of English and art history and chair of the Faculty Executive Committee, wrote to him saying that his behavior was disgraceful, violating faculty member decorum and making faculty self-governance almost impossible.[27]

It was around this time that President Swearer stepped down and Vartan Gregorian took over. To celebrate, Neusner wrote "When a Presidency Changes" in the *Brown University Faculty Bulletin*. One of his points was certainly informed by his recent incident with Cohen:

> If Brown is to have graduate programs, then students who fail in them should not have the power, as they do now, to disrupt the University through a grievance process that favors the aggrieved party by giving the academic failure three or four hearings on exactly the alleged grievances, before one authority or hearing board after another. A grievance procedure that is fair to the professors as well as to aggrieved students is needed to protect academic freedom, integrity and excellence.[28]

Despite all of these events, some of which must have taken an inordinate amount of time to deal with, Neusner's work and fame continued to increase. Writing in June 1988, he reflected on the Cohen affair and offered insight into the problems that it and others had caused him. He had now stopped accepting graduate students and was even frustrated with teaching undergraduates: "I never minded the time, I minded the rest, and now I have back, even, the time. Consequently my work goes forward at a stunningly successful pace, and after a couple of years of fearing that I would run out of ideas, I find that has not happened, and is not apt to happen."[29]

Attempts to Leave

While all of this was going on at Brown, Neusner tried desperately to leave. In one letter, he lamented that he had not left after his first couple of years. He surely would have, he said, if his children's Jewish education in a stable and large enough Jewish community had not been a concern. While his academic writing and his methodological advances were certainly well known and respected in certain circles, also well known was his penchant for stubbornness and creating problems wherever he went. He wrote in right-of-center publications, many of which were openly hostile to the liberal values of the academy. In addition, his public attacks against his colleagues and the academy in general would certainly have preceded him as he sought employment at other institutions of higher learning in the country.[30]

He had been encouraged to apply, for example, to the newly created List Professorship at Harvard, his alma mater. Neusner, wanting to leave Brown once and for all, applied but was subsequently informed that the principal virtues that the university was looking for in their ideal candidate were "an irenic personality and acceptability to all segments of the Jewish community at large." This seems to have been code, and certainly Neusner took as such, that they were looking for someone who was more interested in fund-raising among alumni and local community than in building an academic program of excellence. Neusner subsequently withdrew his application and wrote to John Strugnell, an expert on the Dead Sea Scrolls, who had encouraged him to apply:

I believe I am not qualified for the position and herewith remove my name from any further consideration. The position appears meant to serve ecumenical, rather than academic purposes, but ecumenism surely is entirely legitimate at the Harvard Divinity School. Nothing in your report suggested that the Divinity School faculty has in mind the development of a major center for the religious study of Judaism, among other religious traditions. So those qualifications that I believe I do bring to the position in no way prove relevant.[31]

He ended this letter with a cheeky wager that, I believe, reflects Neusner's principles:

So let us now inaugurate a friendly competition between Harvard University, in its nascent interest in Judaism as a religion (within a divinity faculty, to be sure) and Brown University, and twenty years from now, we shall all be retired, let us see which University has accomplished the goal of defining the field, in education, scholarship, and academic standards. The beneficiary of this friendly competition will be the humanities and higher education in America.[32]

In his February 2, 1985, On Language column in the *New York Times*, William Safire, a fellow conservative and friend of Neusner, wrote an article titled "Good Night, Irenic," wherein he shared with readers the entire affair at Harvard.[33] Over thirty years after Neusner's friendly wager with Strugnell, we can ask who won. But it may be that no one has. Both Neusner's and Harvard Divinity School's approaches to Judaism still exist. Whereas Neusner sought to bring the study of Judaism into the secular university, many today still want to treat the tradition benignly. Whereas colleagues at other universities were more interested in collegiality and administrators desired, first and foremost, to establish and maintain peaceful relations with potentially wealthy donors, Neusner always put the academic aspect of the field front and center. He deserves credit for this. Was it disingenuous, though, for Neusner to believe that what many universities wanted was ecumenism, on all levels, as opposed to hiring an individual notorious for his mercurial personality? Probably, yes. If Neusner had had a different personality, he probably would have been poached by any of these universities. However, and here is the paradox, his personality is precisely what drove him to accomplish what he did.

Another case in point, something that happened at around the same time, was his withdrawal from the Koshland Chair that had been recently established at Stanford University. Neusner had applied for the position and written a fairly detailed description of how he conceived of the chair, its relationship to the university and the field more generally, and why he was a perfect fit for it. He was invited to campus for an interview and told that, in addition to the usual faculty and deans, he would have to meet with both Hillel and faculty members involved in the local Jewish fund-raising effort. When he returned home, Neusner wrote the following to the chair of the Search Committee:

> While I personally share the goals of Hillel, on the one side, and the UJA and Jewish community organizations, on the other, I do not believe that it is appropriate to join these activities to a candidacy for an academic professorship. Perhaps in your context I take too strict a view of the severely academic definition of the work of a professor of Judaic studies, and, on that account, I believe I would not be a suitable candidate for your consideration. In any event I have to conclude that the interests of those involved in defining the chair involve matters inappropriate, in my view, to the tasks of an ordinary professor and scholar, and that my goals in building Judaic studies as an academic field do not entirely cohere with the goals of yourself and your colleagues for the position at hand.[34]

Again, to his credit, Neusner was trying to distinguish Jewish studies as an academic field and celebrations of ethnic pride, whether for students or local community members. He never vacillated once from this vision.

Another humorous encounter, at least in retrospect, happened at Northwestern University, where he interviewed for the Klutznick Chair in Judaic Studies. Neusner walked out halfway through the process and returned home. His reason, as he explained in a letter written to the president of Northwestern as soon as he returned home, was that he discovered the donor was a good friend of another candidate's father. The donor went to the lecture and out to dinner with that candidate, but not the other two, one of whom was Neusner.[35] Again, for Neusner, this was yet another example of the unsavory and incestuous nature of Jewish studies.

Judaism and the Humanities: Toward a Jewish Humanities

Neusner, as we have seen, was unique in his desire and ability to bring the academic study of Judaism into conversation with the larger themes in religious studies in particular and the humanities in general. This was inspired, I have suggested, by his lack of a traditional yeshiva education, his doctoral training in religious studies, and the sheer force of his personality. All of these combined to produce a fresh outlook on what it meant to study Judaism in the academy. Jewish texts were not worthy of study simply because they were Jewish texts, written by Jews in different times and places. If they were self-evidently important, according to Neusner, then they would not need to be analyzed, but simply described. Rather, according to Neusner's model, such texts, like any texts, had to answer or point toward a particular problem that was raised by larger questions posed by entrenched disciplines. If Jewish scholars of Jewish data did not or could not answer larger disciplinary questions, according to Neusner, Jewish studies risked becoming little more than a vehicle of special pleading or ethnic pride. These were two things that might well appeal to local communities, donors, and students, but made Jewish studies the laughing stock of the rest of the university.

Another feature that contributed to Neusner's desire to connect Jewish data to the humanities was his work with the National Endowment for the Humanities (NEH). Writing in the *Chronicle of Higher Education* a few months after his appointment by President Carter in 1978, he remarked that humanists, in general, were not good at addressing what it is they do or emphasizing the larger questions that they should be asking. "What will they deem important?" he asks. "What are the urgent questions, and what are the trivial?"[36] He reinforced this point with a letter he circulated to his colleagues on the National Council on the Humanities in 1981 in which he argued that the organization needed to define clearly what it meant by "the humanities." Conservative critics, many of whom were Neusner's personal friends, had argued that the Council and the NEH had been responsible for all "the sins of liberalism" since 1933. In the circular, Neusner argues that there are two distinct ideas about what we mean by the humanities. The first is that there are academic disciplines (history, literature, religion, philosophy, art, etc.) that constitute a subject within the humanities. The second idea is that there is "the humanities" in general, something that transcends the various disciplines: "an attitude, a way of mind, a mode of perception." Neusner, given his own training in a discipline, and given the fact that so many in Jewish studies were not interested in questions of disciplinarity, gravitated to the first of these two ideas, realizing that the second was what the NEH had traditionally supported and funded. At the same time, however, Neusner was cautious that we retain some sort of vision of the whole so that we do not see each discipline of the humanities as a complete field in and of itself. The major way to counter conservative criticism that sought to dismantle the NEH (and the NEA), according to Neusner, was to explain to the public sector what it is that humanists do. Whereas today we speak of a crisis in the humanities, Neusner spoke of a crisis of self-definition.[37]

It seems that one of the overarching goals of Neusner on the NEH was both to reward and to advance what he considered to be sound projects grounded in disciplines. In so doing, he contributed to the larger conversation of how to advance pathbreaking scholarship at the national level that was akin to what he was doing at the local level in Jewish studies at Brown. For him, the task of a national endowment devoted to the humanities should be "(1) the nurture of academic learning in the various disciplines of the humanities; and (2) the dissemination at various levels of education, as well as in the community at large, of the results of humanistic learning."[38]

While such an approach might put him on the more conservative wing of the Council, he nonetheless thought that the endowment ought to show others the values that humanists espouse and profess, the greatness that inheres in humanity, and the works of beauty created by the creativity of the human mind and emotion. All of this returns us to Neusner's lifework, to show how each statement made about Judaism functions as an example of some point or question that is common to all those working in the humanities. The particular, in other words, illumines the general in such a way that the study of Judaism becomes relevant to our larger understanding of the human condition. In his *Judaism in the American Humanities*, for example, Neusner reflected on his time on the National Council on the Humanities. He writes in the preface,

> Two issues, in particular, engaged my attention. First, I wanted to know what we mean by "the humanities," and why there should be a public program aimed at the nurture and dissemination of humanistic learning and expression. Second, I wished to learn how the humanities might reshape my understanding of my own field of study, so that I might become a better teacher and scholar.[39]

It is against the backdrop of the humanities that the particular—Judaism, the study of Judaism—moves from the private and the parochial to that which is general and universal. For Neusner, the relevance of the humanities resides in its study of humanity writ large, of which the Jews form but a part. "The importance of the humanities," he writes, "finds its measure in the importance of ourselves, of our significant humanness."[40]

In the essays in *Judaism in the American Humanities* Neusner encourages us to ask tough questions about the intellectual and social worth of what we study and teach. Returning to the problems he had with the traditional study of Judaism that he encountered as a young rabbinical student at JTS, he argues that there can be nothing—no subject matter, no discipline—that is intrinsically interesting. The scholar makes choices, based on taste and judgment, in the service of larger problems. This is the task of the humanities in general and the study of Judaism in particular: it teaches people how to think. The absence of a vocational connection is what justifies and legitimates what it is scholars in the humanities do. This is why he was so critical of affirmative action—he thought it meant people would be allowed in and subjects taught at universities that did not or could not justify intellectually their inclusion. If Jews like him could make it on their own merit, he reasoned, then everyone should.

Yet, for Neusner, the connection of the humanities to Judaism was good not only for the academy and scholar of Judaism, but also for the Jewish community at large. What he calls a "Jewish humanities" had the promise to reinvigorate Judaism at a formative time in its development. Rather than hold on to previous models such as the Holocaust, anti-Semitism, or Zionism, Neusner argued that an understanding of the history, philosophy, literature, and religion of the Jews shows the humanity of Judaism. A scholarly approach to Judaism has the ability to stimulate and to encourage the freedom of imagination—the hallmarks of the humanities—to Jews.[41]

This is in keeping with Neusner's belief that it is the academic study of Judaism—not the Sunday school, not the synagogue—that will be the future of ideas within the Jewish community in this country. This is also a large part of the reason, I am convinced, that Neusner was so hard on contemporary institutions within American Judaism. For him, it was extremely important to get American Jews to respect Jews who learn from books, and who teach from book writing, as opposed to those who perpetuate the myths of insularity and focus solely upon anti-Semitism.[42]

The Israeli Academy

Neusner's relationship to the Israeli academy was aloof at best, and openly hostile at worst. I think it fair to say that its relationship to him was much the same. Neusner had lectured there twice, on the same trip—at the University of Haifa and at the University of Tel Aviv—in 1976. He always felt that Israeli scholars of rabbinics, who largely bought into the traditional paradigm of Talmudic study of which he was so critical, tended to ignore his work. Things took a downward spiral in late 1983, hitting their nadir in 1984.

In 1983, an Israeli scholar teaching at McMaster University in Canada, Albert I. Baumgarten, published an article on the origins of the name of the Pharisees in the *Journal of Biblical Literature*, the preeminent outlet in the field of biblical studies. In that article he did not once cite the extensive work of Neusner but did cite favorably those of whom Neusner was critical, for example George Foot Moore, and those who were critical of Neusner, including Saul Lieberman, Morton Smith, and E. P. Sanders.[43] In a personal letter to Daniel Schwartz, in the Department of History at the Hebrew University of Jerusalem, Neusner wrote that this oversight was intentional and an international scandal, "one from which the Hebrew University will benefit not at all":

> Specifically, scholars do not engage in theologico-political boycotts. They disagree with one another, criticize one another, but, so long as they wish to be regarded as scholars and not politicians, theologians, or clowns, they do not *ignore* one another as if the other does not exist. Now so long as you people are kept in your cages in Jerusalem, the rest of the world was not forced to confront your elaborate and ostentatious "ignoring of Neusner" campaign. . . . In Hebrew you can play that game; no one reads what you write in Hebrew anyhow, and no one takes seriously anything your sect does. But in English it is a circus, and there is now an enormous public reaction.[44]

Neusner took Baumgarten's failure to mention him or any of his work (or that of his students) to be symbolic of his treatment at the hands of Israeli scholars. It would be one thing, he argued, to take him and his ideas to task in a public venue such as an academic journal. However, to ignore completely his ideas was not only to treat him as nonexistent, but to imply that his many writings devoted to this topic were completely irrelevant.

Things got even worse in the following year. The Historical Society of Israel invited Neusner to Jerusalem to lecture in celebration of the fiftieth anniversary of its journal, *Zion*. The organizers of the event asked him for his paper in advance, with the understanding that they would translate it into colloquial Hebrew for him to read at the conference. Neusner penned, in English, a lecture that examined the Israeli tradition of scholarship on Jews and Judaism as presented in *Zion* over the past fifty years. He titled the lecture "Methodology in Talmudic History." His argument was typical: he accused the Israelis who wrote in *Zion* of believing everything the two Talmuds said, and not applying any critical methodology. In the published version, Neusner raised several uncomfortable, yet important, questions, putting the study of Talmud in counterpoint with the more critical non-Jewish approach to biblical studies:

> From the very beginnings of Talmudic history, the critical program of ancient history and of biblical studies remained remote. By the 1850s, biblical studies had attained a quite critical program. From the time of Geiger, Graetz, and Frankel, down to nearly our time, by contrast, it has been taken for granted that a story in a holy book about an event accurately portrays exactly what happened. The story itself has no history, but is history. No special interests or viewpoints are revealed in a given historical account. Everything is taken at face value. Since historians and story-tellers stand together within the same system of values, it was unthinkable that anyone would either lie or make up a story for his own partisan purposes. No one would wonder, *cui bono*? To whose interest is

it to tell a given story? Obviously, if a learned rabbi told a story, he said it because he knew it to be so, not because he wanted to make up evidence to support his own viewpoint.[45]

Neusner here illustrates what a critical approach to rabbinic literature ought to look like and compares it with what he regarded to be the largely uncritical approach in Israel, as represented in *Zion*, the very journal whose jubilee the conference was to commemorate. If the Talmud says that a rabbi said something, then he really must have said it. Why, after all, would rabbinic sages lie or fabricate things for political or other ideological purposes? This is the approach, it will be recalled, that Neusner originally adopted in his own doctoral dissertation, before repudiating it as naïve and little more than fiction. *Zion*, now taken as a symbol of Israeli scholarship, was, for Neusner, not about analysis, but about the collection of "facts" about rabbis and other Jews who lived in the land of Israel and Babylonia. There was little or no interest in basic critical questions with which normal historical study commences. The lecture he sent to the Historical Society of Israel basically scolded Israeli scholars for their naïveté. Several months later, on March 5, 1984, he received a one-paragraph note from Zvi Yekutiel, the director of the Society:

> Dear Prof. Neusner,
> As a result of changes in the last minute in our program, we had to change the character of the convension [*sic*]. According to the new program, it will be an internal Israeli meeting and we appologize [*sic*] to all participants from abroad for the inconvenience we have caused them.
> Sincerely Yours,
> Zvi Yekutiel,
> Director[46]

Neusner was livid. He took the "change in plans" to be a personal affront and a rebuke to his work. Writing to Lawrence Schiffman, he claimed,

"We are not talking about personal insults or mere whims. We are talking about a boycott of twenty-five years standing. We are talking about a systematic denigration of everything I have done, on the part of people both in Jerusalem and in nearly all centers of Jewish studies in this country."[47] For him, this episode symbolized all that was wrong with the Israeli academy. It was too conservative, too methodologically unsophisticated, and so hostile to his own approach that it would rather ignore or censure him than listen to his viewpoint. He never forgot this event, even though he and Yekutiel seem to have reached at least a détente in the following year. Even some twenty years later, as the old guard had largely retired or passed away and he was beginning to find an audience among a new generation of Israeli scholars, he still referred to this as "the world famous Jerusalem boycott."[48]

The rationale for the dis-invitation was that the nature of the conference had changed from international to national. Despite this, two Americans, Isadore Twersky and Arthur Hertzberg, were still welcome on account "of the special connections these scholars have with the Hebrew University."[49] The president of the Historical Society of Israel, Menahem Stern, wrote to Neusner, basically saying that the conference organizers did not like his angry outbursts surrounding the Baumgarten article published earlier in the year:

> It has been admitted that the organizing committee could have considered you also as an exceptional case. However, it seems that the scandal attached to the JBL article of Baumgarten in which you involved active participants of the conference and of the organizing committee led people to think that you were not interested in coming. Nobody could understand why such people as Levine, Schwartz and Herr are to blame for an omission of a reference in Baumgarten's article. They have not written the article and are not responsible for its contents.[50]

Neusner responded to Stern's letter with two of his own over the next two days. The first was a one-page "public reply" that was formal and concluded with the statement "I do acknowledge with thanks the letter that you have written, which is important evidence toward the establishment of the facts of the matter."[51] The second, written on the following day, was a three-page "personal note" that was much more accusatory. In it, he accused Stern of trying to "exculpate your junior colleagues, who have made use of the Historical Society of Israel for a personal vendetta against me."[52] He claimed that the invitation and subsequent dis-invitation was less about personal anger than methodology, that is, the Israeli versus the Jacob Neusner way of doing things:

> In point of fact, "if" I am right in my statements on method then your colleagues cannot do the work they wish to do, since, in my view, the evidence at hand does not sustain the types of inquiries they propose to undertake. . . . Schwartz writes articles on what time of day Pontius Pilate went to the toilet (so to speak). Heer writes articles telling us the motives and intentions of figures of ancient fairy tales, as though he knew what they were thinking as they went about their affairs. Levine writes articles on the politics of Rabbi Judah the Patriarch, as though the sources at hand were stenographic reports of things people really said, or a TV camera recording of things people really did.[53]

He ended the letter by saying the way to refute him is not through humiliation or ostracism, but through intellectual refutation. "Write a better book," he says, "I'll be impressed. I'll be the first to say so. That is what scholarship is about."[54]

Neusner nourished this hurt for a long time. He was always critical of Israeli scholarship on rabbinics in general, and that carried out at the Hebrew University of Jerusalem in particular. Neusner would always remark that at the university's library his books were not kept open on the shelf, but behind the desk "under lock and key, along with the pornography"—I am never sure if this is a metaphor because the Hebrew National Library at the Givat Ram campus has closed stacks, wherein patrons request books that are then fetched, or if he is referring to the fact that his books were not in the open shelves in one of several of the library's reading rooms.[55]

A case in point might be the acerbic comments he levels at Eliezer Segal, a Canadian scholar of rabbinics who received his training at the Hebrew University of Jerusalem. Writing in 1995—a period that witnessed him produce numerous polemical books devoted to attacking those who disagreed with him, often in very personal terms—Neusner had the following to say of Segal and what he considered to be his methodological lack of sophistication, even though, and it is worth noting, Neusner published the book in his own series:

> Now why this claim that Jerusalem is now *hors de combat*? It is because Segal's allegation that I have provided no evidence on behalf of the method contains a confession of not bankruptcy but mere incomprehension and sheer ignorance. And it is an ignorance for which Segal's education in Jerusalem bears the burden of guilt, since for decades my books were kept under lock and key, along with pornography, and not given a place on the open shelves of the reading room of the Jewish National and Hebrew University Library of Jerusalem! So, in Segal's defense, it must be said, he may simply not have had access to educate himself in a university in which ideas do not circulate freely and come under responsible debate at all. But that is responsibility enough for making so stupid a statement as we shall take up in Chapter Two.[56]

For Neusner, the Israeli academy in Jewish studies in general and of rabbinics in particular represented an extension of the yeshiva approach to the texts. It was an approach, moreover, that we have seen Neusner rejected and fought vociferously for his entire academic career. His debate with the Israeli academy, symbolized so clearly in his invitation and subsequent dis-invitation from the Historical Society of Israel, was personal, scholarly, and ideological—all at the same time.

Neusner would claim the same year that his ostracism was not unique to Israel. When Steven T. Katz published an article titled "Issues in the

Separation of Judaism and Christianity," also in the *Journal of Biblical Literature* and only several months after Baumgarten's piece, Neusner accused him of also ignoring his entire corpus.[57] Writing in "Orwell's 1984—and Mine," Neusner proclaimed that Katz's article

> took up the problem of what happened in the Jamnian period of Judaism in respect to the treatment of Christians. In that article Katz, like Baumgarten, ignored every word my students and I have ever written on the problem of Jamnia in general and on the Christians in that age in particular. . . . Worse still, Katz made use of the sources in ways which I have argued are not appropriate to a critical approach to learning, but he ignored that criticism, as though it did not exist. He made no effort to answer or to deal with the issues of the critical use of sources. He just pretended nothing had been said about quoting sources as though trained reporters recorded everything said and done—when that is not what happened in ancient times. (I of course was not asked to vet the article.) I slipped further down the memory-hole.[58]

The end of 1983 and the beginning of 1984 thus signaled to Neusner that his novel approach to rabbinic sources was so revolutionary that others either did not want to deal with the fundamental issues it exposed or were quite simply incapable of so doing. Although Neusner reacted angrily to what he perceived to be his ostracism by Baumgarten, the Historical Society of Israel, and Katz in separate incidents, they were in retrospect three versions of the same theme. What Neusner wanted, though, was engagement with his work. Instead he encountered a situation in which he believed that others did not feel they even had to acknowledge his criticism or reply to it. Little did he know at the time, however, that things were soon to get much worse.

Lieberman's Review

At around the same time that Neusner had his invitation from the Historical Society of Israel revoked, one of the most scathing reviews of his work appeared in the pages of the *Journal of the American Oriental Society* (*JAOS*). Neusner, as we have seen, was certainly not immune to criticism, and he never hesitated to incorporate, if possible, the positive, while responding, often in kind to the negative. This review, however, was somewhat different and particularly painful because, as we have seen, not only did it come from his old teacher of Talmud at JTS, Saul Lieberman, a person whom he had thanked for support early in his career, it was also published posthumously. Although many previous reviews of Neusner's work had accentuated what they perceived to be his sloppiness and poor translations that did not properly understand the nuances of the text in question, let alone the literal level of the Aramaic or Hebrew original, it was Lieberman who elevated this criticism, and indeed his review represents one of the most extended critiques of Neusner's translative ability, throwing, for many, his entire project into doubt.

Even though the review article, "A Tragedy or a Comedy?," was published after Lieberman's death—it will be recalled that he had died of a heart attack en route from New York to Tel Aviv on March 23, 1983—it seems to have circulated even before his death. An editorial note by Jack Sasson, the Near Eastern and Bible editor of the journal, immediately followed the article and informed the reader that Lieberman "had promised the *JAOS* the above review and had mailed to Jerusalem a handwritten manuscript which he had prepared for submission. Under the present circumstances, my role as editor has been limited to preparing it and sending it to print. Professor Neusner has declined an invitation to respond." Neusner, however, had wanted to respond, and he wrote the editors telling them as much, to which they did not reply. Neusner, it seems, was aware of its existence, if not the actual contents, even before it appeared in print. As for the contents of the actual review, which offers an assessment of three tractates of Neusner's then recently published *The Talmud of the Land of Israel: A Preliminary Translation and Explanation*, Lieberman strongly criticized Neusner's ability to translate. He begins by claiming that Neusner did not fully understand the manuscript tradition of the texts he purported to translate, "a fact with which any rabbinic student is familiar."[59] For Liebermann this leads to problems on the part of the translation:

> Hence one begins to doubt the credibility of the translator. And indeed after a superficial perusal of the translation, the reader is stunned by the translator's ignorance of rabbinic Hebrew, of Aramaic grammar, and above all of the subject matter which he deals, as we shall presently demonstrate.[60]

From this initial assessment, Lieberman goes on to catalogue select mistranslations and other blunders as a way to discredit the whole. He calls some of the translations "pure inventions," "senseless," and "almost unbelievable that a modern student of rabbinics should be entirely uninformed regarding a document which was treated in detail by many scholars for over a century. And behold, how much the document is being distorted and mutilated!"[61] Lieberman acknowledges that some of Neusner's non-translative works are "meritorious," and that "they abound in brilliant insights and intelligent questions." However, lest the reader believe that this is praise, he immediately counters, "In the beginning, when he was well aware of his ignorance of the original languages, he relied on responsible English translations of rabbinic texts (like those of Soncino Press)." However, once he began to think that he could do the translations himself, Lieberman opines, he ran into serious difficulties. Lieberman then concludes the article with the following statement:

> As I have previously stated I have presented only a few examples of our translator's learning and I conclude with a clear conscience. The right place for our English translation is the waste basket. A preliminary trans-

lation is not a mockery translation, not a farce of an important ancient document.[62]

This damning indictment, what Neusner later called a "Parthian shot," created a considerable response. There was a failed campaign mounted, by whom it is unclear, to persuade the University of Chicago Press to take the entire Talmud translation out of print. The dean of faculty at HUC-JIR apparently sent a copy of the review to all the faculty in the Cincinnati, Los Angeles, and New York campuses, presumably as a way to discredit Neusner's reputation and stature in the field.[63]

Neusner responded in three ways. The first was through his long-time lawyer, Norman G. Orodenker, of Providence. Orodenker wrote to Wolf Leslau, the president of the American Oriental Society, which published the *JAOS*, putting the society "on notice that we are examining that article in accordance with the well-established case law of the United States on scholarly criticism to determine what further action, if any, we shall recommend to Dr. Neusner." Orodenker had in mind the issue of what constituted the bounds of fair criticism as permitted in *Ollman v. Evans and Novak* (U.S. Court of Appeal, District of Columbia Circuit, March 6, 1984). In this case Ollman's offer of chairmanship of the Government Department at the University of Maryland, College Park, had been rescinded on account of a libelous article written by the columnists Rowland Evans and Robert Novak. They accused Ollman of being a Marxist and of indoctrinating rather than teaching students. Orodenker certainly would have known, however, that Ollman's suit was defeated in the District of Columbia Circuit Court, which held that Novak and Evans's column was protected speech. Needless to say, the letter was more, as it says in so many words, about putting the American Oriental Society on notice that Neusner and his lawyers were not happy with the review and the situation surrounding it.[64]

Neusner's second response to Lieberman's review was scholarly. He incorporated Lieberman's criticisms of the actual translation into an appendix of volume 23 of his *Talmud of the Land of Israel: A Preliminary*

Translation and Explanation. This is in keeping with Neusner's stated goal of always learning from and incorporating the criticism of others. The third was to launch his own attack against Lieberman, which in characteristic fashion came in the form of a monograph with the polemical title *Why There Never Was a "Talmud of Caesarea": Saul Lieberman's Mistakes*, which he published in 1994, to mark the ten-year anniversary of the original review. He opens the introduction with the claim that Lieberman

> teaches us nothing about what we should do, but only how we should not undertake the work at hand. As we shall see, out of Lieberman's one ambitious monograph on the dating of documents, one could compile a handbook of obvious errors of method, blunders of logic, and above all, failures systematically and conscientiously to accomplish the tasks of serious research. So far as, in time to come, he has any reputation at all, it will have to rest on something other than the work we examine here.[65]

Whether or not this amounts to a revenge attack to compensate for Lieberman's scathing criticisms ten years earlier is difficult to say. Neusner would certainly deny it, and instead remark that the intent of this work was simply to reveal the shortcomings of the closed-mindedness of the yeshiva world, which is less interested in ideas than it is in matters of philology. Neusner took Lieberman's criticisms to be a sign that he was ruffling feathers in that world precisely on account of the novelty of his own approach, something that was actually based on a critical methodology.

The Fallout: Smith's Revenge

Perhaps the most bizarre use to which the review was put occurred at the annual meeting of the Society of Biblical Literature (SBL) in Chicago in 1984. The previous year Neusner had been invited by the executive secretary of the organization, Kent Harold Richards, to be the third scholar in a new series that the SBL was implementing for the coming year. The series was titled "How My Mind Has Changed (or Remained the Same)" with the idea of having major scholars in the field reflect on their careers, and how they had changed (or not) over the years. The session would have involved Neusner giving a twenty-minute lecture, to which two scholars would respond for fifteen minutes each, and Neusner would have the final word in the final ten minutes, before a question-and-answer session.[66]

Neusner agreed and the session was advertised in the annual program for the meeting as follows:

> Formative contributions to biblical studies provoke years of discussion. This program unit provides a forum for retrospective and prospective reflections by the scholars who produce these seminal works. Raymond E. Brown and Frank Moore Cross, Jr. have been recognized previously in this important series. Professor Jacob Neusner of Brown University, whose works are numerous and pivotal, is the third scholar in the series. The session will focus on two of his books: *Judaism: The Evidence of the Mishnah* and *Judaism in Society: The Evidence of the Yerushalmi*. A paper for this session is published in *SBL 1984 Seminar Papers*. You are encouraged to take advantage of this significant opportunity.[67]

The event was to take place on Monday, December 10, from seven to nine o'clock in the evening in one of the large and ornate ballrooms in the Palmer House Hotel, where the meetings were being held. A. T. Kraabel, a specialist in Hellenistic Judaism, of Luther College and Anthony J. Saldarini, a leading Christian scholar of Late Second Temple and Rabbinic Judaism, of Boston College were to serve as the respondents. Well over six hundred people attended, including a variety of scholars and graduate students from many fields of both the SBL and the American Academy of Religion, which met concurrently.

At the beginning of the session, Morton Smith, Neusner's former teacher, walked stiffly and quickly to the first row immediately facing the lectern. Beside him was a large shopping bag with two boxes inside. He sat upright throughout Neusner's comments and the two responses, and when comments and questions were invited from the floor, his hand shot up. Recognizing him, W. D. Davies of Texas Christian University, the chair of the session, pointed to Smith, who stood and proceeded to the lectern. After a few rambling comments about the inaccuracies of Neusner's translation—and not the books that were supposed to be under discussion—and the danger they posed to the future of the field, he proceeded to open the boxes in his shopping bag and hand out copies of Lieberman's review to the audience. Davies pleaded with Smith to desist until the end of the session, but Smith ignored him and continued to pass out the reviews. Neusner, needless to say, was dumbfounded.

Davies then asked Neusner if he would like to respond. With Smith still passing out the reviews, Neusner went up to the lectern and said, "Things do not always turn out as planned. Professor Smith was my teacher, and I honor him. He has helped me in difficult times. I honor and respect his criticism, and I am always happy to hear it." He then sat down to subdued applause, while Smith finished handing out the Lieberman review. The session subsequently ended without any further discussion.[68]

This event was for Neusner, as he later confided to me, the lowest point in his academic career. It is unclear what precipitated these events in Chicago. According to Neusner, it resulted from a falling out between the two over their differing interpretations of the Pharisees. Smith at the point of the SBL fiasco was, according to Neusner, "a very bitter and angry man." Neusner also believed that Smith was mad at him because he refused to endorse Smith's reading of Jesus as found in the latter's *Jesus the Magician*, which included the idea that Jesus engaged in magical procedures of initiation that were sexual in nature. Others have suggested that the falling out occurred over Neusner being one of the principal accusers in the fraud charge against Morton Smith's supposed discovery and publication of a letter he found in the Mar Saba monastery in Israel written by Clement of Alexandria, otherwise known as the Secret Gospel of Mark.[69]

To make matters worse, Hershel Shanks, the editor of *Biblical Archaeology Review*, published the ramblings of Smith, who also served on the editorial advisory board of the journal. By the time they found their way into print, Smith's largely extemporaneous ramblings had been transformed, according to Neusner, so that they no longer resembled the original claims. Smith said the following about Neusner:

> Since I have often and deservedly recommended Professor Neusner's earlier historical works, so that his reputation reflects to some extent my sponsorship, I now find it my duty to warn you that his translation of the Palestinian Talmud contains many serious mistakes. It cannot be safely used, and had better not be used at all. . . . The translation is a serious misfortune for Jewish Studies, because the people who use it will not only repeat Neusner's mistakes, but make new ones based on the misinformation his work will provide them. Therefore please warn your colleagues, your students, and your librarian. In Lieberman's words, the place for this translation is the "waste basket," an opinion with which I completely concur. So you can see for yourselves that the mistakes are not mere trivialities but often major matters—entire textual sources ignored, critically important passages omitted, assertions translated as negations, unknown rabbis invented, and so on—to show you the importance of the mistakes, I have brought Xeroxed copies of Lieberman's review, and these I shall now pass around in the hope that they may do something to diminish the coming crop of Neusnerisms.[70]

The *Biblical Archaeology Review*, however, did not mention the contents of Neusner's lecture or the comments of his two respondents. Yet, for some reason, Shanks felt free to mention previous critical comments by Lieberman and Shaye J. D. Cohen. In response to this publication, Neusner had his lawyer, Norman Orodenker, send a letter to Smith informing him that they were also "putting him on notice that we are examining your statements as reported in the *Biblical Archaeology Review* (March/April 1985) in accordance with the well-established case law of the United States on scholarly criticism in order to determine what further action, if any, we shall recommend to Dr. Neusner." Perhaps in response to the threat of a lawsuit, Shanks published an apology of sorts in the next edition of *Biblical Archaeology Review*: "Perhaps we should not have reported the incident at all, either because we are so widely read by lay people or because the subject matter is not sufficiently close to Biblical archaeology. If we have wronged Neusner, we apologize." Shanks, then, goes on to say, "He surely asks the right questions, which in our judgment, is more important than whether he always comes up with the right answers."[71]

Nothing legally came of the threat to either Smith or the *Biblical Archaeology Review*. And, again, Neusner would respond, in scathing fashion, to Morton Smith in 1998, long after the latter had died, this time in his preface to the reprint of a work by Birger Gerhardsson, a Swedish scholar of the Christian origins:

Like Arthur Darby Nock, but lacking his perspicacity and cultivation, Smith made his career as a ferocious critic of others. Smith thereby surrounded himself with a protective wall of violent invective; what he wished to hide, and for a while succeeded in hiding, was the intellectual vacuum within. Of his entire legacy one book survives today, quite lacking influence but still a model of argument, and a handful of suggestive but insufficient articles. In all Smith wrote three important contributions to scholarship, one a model of argument and analysis though broadly ignored in the field to which it was devoted, another a pseudo-critical but in fact intellectually slovenly and exploitative monograph, and the third an outright fraud. . . . As to the scholarly fraud, who speaks of it any more, or imagines that the work pertains to the study of the New Testament at all? I need not remind readers of this reprint of the scandal of Smith's "sensational discovery" of the Clement fragment, the original of which no one but Smith was permitted to examine. Purporting, in Smith's report, to demonstrate that the historical Jesus was "really" a homosexual magician, the work has not outlived its perpetrator. In the end many were silenced—who wanted to get sued?—but few were gulled.[72]

The Next Step: The Talmudic Representation

Because the Mishnah focuses on why things are the way they are, and attempts to arrange all of existence within a great chain of being, with the God of Israel at the top, Neusner claimed that it was systematically philosophical and only rarely theological. If the Mishnah was a work of philosophy, however, it would gradually have to be put within a different frame of reference—or at least be interpreted within a different frame of reference—in order to win broad appeal. Later literature, in particular the two Talmuds, was responsible for this and succeeded in re-presenting the Mishnah theologically. The two Talmuds—the one codified in the land of Israel, approximately 400 CE, and the other in Babylonia, around 600 CE—provide not only clarification and amplification of the Mishnah, but also theological "representation." The latter Talmud, the so-called Bavli, would form the conclusive statement of Rabbinic Judaism and is its reference point from its closure until the present day. It is in this work, above all, that we witness the final phase of Judaism the religion, what Neusner called "the Judaism of the dual Torah."[73] The Talmuds, combined with the various midrashic collections, succeed in allowing the sages to make Scripture into their own work by framing it within their own unique terms of reference.

Whereas the Mishnah rarely referred directly to Scripture, the later presentations of rabbinic Judaism allowed these sages, or rabbis, to write with it and engage it in a manner that spoke to their own existential concerns. This was not mere commentary, but active participation. Neusner compared this to art, as the rabbis used "Scripture as an artist uses the colors on the palette, expressing ideas through and with Scripture as the artist paints with those colors and no others." Scripture now became the locus wherein these individuals found the wisdom and truth that guided them. This provided them with the language and syntax to work out a set of issues that were of contemporaneous relevance to them. They did not write about Scripture, according to Neusner, but wrote with it. It is within this context that they began to think about topics that are referred to as theological: Israel and its relations to God, other nations, and so on.[74]

Neusner defined theology in the following terms:

> Theology is the science of the reasoned knowledge of God, in the case of a Judaism made possible by God's self-manifestation in the Torah. Seen in its whole re-presentation in the Talmud of Babylonia, the theology of Judaism sets forth knowledge of God. This is in two ways. The first is to know God through God's self-revelation in the Torah. This requires that we know what the Torah is, or what torah is (in a generic sense which can pertain to either message or media or modes of thought). Then knowing how to define and understand the Torah afford access to God's self-revelation. The second is to know through that same self-revelation what God wants of Israel and how God responds to Israel and humanity at large. That specific, propositional knowledge comes through reasoned reading of the Torah, oral and written, the Mishnah and Scripture, represented by the Talmuds and Midrash-compilations, respectively.[75]

If previous studies had worked on the documentary approach to understand the various works of literature on their own terms in order to elaborate *historical* theology, Neusner now moved from the discrete parts to the whole. This led to one of Neusner's famous mantras that "it is not the system that recapitulates the documents, but the documents that recapitulate the system."[76] In other words, these diverse writings constantly refer back to and take for granted a coherent and generative system that is composed of a set of interlocking paradigms.

Jewish theology, for Neusner, becomes the later theological representation of the Mishnah's philosophy that witnesses the development and articulation of a set of themes that provide information about what the faithful can know rationally about God. The result of this is decidedly *not* philosophical, but religious and theological, in character.

* * *

The mid-1980s found Neusner at an important place in his career. He was roundly recognized by his supporters as a pioneer in the field, someone who refused to repeat the traditional and religiously based approach to rabbinic texts. Even his critics, including Lieberman, acknowledged the novelty of his approach. But it was so novel his critics did not know what to do with it. If his approach was largely rejected in Jewish studies, it did find a ready hearing—as the SBL panel indicated—in the world of non-Jewish scholarship.

As he was receiving critical acclaim, and the concomitant criticism that went with it, however, his position at Brown was becoming increasingly tense and precarious. By the mid-1980s his children were growing up and looking to go to college. If previous attempts to get out had ended in failure, things would now become so bad, in part because of his own making, that by the late 1980s they would reach a tipping point. But 1984 was, for Neusner, a symbolic year. At the end of "Orwell's 1984—and Mine," he writes,

> Judaic Studies are not going to be forced back into the ghetto by threats or curses. These medieval methods provoke only amusement. Anathematize books? Ostracism and boycott? These things do not work any more. If they did, I would have disappeared long ago.
>
> The texts now are there for all—Jew and gentile—to study. The issues have been framed systematically and rigorously. We who draw upon the critical agenda of Spinoza and the Enlightenment have had our say and

will continue our work. If others wish to disrupt or impede our work, they will find only disappointment, as they did last year.

1984 was not their year. It also was not the first tough year I have known, nor in any way the most difficult. In fact, for me it proved reassuring. The enemy had its say, and turned out to have nothing much to teach anybody. . . . *1984 brought into the open things that for many years had been said and done in secret.*[77]

7

Political Intrigue

Neusner's last years at Brown were very difficult. He was determined to leave, but uncertain where he would end up. He even contemplated taking early retirement if nothing worked out. His personal correspondences from this time reveal a real frustration with his situation at Brown, and growing conflicts with colleagues. I suspect that many of these conflicts were exacerbated by the political culture in Washington, to which he was increasingly exposed during the 1980s and early 1990s. Everything now became political: Brown and his colleagues there represented the excesses of liberal values to the increasingly politically conservative Neusner. If he had battled the status quo in Jewish studies, he now sought to wage a similar battle against what he considered to be the special interests and identity politics that he believed posed a real threat to American higher education.

There is, however, a real contradiction here. Although his work on Judaism was exceedingly revolutionary, his political beliefs—on what constituted art and scholarship, for example—might strike us today as extremely conservative and even old-fashioned. Nevertheless, his beliefs seem to have been motivated by his extreme dissatisfaction with affirmative action, something that he believed led to intellectual laziness and identity politics. These were two features of which he was extremely critical in Jewish studies. Since Neusner had entered Harvard, Oxford, and Columbia based on his own merit and sheer hard work, he contended that Jewish studies, or any other area or ethnic study, had to do the same. A balkanized university in which Jewish studies existed for Jews, women's studies for women, African American studies for African Americans, and so on was bound to collapse under the sheer weight of identity politics. Such a compartmentalized university, he argued, would not be a place where one engaged in pure scholarship or asked difficult questions. It was these difficult questions, Neusner believed, that were foundational to his own transformation of the study of Judaism in ways that were consistent with traditional disciplines. Without these disciplines, he reasoned, the modern university is little more than a place where traditionally excluded groups simply celebrate themselves and their contributions.

His political conservatism ultimately emerged out of this milieu. While it may be difficult to square with the daring of so much of his scholarly work, it is nonetheless informed by the same desire to maintain intellectual standards across the board. That he could support legislation for art censorship when he was on the NEA that was even more radical than that proposed by Senator Jesse Helms, his friend, is a corollary of this. Neusner, while a political conservative, was certainly not the equivalent of today's "tea party" wing of the Republican Party. Unlike them, he believed in the two national endowments, but he did have distinct ideas about what they should and should not fund.

The Culture Wars

The 1980s and 1990s were turbulent times in American political culture. The so-called left and right were increasingly at odds with one another over what each considered to be the proper direction for the country. In the world of arts, literature, and scholarship this meant that many conservatives were critical of government subsidies funded by taxpayer dollars, especially those that seemed to undermine what they perceived to be so-called American values. For many liberals, however, art, literature, and scholarship were less about jingoistic nationalism than they were about undermining the values and normativity of the status quo. Anything else amounted to censorship. The virulence of the debate is perhaps best summed up in a speech at the 1992 Republican National Convention in Houston, Texas, given by Pat Buchanan, the American conservative political commentator. He proclaimed to his like-minded audience, "My friends, this election is about much more than who gets what. It is about who we are. It is about what we believe. It is about what we stand for as Americans. There is a religious war going on in our country for the soul of America. It is a cultural war, as critical to the kind of nation we will one day be as was the Cold War itself."[1] Buchanan would later claim that this cultural war was about the power over society's definition of right and wrong, and that its main theaters included abortion, women's rights, sexual orientation, and taxpayer-funded art. Neusner would increasingly be drawn into these debates about the future of American values and the relationship of such values to art and scholarship.

Neusner was brought into these debates because of his involvement with the two major national endowments, both created in 1965—one for the humanities, the other for the arts. For their supporters, these two programs were, and still are, responsible for strengthening the teaching and learning about the arts and humanities in schools and colleges across the nation, facilitating research and original scholarship, and providing access to cultural and educational resources. For critics, however, these very same endowments provided taxpayer support to a host of programs and exhibits that not only were a waste of money, but also had the power to undermine the values of American society. If taxpayer dollars were to support such programs, they reasoned, there should be aesthetic standards that conformed to popular taste and judgment. To many supporters of the endowments, this sounded like censorship.[2]

At stake in these debates was the very definition of "arts" and "humanities." Were these two concepts to be stripped of all controversy, sanitized, and made to stand for the best that humans aspired to in the past, thereby serving as a role model for the present? Or was it the goal of the arts and humanities to push boundaries, revealing uncomfortable assumptions about the white, Christian, and male status quo? Supporters of the latter option only needed to point to the fact that the so-called good arts—ballet, opera, and literature—were subversive and new when first presented. Cultural conservatives, however, further argued that the purpose of the arts and the humanities was to reproduce the "true," the "good," and the "beautiful," and do so, moreover, within the context of distinctly American virtues such as democracy and national pride. Arts and culture, on this reading, become the provenance of every American, and those produced by minorities (women, African Americans, Latinos) become, by definition, "special interest" precisely because they are not open to the whole population. "Special interest," it is worth noting in this context, often functions for conservative critics as code for a liberal and multicultural agenda that threatens the "mainstream." The conservative position, not coincidentally, always presents itself as centrist with a goal to protect the "moral majority" from the radical fringe of what is often referred to as the secular left.

Rethinking a Political Allegiance

Earlier we saw Neusner as a Jewish intellectual, a scholar of religion, and a critic; it is now time to turn to his role in some of the intractable political debates of the 1980s and 1990s. In these debates, he was less a critical voice seeking to redefine a field of inquiry than he was a defender of the status quo, someone with distinct ideas about what arts, humanities, and scholarship ought to be and what values they should uphold. Again, I note the paradox mentioned earlier, namely, that a rebel in Jewish scholarship became a political conservative upholding the values of the "moral majority." Perhaps it is easiest to say that here, once again, Neusner broke the mold of what was expected of him. If most academics are notorious for their liberal views, Neusner once again went against the grain. As we saw earlier, Neusner's first political affiliations were with the Young Conservatives while a student at Oxford University. But, as he himself admits, this had less to do with ideology than with post–World War II criticisms of America from the British left.[3] Indeed, in an article written in February 1954 and published in the *Oxford Tory*, the young Neusner explains and contextualizes for his British audience the investigations of subversive activity by congressional committees in the United States. "Mr. Neusner," the editors inform their readers, "is an American, and a supporter of the Democratic Party."[4] He was, as he himself noted, a proud American, and since America's friends in 1950s Britain were the Conservatives, he gravitated to them. When he returned to America, Neusner affiliated with the Democratic Party, campaigning for, among others, Edward Kennedy in his 1962 senatorial campaign.[5] Increasingly, though, he became disillusioned with the Democrats. This disillusionment seems to have begun in the 1970s when he became highly critical of Democratic support for minority quotas, which, as we have seen, was symbolized for him by Brown's New Curriculum. This curriculum, he argued, indulged students by encouraging them to do whatever they wanted as opposed to engage the traditional model that Neusner believed trained them thoroughly in a discipline. What is important to note—and this probably contributed to his thinking on the matter—is that Neusner had successfully expanded this traditional model to include Judaism. The canon of Western civilization would now have to include, thanks to him, previously excluded works such as the Mishnah, the Talmuds, and other works of formative Judaism. Others, he argued, had to make the same case that he had.

By 1972, he firmly supported Nixon's reelection bid. And although it was President Carter who, in 1978, would appoint Neusner as a member of the National Council on the Humanities, the citizen's advisory board to the National Endowment for the Humanities (NEH), Neusner had become, by that point, a committed conservative and card-carrying Republican.[6] Since everything in Washington is about political connections, it seems that Neusner's connection to the White House was Robert J. Lipshutz, who had served as President Carter's national campaign treasurer in the 1976 presidential bid and was subsequently the White House counsel from 1977 to 1979. Neusner had taught Lipshutz's son, Bobby, at Brown and written a letter of recommendation for him in his law school applications. Neusner, pragmatic person that he was, sent a copy of his letter to the father.[7] This was the first of many connections, as he would soon befriend other highly connected individuals, though mainly in the Republican Party.

It was as a member of the National Council on the Humanities, on which he served from 1979 to 1984, that Neusner grew critical of what he called the "special interests" at the NEH, and the petty politics that determined who and what projects were funded. He was, thus, greatly inspired with the election of Ronald Reagan to the presidency in 1981, and his subsequent appointment of William J. Bennett to the chairmanship of the NEH in the same year. Like Bennett, Neusner took a conservative position on affirmative action, curriculum reform, and religion in education. Both supported a classical education that emphasized the accomplishments of Western culture, which for Neusner included Judaism, and minimized the value of multiculturalism or liberalism in the educational curriculum. What Neusner had going for him in all of these debates was his own work in Jewish studies. Not infrequently, he invoked—or others invoked—his other title, that of "rabbi." Rabbi Jacob Neusner could demonstrate to all who cared to listen that the place of area studies, and the place of those traditionally excluded from the education curriculum, was in the heart of the humanities, and not in some program that was based on identity politics and special pleading. If a Jew, a rabbi no less, could speak to the ills of affirmative action and identity politics at the heart of ethnic and area studies at the university, many would take note. His voice thus became more important than, say, that of another white male politician.

Neusner increasingly became a political conservative on the NEH. Supported by powerful and influential friends—such as Lynne Cheney, William F. Buckley, Jr., William Safire, and Jesse Helms, to name but a few—he gravitated toward the highly conservative views of Bennett. Writing in 1983 in the *National Review*, Neusner hails Bennett's credentials and desire to transform the agency in a way that would make it more "publicly accountable" and "transparent." These latter terms function as metaphors in the cultural wars of the 1980s as creating "good humanities," that is, humanities that led to "intellectual refinement and spiritual elevation," but were extremely critical of "special inter-est humanities," symbolized by such fields as women's history or Afri-can American literature. Whereas the so-called good humanities were transparent, so the narrative went, special interest groups using identity politics had hijacked the field to create "special interest humanities." Of Bennett, Neusner writes,

> He came to Washington to speak of greatness: "Great works, important bodies of knowledge, and powerful methods of inquiry constitute the core of the humanities and sustain the intellectual, moral, and political traditions of our civilization." He's one chairman any conservative should be proud to quote.[8]

Neusner would become an even greater conservative voice on the National Endowment for the Arts (NEA). His tenure there was marked by a number of high-profile cases, most notably, public funds that had supported the photography of artists such as Robert Mapplethorpe and Andres Serrano (perhaps most famous for his *Piss Christ*), both of whom cultural and political conservatives had attacked for, among other things, producing offensive art supported by tax dollars.

Change of Heart: From Democrat to Republican

Neusner, as we just saw, did not start out as a conservative. He worked on the 1962 senatorial campaign of Edward Kennedy; he voted for John Kennedy and Adlai Stevenson and, even as late as 1968, for Hubert Hum-phrey.[9] At some point during the Nixon administration, Neusner seems to have changed his political allegiance. In an article in the *Brown Daily Herald* in the fall of 1972, he makes it clear that, unlike his rival, Senator McGovern, Nixon was opposed to minority quotas. Nixon, according to Neusner, had "ended the policy of imposing (minority) quotas in government, university, and elsewhere." Only such an attitude, Neusner believed, could truly stand for "an open, free society." Neusner was also opposed to "the draconian punishment inflicted on universities which cannot show 'enough' black faces, or 'enough' Spanish-speaking people, or 'enough' women.'"[10]

Rather than have such quotas, Neusner called for establishing preparatory fellowships for students who were underqualified for university studies.[11] If this was not done, he reasoned, then such students would be set up to fail, thereby reinforcing traditional stereotypes. The alternative, to accept students without requisite skills and preparation, would create a university with a caste system. Here, it is worth noting, that Neusner was writing during the rise of area studies. He was critical of African American students who would simply gravitate to courses on African American studies taught from insider perspectives as opposed to being more fully integrated with the humanities curriculum. Such courses, he argued, meant that minorities would fester in their own narratives of resentment. Writing years later, in 2000, in a book cowritten with his son, Noam, and dedicated to William Safire, he could write that affirmative action "is reprehensible in a meritocracy, and goes against what universities stood for from the 1930s to the 1960s. Abandoning that meritocracy, which applied to professors and students alike, has cost universities dearly."[12]

In an essay titled "Why the Republicans?," written sometime in 1984, his final year on the NEH and just prior to his appointment on the NEA—a year that as we have seen he referred to as "Orwellian" in another context—Neusner further expatiates on his decision to become a Republican. His explanation, however, is a little different in this piece. Despite the fact that he was appointed by President Carter to be on the National Council on the Humanities, he writes, "I went to Washington a Democrat, and inside of two years the Democrats had convinced me to become a Republican." He goes on to explain that, for him, the NEH, rather than engage in "promoting excellence in the humanities and conveying the lessons of history to all Americans," actually stood for the "corruption of the political process by the Carter-Mondale administration. It stood for vote-buying in the new, improved left-wing way."[13]

Neusner was again bothered by the fact that the NEH was in the business of funding special interest groups as opposed to an overarching theme that was for the good of the entire country. This meant, in his own words, that at the NEH "the women got theirs, the blacks got theirs, the Jews got theirs, the Spanish-speaking got theirs, the unions got theirs, the radical left, the chic left, and the limousine liberals got theirs, everybody got culture—and we spent $175 million on god-knows-what."[14] This is why Neusner thought that the conservative Bennett would be able to turn the agency around. Bennett argued that the humanities were "in the past," meaning all that was relevant to the NEH were things that had happened long ago (e.g., Greek and Roman history, the Renaissance, the Civil War; but not contemporary issues). Bennett, like his successor, Lynne Cheney (NEH, 1986–1993), the wife of the future vice president, was responsible for steering the NEH to the right. Neusner, like Bennett and Cheney, had no qualms articulating what constituted "good" humanities and how it differed from "bad" humanities. Bennett was not interested in funding projects that he deemed inappropriate or opposed to the educational aims for which the NEH had been created. This approach, something that Neusner was highly supportive of, bothered more liberal academics and organizations that deemed such policy akin to waging an ideological battle and censorship.

Writing years later to Sidney R. Yates, a congressional Democrat, Neusner described the problems, as he saw them, at the NEH:

The panels are made up competition by competition; everything is ad hoc; there is no clear system. The panelists are not necessarily (and, in my observation, not routinely) superior to the applicants in achievement; indeed, as I reviewed the names over the years, I did not have the sense that the NEH was looking for the most accomplished scholars. The people were chosen for criteria that were not always self-evident. In having to invent a panel for each competition, moreover, the staff had an enormous burden of inventing the wheel every morning. My sense of the panel results, as a Council member, was that I could not always say why this and not that, that is, I could not always find the prevailing principle of rationality and order in the decisions of the panels—which is why, at the Council-committee level, we so often were astounded both at what was recommended for funding and also what was not recommended for funding. . . . [The] NEH is so distant from the fields of the humanities because it is organized not by field but by function, e.g., research, education, fellowship, and so on. The result is that the NEH has no clear access to the fields as such, there is no on-going relationship, e.g., with history, or religion, or philosophy, or literature, as such.[15]

It is worth underscoring here, lest we lose sight of it, just how hard Neusner worked. Not only was he engaging in revolutionary scholarship on rabbinic Judaism, writing profusely in both academic and public media, undergoing massive political battles with his colleagues at Brown, he was also traveling regularly to Washington for high-level meetings. In addition, he was able to apply his work especially at the NEH to think about where the study of Judaism belonged in the American humanities.

Neusner's time on the National Council under the leadership of the well-connected Bennett afforded Neusner a number of important connections in the world of conservative politics. His letters show fairly regular correspondences with many of the major players of the time. It was William F. Buckley, Jr., for example, who would nominate him to be the librarian of Congress. He also developed a friendship with William Kristol. Kristol—the son of the late Irving Kristol, who was often called the "godfather" of neoconservatism, and Gertrude Himmelfarb—entered the Reagan administration in 1985, serving as chief of staff to Bennett, then the newly appointed secretary of education. Kristol then became the chief of staff to the Vice President Quayle in the George H. W. Bush administration. Writing to Kristol in the latter office, Neusner points out his affinity with Bennett:

In the present controversy on the types of grants made by the National Endowment for the Arts, one issue has not been addressed, but I plan to raise it at the Council meeting next week, if the occasion arises. It concerns defunding the left. When Chairman William Bennett came in at the NEH, he found (as some of us on the council had been pointing out for some time) that pretty much all the dubious grants—e.g., grants that were of no academic value and no clear humanistic interest—turned out to be for left wing political propaganda. Very quietly but firmly, he ended that line of Federal support for partisan politics. Chairman [Lynne] Cheney has been equally reliable to keep the agency non-partisan. She has not funded the conservatives, but she has defunded the radicals. And where genuinely scholarly and humanistic work was proposed, she made grants without regard to either liberal or conservative considerations.[16]

Years later, when he was at the University of South Florida, Neusner approached Kristol again with the hope that Quayle might be willing to accept an honorary degree in the coming years from his new institution. He told Kristol in the same letter that his university was going to award "our own" William F. Buckley, Jr. an honorary degree in 1992.[17]

Neusner was also a big fan and supporter of Lynne Cheney. He wrote to her, for example, complaining about the lack of academic freedom at the Institute for Advanced Study at Princeton, where he spent the 1989–1990 academic year as a fellow-in-residence. Again, though, he seems to have turned what was supposed to have been a pleasant leave away from Brown into a political fight. He believed that the Institute's policy of not advertising a reading group that the visiting members put on to be a clear violation of academic freedom, and since the Institute received money from the NEH, this was to him a clear violation of NEH policy.[18] In a subsequent letter to Cheney, he argued that such little things matter, and can and should be used "to turn our side's political advantage . . . and [if] they're dismissing me and you as right-wing kooks, so be it."[19] Neusner, however, did not see himself as someone on the far right of these conversations. In another letter to Cheney, he sees both himself and her as occupying the center of the political spectrum. "You've done a wonderful job," he writes, "amid enormous pressures, and you will leave much stronger than when you came (and Bill [Bennett] had done a great deal to clean up the mess in which it was in), and you did so, and are doing so, in a time in which the center, which you and I have stood for, has come under siege from the radical fringe."[20]

National Endowment for the Arts (1984–1990)

If Neusner's criticism of affirmative action and minority quotas on campuses put him on the conservative side of the political spectrum, so, too, did his classical definition of what constituted the "humanities." He would bring this conservative temperament into his service on the National Endowment for the Arts (NEA), to which President Ronald Reagan appointed him in 1984 for a six-year term. If Neusner had been critical of the NEH's policy—at least until the reigns of Bennett and Cheney, whom he believed were able to make the agency more "centrist"—he would be extremely critical of the NEA, which, in his own words, "lacked such creative and firm leadership."[21]

The NEA was created in 1965 when President Lyndon Johnson signed the agency into legislation. "We fully recognize that no government can call artistic excellence into existence," he said, "nor should any government seek to restrict the freedom of the artist to pursue his own goals in his own way." Neusner, however, joined the National Council on the Arts, the main advisory committee to the NEA endowment, at a very controversial time. When Reagan came into office in 1980, he had attempted to abolish or defund the agency, but he lacked sufficient congressional support. Even his special task force on the arts and humanities, which included close allies, agreed that the NEA served a purpose in promoting the arts. In 1989, in particular, many conservative Christians and other social and political conservatives were up in arms and denounced the agency for funding "anti-Christian bigotry." They had in mind an exhibition of Andres Serrano's work, which included *Piss Christ*, a photograph of a crucifix submerged in the artist's urine. The controversy later expanded to include the work of other artists, especially the photography of Robert Mapplethorpe. Republican Senators Jesse Helms and Alfonse D'Amato denounced the work of Serrano and Mapplethorpe as morally reprehensible.[22]

In 1989, Senator Jesse Helms introduced an amendment that would ban taxpayer-funded grants from being used to "promote, disseminate or produce obscene or indecent materials, including but not limited to depictions of sadomasochism, homoeroticism, the exploitation of children, or individuals engaged in sex acts; or material which denigrates the objects or beliefs of the adherents of a particular religion or non-religion."[23] Also banned was art that "denigrates or debases or reviles a person, group or class of citizens on the basis of race, creed, sex, handicap, age, or national origin."[24] In early October 1989, Reagan's last year in office, Congress reached a compromise, which rejected the controversial Helms amendment but still contained restrictions on NEA granting procedures. The new bill, 304(a) of the 1990 Interior Department and Related Agencies Appropriation Act, was approved by both the House and Senate, and prohibited funding for projects that "promote, disseminate or produce materials which in the judgment of the National Endowment for the Arts or the National Endowment for the Humanities may be considered obscene, including but not limited to, depictions of sadomasochism, homoeroticism, the sexual exploitation of children, of individuals engaged in sex acts and which, taken as a whole, do not have serious literary, artistic, political, or scientific value."[25]

Neusner was a tireless supporter on the conservative side of these debates. During the height of the Serrano and Mapplethorpe controversy, he wrote a letter to John O'Sullivan, editor of the *National Review*, asking him for his support:

> Now I have a public, as distinct from a purely private, complaint to address to you. I think you have not helped us on the NEA controversy, since we required much more than an occasional editorial or cartoon, but an up-front, major philosophical statement of the position of the right

on the entire issue of the arts, such as *The Spectator* has been providing British conservatives in their context. The issue is not NEA, it is the shape and future of cultural life, and *NR* has been silent.[26]

In a subsequent interview with the *Philadelphia Inquirer*, Neusner spoke publicly about his work at the NEA. He explains how its Advisory Council, of which he was a part, had voted to reverse the recommendations of its panel of art experts and deny funding for two projects proposed by the University of Pennsylvania's Institute of Contemporary Art, which had the year before mounted a controversial exhibit of Mapplethorpe photographs. "The issue is what tax money should be used for," he said. "[T]he message we have been trying to express is that we have heard our critics. We think they have a very righteous criticism, and we're trying to respond to it in a constructive way without censoring." And, quoted in the *Los Angeles Times*, he declared the vote to turn down the two grants to the Pennsylvania institute as "an enormous victory."[27]

Neusner would prove to be one of the most conservative voices on the Advisory Council of the Arts. In the summer of 1990, his final year on it, Neusner proposed a resolution that would go even further than that proposed by Jesse Helms to restrict NEA funding. He proposed that the NEA's obscenity guidelines should deny funding that utilizes any part of an actual human embryo or fetus or to art that denigrates religion or defaces the American flag, something that struck many as tantamount to censorship. His resolution for sweeping restrictions, however, was defeated by the rest of the Advisory Council, ten votes to two, with one abstention. John Frohnmayer, the chairman of the government arts endowment, said he strongly opposed the restriction because it represented "the highest degree of insensitivity."[28]

Writing to Frohnmayer, who had been critical of Neusner's desire to speak publicly about NEA business, Neusner disagreed. Rather, he told him that he had a duty, as a public servant, to speak publicly about the NEA. Although Frohnmayer had stated in a letter, widely circulated, that he would "fire [Neusner] if I could," Neusner responded that "I am (1) for the Endowment and the arts; (2) against using public funds for things that are patently offensive to a vast body of taxpayers and citizens; and (3) against censorship of the arts."[29]

Again, unlike many of today's "tea party" Republicans, Neusner was not opposed to the public funding of either the arts or the humanities. However, his understanding of both was extremely limited owing to his conservative leanings. Writing to O'Sullivan, Neusner sums up his politics:

> My theory in general, as an instinctive conservative, as against either a paleo- or neo-conservative, is that the conservative movement is in two large parts, the neo-conservatives, nee the Rockefeller wing, which cares about the economy and foreign policy (and which handles that brilliantly in general), and the paleo-conservatives, nee the Goldwater-Reagan wing, which cares very deeply about cultural and social issues. . . . When attitudes shift, public policy is affected; and the pragmatic wing of the conservative movement cannot take for granted that the ideological wing will always be there.[30]

For Neusner, the NEA should not be in the business of funding projects that "invariably favor the left, indeed the far and sectarian left." Rather the role of the NEA should be to fund projects that "the people of this country can support without regard to partisan political commitments." Neusner had in mind regional theaters, ballet companies, orchestras, and on and on. These are all organizations that make life, in Neusner's words, "more pleasant" and—for him, at least—are not encumbered by political ideology.[31]

Writing in an essay titled "We Won," Neusner explains what exactly he and the Republicans accomplished at the NEA: They created

> [g]rants mostly for institutions, e.g., schools, community organizations, international exhibitions, museums and theaters, which can be trusted

not to blow up Pittsburgh, and not so much for individual artists, who cannot.... The chairman's reiteration of magic words conservatives heard so little in the past eighteen months—"accountability," "taxpayer," "no longer solely for the arts community"—tells us that the NEA has capitulated to what I regard as good sense. It aims at a long future as a Federal agency devoted to building audiences for the arts and institutions for the arts—but not the careers of artists. So no more politics in the guise of "art," no more thousands of dollars of grants for bottles of urine, no more performance art that replaces Shakespeare with chocolate covered shriekers, no more hysteria about censorship and no more Federal subsidies to the sectarian-left. The other side has lost and lost big.[32]

Even after his time on the National Council on the Arts had ended, Neusner remained involved in a variety of conservative causes. He became associated, for example with the Rockford Institute, which was founded by John A. Howard, the president of Rockford College (Illinois), in 1976 as a response to American social changes of the 1960s. Its goal, as stated on its website, is to work to "preserve the institutions of the Christian West: the family, the Church, and the rule of law; private property, free enterprise, and moral discipline; high standards of learning, art, and literature." Neusner was also a regular contributor to its journal, *Chronicles*. In addition, he presented a lecture, "Melting Pot or Mosaic: The Roots of Moral Order in an Increasingly Multicultural America," at the Rockford Institute's conference devoted to "For What Does America Stand?" on April 23 and 24, 1992. It also seems that it was through his work with this organization that he first encountered Cardinal Ratzinger, later to be Pope Benedict XVI, who gave a lecture to the organization in New York in January 1988. The two would go on, as we shall see, to become friends and letter writers to one another.[33]

In 2000 Neusner was a signatory to the conservative Cornwall Declaration on Environmental Stewardship. This organization, according to its website, contends that "some environmental concerns are well founded and serious, others are without foundation or greatly exaggerated." The latter would seem to be code for climate change, something that the Cornwall Alliance believes is religiously and scientifically unfounded. Its executive summary claims that "[w]e believe that the idea—we'll call it 'global warming alarmism'—fails the tests of theology, science, and economics. It rests on poor theology, with a worldview of the Earth and its climate system contrary to that taught in the Bible. It rests on poor science that confuses theory with observation, computer models with reality, and model results with evidence, all while ignoring the lessons of climate history. It rests on poor economics, failing to do reasonable cost/benefit analysis, ignoring or underestimating the costs of reducing fossil fuel use while exaggerating the benefits."[34] Rabbi Jacob Neusner is upheld on the website as one of the preeminent Jewish leaders who have signed on to the ideas behind the Cornwall Alliance.

Reaffirming Higher Education

Perhaps Neusner's most articulate expression on what he considered to be the failure of American higher education may be found in his *Reaffirming Higher Education* (2000), a work that he again coauthored with his son, Noam. His main criticism in this work is with what he calls the "new Humanities," code for the insular study of minority and ethnic groups outside of preexisting disciplinary structures, what he refers to as the "old Humanities." As a Jew, Neusner is certainly aware of the white, Christocentric, and male nature of the traditional canon in the humanities—a canon that traditionally made no room for Jews, women, or other minorities. The positive aspect of the revolution in the late 1960s and early 1970s was to expand the established canon of humanistic learning in the United States. This is certainly something to which Neusner saw himself contributing. This meant that disciplines had to take into consideration the narratives and contributions of traditionally excluded others. Departments of history, for example, could no longer concentrate only on American and Western European history but now had to make room within their curriculum for African,

Asian, and Middle Eastern history, to name but a few examples. The same is the case for literature, in which catalogues had to be expanded to teach not just great American and European literature, but now also African American and Lain American literature. The same is also true for departments of religious studies, which could no longer be content simply teaching about Christianity (which included, of course, the "Old" Testament), but now had to make room for religions of the East, in addition to Islam and Judaism.[35]

All this, for Neusner, is for the good. His objections begin when special interest groups ignore the universal questions supplied by the disciplines that form the traditional humanities curriculum. In this "new Humanities," Neusner writes, "special pleading replaces learning, politically correct opinions substitute for free debate, proscribed attitudes substitute for free inquiry, and a reign of intellectual terror has descended on those who dare to deviate from accepted scholarship, particularly at the most expensive and liberal universities."[36] Neusner had at least two things in mind here. The first is when, say, Jewish studies or African American studies are framed solely by their own internal terms of reference so that they become divorced from larger and more entrenched disciplinary units. The second thing, according to Neusner, is that even when such courses are taught within disciplinary confines they still tend to gravitate toward the "insider" perspective. "Professors of Jewish Studies," for example, "routinely assume that most of their students will come from Jewish families, whole or in part. And they orient their instruction to one notch above the quality of most extracurricular synagogue schools. They dwell on ethnic resentment and its quite reasonable provocation, the Holocaust."[37] It is important to be clear, then, that Neusner is not opposed to the inclusion of the study of women and ethnic minorities, he is just concerned about the place that such topics should be studied within the institutional context of the modern university.

The ideology of the subject, he concludes, has the potential to obscure its rationality and, just as important, its universality. When this happens, Judaism no longer becomes teachable to non-Jews, but festers in its own resentment (over, for example anti-Semitism and the Holocaust) and ethnic pride (for example, the formation of the State of Israel in 1948). When special interests are taught over universal norms or applicability, we cease to have an academy and, thus, a shared language of reason. The result is the balkanization of the modern university: Jewish studies, women's studies, African American studies, Latino studies, gay and lesbian studies, disability studies, and so on. Rather than add to the traditional curriculum, such special interests attempt to dismantle it. When this happens, Neusner contends, we no longer "preserve the notions that keep democracy healthy."[38] Within this context, he cites positively the work of neoconservative thinkers such as Allan Bloom, William Bennett, and Dinesh D'Souza, and warns that "the new multiculturalists" threaten to undermine that which has made America great.[39]

This, again, returns Neusner to the theme of the decline of American higher education. The movement from learning and teaching based on meritocracy to affirmative action and from studying minority traditions in entrenched disciplines to identity politics, he argues, has created a diminution in scholarship across campuses. According to Neusner, criticism and conflict are needed to form a necessary component of scientific process. Rather than sweep uncomfortable topics under the academic carpet, Neusner instead argues that such topics necessarily lead to further analysis, which will mean jettisoning prior theories through rational and scientific argument. Unless this happens, the personal is elevated to the universal, and the political masquerades as truth. This creates real intellectual dangers:

> Scholarship driven by personal and ethnic identity-considerations does not permit such revolutions. In the scholarship of personal identity, the characteristics of the scholar begin to determine not only the questions that are asked of a subject, but also the answers reached. That explains why, without fail, the study of blacks, black history, and issues relating to race are beyond the pale of normal scholarly debate: most of it is extrapolated politics.[40]

Neusner is certainly correct to point out the elevation of the personal and the political. However, his proposed solution—that courses on civil rights in the United States, for example, should not focus all their time on the protest movement of the 1960s, but should involve "a careful reading of the Declaration of Independence and the Constitution"—might not appease everyone, to say the least.[41] It is here that his conservative ideology is on firm display.

Neusner's writings on education vacillate between a conservative attempt to keep the great books of Western civilization, although to which he has no problem adding great books from other cultures, and the need for standards in a liberal arts education. It is a balance that, at least in the contemporary and increasingly polarized political moment, is difficult to maintain. Many (neo)conservative thinkers decry humanities-based scholarship, let alone a great books curriculum. For Neusner, the foundation, and indeed future, of the university is its analysis of possibilities and probabilities for the nation. It is, and here Neusner would seem to use his own work in rabbinics as a template, a process that takes inherited paradigms and transforms them so that they can be rethought and reconfigured for a new generation. The goal of the university, and here Neusner invokes Allan Bloom's *The Closing of the American Mind*, is to warn of the pitfalls of historical revisionism and get people to think about democracy with the same force as previous thinkers, such as Aristotle, Plato, and Socrates.[42]

Librarian of Congress

In 1987, midway through his term on the National Council on the Arts, Neusner was nominated for the position of librarian of Congress. The librarian, a presidential appointment in tandem with the advice and consent of the Senate, heads the Library of Congress, and serves as its chief librarian. Neusner's situation at Brown was getting worse, and he admitted that his time in Washington had provided him with a pleasant "escape" from the various interpersonal conflicts that he was involved in

there. He was still looking for a way out of Brown. In addition to applying to, and then often rescinding his application from, places such as
Harvard, Stanford, and Northwestern, he was also applying to smaller
and less prestigious institutions, such as the University of Memphis in
1986.[43]

Neusner asked William Buckley and William Bennett to nominate
him for the position. He also had the support of others, such as Caroline
Ahmanson, a wealthy philanthropist from California, whom Reagan
had appointed to a post on the President's Committee on the Arts and
the Humanities, and Rita Ricardo-Campbell, an economist and, from
1982 to 1988, a member of the NEH.[44] Writing to a colleague, he gives us
the following insight into why he wanted the position:

> I have made it clear at the outset that—to state matters negatively—I
> would not want the job either as a partisan or a non-partisan, but only as
> a bi-partisan candidate. That is to say, I regard the Librarian of Congress
> as an important agency within the Federal cultural establishment, I see it
> as part of that enormous and potentially effective instrument, along with
> the two Endowments and other agencies. I would want the job only if I
> could enjoy the confidence and support of both parties, on that account
> I have asked Claiborne Pell [a Democrat from Rhode Island] and Sidney
> Yates [a Democrat from Illinois], as well as Warren Rudman [a moderate
> Republican from New Hampshire] and John Chafee [a moderate Repub-
> lican from Rhode Island], for support, and requested that, if they feel that
> I can credibly do the job, they write to the White House as well.[45]

Neusner was—along with James H. Billington (director of the Wood-
row Wilson Center), Jaroslav Pelikan (a scholar of religion from Yale
University), Robert Wedgeworth, Jr. (dean of the School of Library Service at Columbia University), and Gertrude Himmelfarb (a historian
from City University of New York, and wife of Irving Kristol)—a finalist
for the position. He interviewed in Washington on February 24, 1987,
and returned for a second interview on March 9 of the same year. In a

letter to his good friend, William F. Buckley, Jr., he admitted that, should he get the position, "it would mark a move from a quite private life, public only by choice, when and where I want, a life focused essentially upon learning and inner growth through learning, to a quite public life—a life of service to others."[46] His worry was unfounded, however, as the position went to Billington. He was appointed, though, by the chairman of the NEA, Lynne Cheney, to serve on the Selection Committee for the National Arts Medals for 1988.[47]

The Price of Excellence: Leaving Brown

Neusner's biggest academic struggle, in addition to reframing an entire field of study, was with the watering down of the educational curriculum. Brown most acutely symbolized this switch when it went from having a distinct curriculum that all undergraduates took to a "demolished" one, "leaving only episodic courses (many of them student-organized and taught, or self-taught) and inchoate, dubious majors."[48] If Neusner had grown up a Jewish kid from West Hartford who, through his own hard work, went to Harvard, Oxford, and Columbia, he now stood among the ruins of what he considered to be a once glorious educational system run amok—though, as noted, he always complained about these other institutions. Neusner argued that behind the demise of American higher education, perhaps not surprisingly, was the American left. Whereas a generation before academics were content to go about their business as scholars, a new generation—energized by the Vietnam War, the call for civil rights, and the Watergate affair—had politicized the classroom. Faculty became antiestablishment and critical of traditional institutions. They, in Neusner's own words, "forgot their national purpose," which was to educate.[49]

As we have seen, the other problem with the new American academy was affirmative action and minority quotas. English faculty, for example, went from teaching Western civilization's great literature to basic literacy once campuses were open to "a philosophy of inclusion." Most symptomatic of this new policy, for him, was the place of African American students. The need for their inclusion, according to Neusner, quickly replaced protest against the Vietnam War among the now liberal American intelligentsia.[50] Neusner writes,

> The crucial issue, however, for blacks was not simply curriculum [in the form of African American studies programs], but access: like Catholics, Jews, and women one generation before, blacks faced a demographic underrepresentation in colleges. But unlike those other minorities, many blacks had not demonstrated, as part of the routine and objective process of application, the capacity to excel and survive in college.[51]

Neusner and his son, Noam, explicate this in great detail in *The Price of Excellence* (1995), a quasi-memoir, quasi-*apologia* for leaving Brown, and a quasi-conservative reaction to the perceived excesses of liberalism on American campuses. In another context, he called the work his "auto-obituary." Even the title is significant. Did Neusner perceive himself to pay the "price of excellence"? Or is the title an allusion to the price that a once-great postsecondary educational system paid for inclusion?

While Neusner was involved with all the political issues surrounding the NEA, his problems continued at Brown. President Swearer, who seemingly was not particularly liked at Brown, had announced that he was stepping down. His unpopularity seems to have been the result, in part, of his 1985 "roadmap" for future hires. This plan would limit hiring in some departments, while increasing it in others, with criteria based on current and potential enrollments. In addition to this preferential increase and decrease in departmental hires, Swearer also proposed creating "undesigned" positions that, he believed, would meet changing needs in the future. Given the fact that over half of Brown's full-time faculty would retire by 2000, Swearer's plan for rebuilding had angered a lot of people, not the least of whom was Neusner, someone who, as we have seen, was committed to traditional disciplinary boundaries, at least within the humanities.[52] Neusner was opposed to wishy-washy interdisciplinary appointments, thinking that students, the faculty of tomorrow, needed to be trained traditionally.

Neusner was particularly irascible at this point. In a letter to Rabbi Baruch Korff, a well-connected rabbi in Massachusetts, he announced his desire to fight plans to create an endowed chair in Holocaust studies that had just been announced in the *George Street Journal*, the weekly publication of the Brown News Bureau:

> I do not regard "Holocaust studies" in that formulation as an academic subject, though a vast amount of important academic study of the events of Europe in the twentieth century, from the viewpoints of the disciplines of history, political science, sociology, anthropology, and the like, is to be done, with consequent work of a critical order on the annihilation of the bulk of European Jewry. But a subject is not a chair, and a subject taken out of its broader context cannot form the definition of a scholarly enterprise such as is represented by an endowed chair.[53]

He ended the letter by claiming that, while he could not fight the creation of such a chair, he would do his utmost to persuade his colleagues to reject it should it be offered to any academic department at Brown. This, of course, would have been unlikely, because Neusner was systematically alienating himself from much of the faculty. In a memo to Kurt Raaflaub, in the Department of Classics at Brown, he wrote, "*In a university in which there is no honor or dignity, there can be no collegiality either. Such a university is merely a place of employment, and a job is a job—not a commitment or a calling.*"[54]

Swearer stepped down in 1988. In *The Price of Excellence*, Neusner characterizes his administration in the following terms: "solid scholarly achievement no longer would make a difference to careers or the conduct of universities."[55] For Neusner, "Swearer carried no academic philosophy and found guidance in no academic goals. He did not measure success in terms of scholarly greatness he might bring to campus but only in crass terms, if possible, fundraising, or, at all costs, popularity."[56]

Neusner seems to blame Swearer for all of his negative feelings toward the university. Everyone there—from Swearer to Provost Glicksman to the Department of Religious Studies—failed to recognize Neusner's contributions to scholarship, his "excellence," for which he paid the price. Neusner believed that he alone stood for academic excellence at Brown. Whereas his colleagues there saw him as volatile and difficult to work with, Neusner framed the impasse ideologically, as his memoir clearly reveals.

One of the last things that Swearer did before leaving, in the fall of 1988, was grant an honorary doctorate to Gore Vidal. Neusner protested this event, both in private and in public, arguing, as others had, that some of Vidal's writing bordered on anti-Semitism. Neusner was also upset that Vidal was a "notorious leftist." There was, however, nothing that he could do. Vartan Gregorian succeeded Swearer, and he seems to have done much to try to placate the aggrieved Neusner. He even went so far as to ask Neusner to march at the head of the faculty along with the other university professors and named chair holders on the occasion of his inauguration as president. Neusner, however, declined, stating that "as a matter of personal policy, I do not attend public events on Brown campus. The simple reason is that I have been condemned, by a Faculty Committee in the name of the Faculty Executive Committee, as a liar and a thief. . . . [A]s an act of self-respect and dignity I will not appear in any public role on this campus so long as my honesty as a professor and a scholar and a human being is called into doubt by any body or office at Brown University."[57] When Gregorian tried to make amends and get Neusner to attend the Saturday event, Neusner informed him that "I never conduct secular business on Saturday mornings."[58] Gregorian then offered to move it to the Sunday, but Neusner still refused to attend.[59]

In the meantime, Neusner had applied for and received a fellowship from the Institute for Advanced Study at Princeton. This would take him out of Brown for the 1989–1990 academic year. It is important to be clear that Neusner knew full well that his residential status there would be for only one academic year. He did not, as some wrongly contend, think that it was a new full-time position. He left Brown the summer of 1989 with the realization that, if he came back, it would be under different circumstances. He was contemplating either taking early retirement from Brown or working out an arrangement wherein he would teach one semester at Brown and remain the other semester at Princeton.[60]

All of these plans, however, would change due to a job offer that he received from the University of South Florida in the fall of 1989, while he was in residence at Princeton. This came about through his service on the National Council on the Arts, where he had met and befriended a Florida state senator from Sarasota by the name of Bob Johnson. Ronald Reagan had placed Senator Johnson on the council in 1986, and he and Neusner were in firm agreement about how public programs in the arts should be conducted. Johnson also served in the Florida State Senate on the Committee on Higher Education, and he encouraged Neusner to join the Florida system.

The only problem was that Neusner, at this time, was only fifty-seven, and eligibility for the Brown retirement system did not begin until age sixty. Neusner, however, was able to work out with Brown that they would pay him 30 percent of his 1989–1990 salary for the 1990–1991 academic year, to be increased by 5 percent every year for the following four years. Neusner joked that this was the first time he had received a prompt and favorable reply from Brown in all of the years that he had worked there. Gregorian, however, did make a modest counterproposal that would have seen Neusner remain at Brown half time as a distinguished professor, "the only such title and designation at the University." But Neusner declined and opted to take early retirement beginning in the summer of 1990, at which time he would move down to Tampa and teach at the University of South Florida with the title Distinguished Research Professor of Religious Studies.[61] Neusner admitted that the University of South Florida gave him "one course per semester, a big salary, and general recognition."[62] It was, however, his first time at a public institution since the debacle at Milwaukee, and there would certainly be growing pains.

Writing to Richard Scheuer, one of Neusner's benefactors over the years, he describes his new situation:

I see USF as a very exciting challenge and a great opportunity, not only because of the quality of the people with whom I have been dealing in the department, administration, and board of trustees, but also because of the exemplary character of the University. Specifically, USF is one of those new and vital state universities that have been taking shape since World War II, they have reached a level of maturity and are now moving on to achieve excellence, I found Brown pretty stagnant and took early retirement and then found out that there were opportunities, among which I chose USF, for a whole new career.[63]

In the same letter Neusner asked Scheuer for a half million dollars—at the rate of one hundred thousand to be paid over five years—with the aim of developing a program of national significance "to show how the great universities may shape the cultural life of Jewish communities, among other local communities, through sustained programs of public service of a cultural and educational character." This would involve Jewish education and teacher training, public education, and the "creation of permanent resources of culture and education for the community at large." This new goal of Neusner was undoubtedly inspired by his public service on the citizens' advisory councils of both the NEH and the NEA. This also seems to be in keeping with his newfound notion that public education, not the elitism of the Ivy League, was the future of higher education in the United States.[64]

But before Neusner would leave the world of elite private universities on the East Coast for the public ones of the South, he would spend a year in Princeton.

Institute for Advanced Study (1989–1990)

Neusner went to the Institute for Advanced Study (IAS) full of hope and the belief that, at long last, here was a place that would recognize his many contributions both to the study of rabbinic texts and to the academic study of religion more generally. This expectation—like at Harvard, like at Oxford, like at Columbia, like at JTS, like at Brown—proved to be illusive, however. Within a month of his arrival, he wrote a letter to Marvin ("Murph") Goldberger, the director of the IAS, complaining of the poor state of the Institute's collection of books in antiquity. "But the embarrassment to the Institute," he writes, "which claims to work in antiquity and in the humanities, is what they do have: half is simply *dreck*, not of scholarly interest at all. I could take you to any tenth rate synagogue in back-country Pennsylvania and show you less *dreck* than you have here."[65] Neusner was particularly insulted because, according to Institute policy, members were requested to donate to the library books that they had published or worked on while at the Institute. Neusner had given them three books that had just come out, two monographs and one trade book—and the library kept the trade book, but returned the other two with a curt note declaring that they did not need them. Neusner took this as an insult, and ended his letter to Goldberger with the claim, "So there is a snake in Eden."[66]

No doubt aggrieved by his treatment from the library, he also wrote a letter of complaint—again within his first month of arrival—to the librarian, Elliot Schor, about the Institute's propensity for subscriptions to liberal magazines and papers. Neusner wished to correct this and informed him that he would gladly pay for "[c]onservative intellectual journals of opinion," such as the *National Review*, *Commentary*, or *Chronicles*. He offered to use funds from the Max Richter Foundation, to "cover whatever subscriptions you decide you want to order, and will pay now for five years (1989–1994), renewable in five-year units as long as we both shall live."[67]

In another letter to Goldberger, written in November, he complained about the treatment of visiting members, such as himself, by the support staff: "The Members—your guests—are all reputable scholars and ought to be treated with respect and even dignity, as they are, after all, in their home institutions." He was also critical of the weekly dinners for members: "Remove from your announcements the matter of your Wednesday and Friday dinners, or indicate that they are *not* for all Institute Members, only those who conform to the dietary rules of your (German) cuisine. That again will save you from the now-just accusation of not wishing to accommodate difference among members, which surely affects not only Jews who practice Judaism by any means (though that would suffice)."[68]

In a letter to his son Eli, he called the Institute a "shtetl" and said that he "would not want to be in a place like this permanently." He further claimed that the full-time members are largely uninterested in his work: "In the humanities you need colleagues," he wrote to his son, "and these guys don't want or have colleagues; and I think you benefit from students, and of students they know nothing." This led him to complain about the Institute and its policies, as we have seen, to Lynne Cheney, then the chairwoman of the NEH.[69]

In *The Price of Excellence*, written five years after his departure, Neusner is extremely critical of the IAS:

> I was struck by the arid and self-absorbed life of those who remained on the permanent staff of research institutes. At IAS I found the permanent "professors" disdainful of the work of others and uninterested in learning from others; but also, I noticed, they did not find themselves driven to share what they knew with others, the social scientists and historians at IAS had all done their best work before they got there, and, palpably and measurably, their own work over time can be shown to have faded into triviality. Reading the writings of permanent staff as these unfolded over the years, both before joining the institute and after arriving, I noticed a decline in vitality and originality—and even in sheer volume. So a life of

research divorced from teaching in the social sciences and humanities exacts heavy costs.[70]

Despite his criticism, both at the time and later, Neusner did nominate himself to be director of the Institute, presumably with the desire to reform it, when Goldberger announced his retirement in the summer of 1990.[71]

Neusner would spend one other academic year in a solely research-based environment. For a semester in the academic year 1992, he was a fellow at Clare College, Cambridge. This semester started better than his time at the IAS. At the beginning, he described the place to Anthony De-Palma of the *New York Times*, as the opposite of the IAS: "They have no money and IAS is rich; but they have something rarer and more precious: intellect and humility and concern for not what other people think but what they themselves accomplish."[72] Eventually, however, Neusner seems to have had a falling out not just with Clare Hall, but also with all of Cambridge. This had to do with his treatment by Cambridge University Press. Writing to Morna Hooker, the editor of the *Journal of Theological Studies* and fellow at Robinson College, Neusner complains that

> [d]espite the wonderful time we had in Clare Hall, I shall not come back to Cambridge. Their Press's rejection of the book I wrote at Clare Hall was couched in such violent, personal terms, with no attention at all to the argument of the book and what is fresh and important in it (questions their dismissive "reviewers" do not raise) that I have now to dismiss Cambridge as a place of serious learning, at least, where I work. I can't take a place seriously that can't run a press with an academic, as distinct from a political, purpose; admittedly, Cambridge has the best academic library in the world, and I certainly met people I thought quite interesting (one of whom is reading this letter), but the Press's report on my book (already accepted elsewhere!) was so savage and uncomprehending that I just see Cambridge as an unattractive academy.[73]

It would seem that Neusner held all of Cambridge responsible for his treatment by two external readers for Cambridge University Press. Later, in 1995, again writing in his *The Price of Excellence*, Neusner lumped Clare Hall in with the IAS. He was particularly critical of the graduate students who also were allowed to spend time at the institution. These individuals were "like the permanent members of the IAS, they banded together to the exclusion of the outsiders who had come for a semester; they wanted nothing to do with mature, working scholars." Summing up his time at both, he acknowledged that research institutes were not for him: "After a year at the one and a semester at the other, I concluded I should never again consider appointment in a research institute."[74]

Brown: Gone but Not Forgotten

Increasingly Brown was behind him. However, he was still bitter about his treatment there. As we have seen, he even wrote a book, *The Price of Excellence*, to attempt to explain what unfolded there. The year after he left for the Institute for Advanced Studies, the *Providence Journal* ran an article titled "Neusner's Parting Shot at Brown." In it, Neusner complained that Brown, like Princeton, was a very "waspy" place that had made little or no room for Jews. Speaking positively now of institutions that he had previously excoriated, he claimed, "Harvard, Yale, and Columbia have done extraordinary things with Judaic studies. [Brown's] model has been Princeton, and they don't need all these Jews around, they just don't want to be all that prominent in the field."[75] Maurice Glicksman, Brown's provost, interviewed in the same article, responded by saying "that is a lie," and suggested that the real reason Brown's program never received departmental status had to do with Neusner's belligerent personality.

Writing two years after his departure, when he was the visiting Martin Buber Professor at Goethe University in Frankfurt am Main, he quipped,

I was so abused in a few places, unfortunately including my own university, that I did not know; but here, where I go, I get enormous audiences,
200–300, regarded as truly amazing, in places like Würzburg and Heidel-
berg and Köln and so on; professors come en masse, and, in general, I am
received as a great man. The abuse I have suffered is over, I think; I don't
need any jobs, and I am now free of Brown. . . . Frerichs & Dietrich & Co
were not only no friends but the bitterest of enemies, and they now show
themselves responsible for much that I would not have imagined they
could have contemplated, let alone done.[76]

Neusner here refers, in particular, to the book series that he had begun
at Brown, and the subsequent appointment of Shaye J. D. Cohen as his
successor. Scholars Press informed Neusner in June 1990—that is, the
same month that he took early retirement from Brown—that Ernest
Frerichs would now be in charge of the series and that all further orders
would come directly from him and not Neusner. Since he had founded
the series and funded it in part with his own money, having received
nothing from Brown other than the use of their name, Neusner took this
as a great personal affront. In a letter to Frerichs written on June 13, 1990,
he officially resigned as editor-in-chief of Brown Judaic Studies, Brown
Studies in Jews and Their Societies, and Brown Studies in Religion. On
the same day he also wrote to Tom Anton, the dean of faculty at Brown,
stating that he refused to take the role and status of University Professor
Emeritus and Ungerleider Distinguished Scholar of Judaic Studies
Emeritus at Brown.[77] This made Neusner, as far as he was aware, the
first person to reject the title emeritus, and he, thereby, severed all ties
to the university.[78]

Neusner looked into his legal options, thinking that Scholars Press,
and not Brown University, owned the series, but this never amounted
to anything. Even before this fallout had happened, he had arranged
with the University of South Florida to begin a new series there, also
to be published by Scholars Press. Before he learned of his dismissal
from Brown Judaic Studies, he had intended the latter to publish more

technical monographs, whereas South Florida Studies in the History of Judaism would publish more scholarly monographs in the areas of history and history of religion. South Florida Studies was to be funded, in part, by Thomas Tisch, who had promised twenty-five thousand dollars per year until royalties from the backlist would sufficiently support the series. When Neusner no longer had anything to do with Brown Judaic Studies, he devoted all his energies to his new series at the University of South Florida, which quickly replaced, in both sheer scope and pages published, anything that he had done at Brown.[79]

Neusner was also bothered by the fact that his colleagues at Brown had hired Cohen, who had previously taught at JTS (now at Harvard). As we have seen, Cohen had been quite critical of Neusner's *Judaism: The Evidence of the Mishnah* and had, according to Neusner, referred to him and his students as *am haaretzim*, that is, ignoramuses. Writing to Frerichs and Dietrich, he reprimands them: "He was dismissing your own students. In making this appointment you repudiate your doctoral alumni and write the epitaph of your careers."[80] Neusner was undoubtedly upset that the program he had started and conceived in a particular way should, within a year of his departure, go to someone with a divergent vision. He felt that his former colleagues had all but repudiated not only Neusner and his work, but all of the students that they had trained together.[81]

By the time that Neusner left Brown in 1990, he was, although little did he realize it at the time, entering into his most prolific period as a scholar. The next twenty-some years would see him both triple his publication record and continue to move his scholarship on Judaism into new and equally pathbreaking areas.

Success and Winding Down

Earlier we witnessed Neusner play a key role in defining both the place and function of the humanities and the arts on a national scale. On a scholarly level, this work coincided with his successful expansion of the humanities to include Judaism and Jewish texts. His motivation was that Jews, like all minorities, had to make a case for their inclusion on both intellectual and aesthetic grounds as opposed to reverting to some inner core of identity that they perceived to be special and that they sought to validate by excluding others. His role in the political debates surrounding the funding of the arts and humanities in this country was certainly not ancillary to his scholarly activity. Indeed, it is important to see his political involvement as an outgrowth of his scholarly production. If the latter had been an attempt to take Jewish studies out of its self-enclosed ethnic ghetto, his political endeavors, at least at the NEH, sought to remove minority quotas that he believed made ghettos possible in the first place. Neusner the scholar and Neusner the politician, in other words, cannot be neatly separated from one another.

In 1990 he moved to the University of South Florida (USF) to take up a position as Distinguished Research Professor of Religious Studies. In 1994 he also began to teach at Bard College in Annandale-on-Hudson, New York, as professor of religion. In 2006 he was named Distinguished Service Professor of the History and Theology of Judaism. He retired from USF in 2000 and from Bard in 2013. The time after Brown was certainly the most prolific and creative of his career, for a number of factors. First, he had much more collegial colleagues at both of these institutions so that he invested less emotional energy in petty internal politics. Second, and this is certainly related to the previous point, he felt needed and wanted at both schools, something he never felt at Brown. Third, this period also corresponds with the height of his international fame. If Neusner felt isolated at Brown, all of this was to change after he left. Within a matter of years his work was celebrated, especially outside of the United States. The 1990s, for example, witnessed him make almost annual trips to Europe and beyond to take up various distinguished positions.

In the summer of 1991, his first year at USF, he was named the Martin Buber Professor of Jewish Studies at the University of Frankfurt; in 1992, he spent a term at Clare College, where he remains a life member; in 1993, he spent the summer as guest research professor at the Åbo Akademi University in Turku, Finland; in the summer term of 1994, he was a visiting fellow at the University of Canterbury in Christchurch, New Zealand; in 1995, he was a Humboldt Research Professor at the University of Göttingen in Germany; and in the spring of 1996, he was a visiting professor of theology at Uppsala University in Sweden. Many of these appointments, it should be noted, were in the area of religious studies, not Jewish studies. The acknowledgment of his excellence, in other words, did not come from those working in the narrow confines of rabbinics, which was carried out primarily in Israel and the United States, two countries that tended to be more critical of the type of work that Neusner was producing, but in the more general field of religious studies, to which he had contributed so much over the years. In 1990, the year he left Brown, he was awarded the Medal of Collège de France, in addition to the Medal of Regione di Campania (Italy). In 1996, he received the Queen Christina of Sweden Medal from Åbo Akademi University in Finland. His work on Jewish-Christian dialogue saw him receive the Ecumenical Medal from Xavier University in Cincinnati in 1992, the Commemorative Medal of the Cardinal of Milano (Italy) in 1993, a Doctor of Humane Letters from the University of Saint Louis in 1993, and, perhaps most important, the Medal of Pope Benedict XVI, about which I shall elaborate below. In addition to these awards, Neusner also received a number of honorary doctorates: from the University of Rochester in 1988; from both Tulane University and Saint Louis University in 1993; and from Dowling College in Oakdale, New York, in 1997.

We now begin to see the mature expression of Neusner's thought as he began to reflect back on a lifetime of working with rabbinic texts. Having redefined the academic study of Judaism in general and rabbinic texts in particular, he now moved to a more philosophical reflection. In terms of his own self-described typology, this represents his "theological" phase, which witnessed a shift from historical and literary reconstruction to showing how all these texts fit together, thereby providing a coherent structure. It was at Bard, in particular the conversations with his new colleagues, especially Bruce Chilton, that Neusner delved into the structure of a set of texts that later came to be designated as "rabbinic." It was also at USF and Bard that Neusner wrote perhaps one of his most famous books, *A Rabbi Talks with Jesus*, a work that caught the attention of Pope Benedict XVI, who wrote that "it is by far the most important book for the Jewish-Christian dialogue in the last decade."[1]

Neusner also worked more closely with colleagues in different religious traditions. This was not to engage in interfaith dialogue so much as it was to take part in a common problem that could be looked at from a variety of different perspectives. Each perspective would illume not only the larger question but also each other perspective. This, it will be recalled, was not unlike what Neusner had tried to do years earlier when he was president of the American Academy of Religion. At both USF and Bard he sponsored with his research funds a number of conferences and collaborative projects that drew scholars of different religious traditions into conversation with one another on a set of common themes and problems. They produced a number of important books on, among other topics, the problem of difference in religion, religion and society, religion and material culture, religion and economics, religion and altruism, and religion and tolerance.[2] These projects not only enabled Neusner to engage with scholars of different religious traditions, but also further contributed to his long-term and overarching goal of bringing the academic study of Judaism out of the seminary, where it was discussed by only a handful of specialists, and into the mainstream academy where it could contribute to a set of larger questions of universal significance. If Neusner had spent the last twenty years working out the relationship of the canonical texts of Judaism to their immediate contexts and to one another, his theological project now afforded him the opportunity to put his work in conversation with other religions.

Neusner's work as a theologian is showcased in the types of activities, and their published products, that he produced after Brown, an institution at which he had spent close to twenty-five years of his academic life. If the first three stages of his career were devoted to a systematic analysis of the historical, literary, and religious dimensions of rabbinic texts, he now gravitated toward their theological message. These four phases, as we have seen, represent four different and overlapping versions of the same project that was meant to map scientifically Jewish texts from the formative period. Within this context, the theological phase emerged out of the so-called religious phase that, it will be recalled, was meant to grasp how the various documents of rabbinic Judaism related to one another despite the fact that they were produced in distinct social and temporal contexts. The texts from these distinct contexts nevertheless were subsequently related to one another by later rabbis, who created what we now refer to with the monolithic term "rabbinic Judaism." Neusner now sought to understand how the parts created the whole. Driving his agenda was the desire to grasp "how the intellects whose writings I study made connections and drew conclusions, what theory of mind told them what they wished to know and how to find it out."[3]

Neusner had a very distinct idea about what constituted theology. He was not interested in using rabbinic sources as a springboard to develop his own constructive reading of Judaism. Nor, as we have seen, was he interested in engaging in interfaith dialogue, at least not in a superficial way that thinly papered over major theological issues between different religions. Instead, Neusner claimed to be doing what he called analytic as opposed constructive theology. "When I do theology," he once told me, "I am interested in how the different theological positions join together and create a coherent body of thought."[4]

Neusner, thus, introduced theology as another tool with which to describe rabbinic Judaism. It represents another method by which to grasp the logic that governs a set of religious texts produced in close proximity to one another. If the "religious" phase of his career sought to understand each text on its own terms, the theological phase sought to uncover the generative principles that produce an all-encompassing structure. As he writes in his *The Theology of Rabbinic Judaism: Prolegomenon* (1997),

> The documents deal with different topics. What reason compels us to look for a coherent structure? They unfolded over long centuries, in different settings and among diverse authorities, and they furthermore drew upon antecedent opinion, going back to Scripture itself. Their authorities lived on the opposite sides of the contested frontier between Roman and Iranian empires of late antiquity. Why therefore should anyone expect to discover a common corpus of shared convictions based upon governing rationality? These considerations explain why we must wonder what justifies our investigating the theology—the sustaining logic, the normative statements and the system that they (allegedly) comprise—of the Oral Torah at all.[5]

For Neusner, since Jews for much of their history have read these documents together, we must ask why, how, and for what purposes this was done. It is important to be clear that Neusner did not want to revert to the old method of "hunting and gathering" statements constructed as "theological" by reading passages out of context with the aim of making them adhere as a cogent statement. For him, theology means ascertaining how Judaism speaks in its own voice, as opposed to the voices of diverse sages within different contexts. If Judaism possessed no system, according to Neusner, it would be little more than a random set of opinions that could be compiled but not analyzed in any systematic manner.[6]

Neusner realized that "historical questions are only one set of things to pursue; whereas theology provides a sustained philosophical reflection on these questions."[7] Theology, instead, provides the logic to understand the historical sources on a much different level.[8] By "rabbinic theology" Neusner meant "the quest for God's rationality" as revealed and uncovered in the sources. Theology, to reiterate, is not what Neusner constructively takes out of the sources, but an analysis of how the sources engage in "reasoned discourse about God and God's self-manifestation in the Torah."[9] Neusner thus made theology address questions raised within the academic study of religion as opposed to constructive theology.

Neusner was also interested in the subject of Christianity, at least as seen from the perspective of Judaism. How, for example, did Judaism emerge as a religious system in argument with Christianity? He attempted to show this not only historically, but also in conversation with Christian scholars, most notably the Catholic priest Andrew Greeley and later the Anglican priest Bruce Chilton. In these conversations Neusner challenged the notion that there has ever been a "Judeo-Christian" dialogue. Even when the two traditions read the same document, he contended that they brought very different questions and answers, and necessarily reached different conclusions. He argued that, despite appeals to the contrary, there has never (in the past or for most of the present) been a desire, on the part of either side, to have such an interreligious or interfaith dialogue. To counter this, Neusner took upon himself in his theological writings to show how such a religious conversation, along intellectualist lines, could be attempted.

In 2006 Neusner became the Distinguished Service Professor of the History and Theology of Judaism at Bard. He admitted to me that, earlier in his career, he would have been uncomfortable with the designation "theologian of Judaism," since he had spent much of his early career stressing more historical and literary issues.[10] This interest in theology, commencing in the 1990s, however, would now play an important role in his remaining years. In 1996, Bard created an Institute for Advanced Theology, imagined and directed by Bruce Chilton. It was one of the reasons that, along with his and Suzanne's desire to be closer to their children on the East Coast, he decided to relocate from Florida to the Hudson Valley.

The Path Back to Reform Judaism

Neusner's relationship to American Judaism was, as we have seen throughout this book, extremely complicated. According to the later Neusner, he had never fully fit within the Conservative movement, which he increasingly criticized as being out of sync with American Jews. He remarked that the movement functioned as little more than a "halfway house" for people transitioning from one wing, Reform or Orthodox, to the other. His relationship to the Reform movement, however, was much less complicated, presumably because he had left the movement when he returned from Oxford in 1954 and took up residency as a rabbinical student at JTS, although, again writing later, he said that he had never really left the movement intellectually; he had only accommodated his Reform beliefs to a new movement to get the best education that he believed he could at that time.

In 2009, Hebrew Union College–Jewish Institute of Religion awarded him a Doctor of Humane Letters. Neusner used this as the occasion to repudiate formally his connection to the Conservative movement. Writing in the *Forward*, he claimed that "after a half-century of apostasy, I affirm Reform Judaism as the American Judaism both of my personal choice and of our communal necessity." In order for the Reform movement to carry the day, Neusner continued, it must

> reaffirm the tradition of reason and criticism that has characterized Reform Judaism from its inception. Reform Judaism founded modern learning in Judaism. Its Scripture was not dictated word for word by a supernatural being from outer space. Its theology does not promise pie in the sky when you die. The power of Reform Judaism from its 19th-century origins has been its courage to say it stands for the Judaism of today.[11]

Neusner argued that Conservative Judaism—which claims to position itself as the middle path for contemporary Jews, somewhere between Reform on the one hand and Orthodox on the other—can no longer hold in an era of contested religious polarization within the tradition. With Orthodoxy—and, by extension, ultra-Orthodoxy—representing the "self-segregationist" wing of the tradition, Neusner maintained that Reform represented the "integrationist" wing. Because of these two clearly defined wings there can be little room for a movement that wants to be all things to all people. On account of its middle ground, Conservative Judaism comes under threat from its two flanks. The result is that it increasingly loses those who privilege the Judaic component of its message to Orthodoxy, and those who privilege integrationism to the Reform movement. This means that, according to Neusner, "the center has not held and will not hold."[12]

This honorary degree from the Reform Seminary is fitting because it recognizes Neusner's lifetime of achievement to Jewish public discourse in the United States. Neusner's contributions to these debates have frequently been unpopular, and he has often said things that many did not want to hear. But they needed to be said. He has never been afraid to air grievances in the full display of the public, and has never relinquished this role. While he has certainly changed his opinions on a given matter, he has never shied away from the public domain. Neusner has consistently, throughout his long career, functioned as a warning sign to American Jews, arguing that they must not rely on nonintellectual mechanisms, for example, ethnicity or the Holocaust, for survival in the present. What is needed, rather, is a serious engagement with the tradition in ways that are intellectually honest and sophisticated. For Neusner, this is the reason why it is in the secular academy, and not in the traditional yeshiva, that this engagement now takes place. The latter, he maintains, has largely failed American Jewry. It was an unpopular position, to be sure, but one that needed to be said, then as now.

On the topic of Hebrew Union College, William Scott Green had nominated Neusner to be its president in 1995. Neusner wrote to Stanley

Gold, president of HUC-JIR's Board of Governors, saying that Green did so with his permission, and that he was willing to establish his candidacy for the position, which would have included becoming a member of the Central Conference of American Rabbis, that is, he would have to become a Reform rabbi. Needless to say, Neusner did not receive the job, nor was he even short-listed for the position, which ultimately went to Rabbi Sheldon Zimmerman.[13]

Neusner expressed his displeasure with the choice of Zimmerman and his lack of academic qualifications in an essay titled "The Wrong Man, in the Wrong Job, at the Wrong Time," wherein he writes that the Board of Governors of HUC-JIR has declared the organization "something other than a center of formidable, academic scholarship and teaching that it once was by saying that these things do not matter in the choice of President."[14] Neusner went on to discuss in detail that although Rabbi Zimmerman might have administrative and fund-raising skills, he lacked intellectual and academic ones. The president of HUC-JIR, Neusner reminded them, is also the leader of an academic institution that, among other things, awards tenure and grants doctoral degrees. The president must oversee these matters, in addition to maintaining the general spiritual and financial health of the movement worldwide. Speaking more generally, Neusner remarks that

> American Judaism cannot flourish on a leadership of good old boys. Ego-massaging may be necessary for the pulpit, but it is insufficient for the serious, first-rate intellectual community that the Jews in this country constitute. That community responds to ideas, rigorous and well-crafted systems of thought and theories of things—and not to cliches and appeals to sentimentality and a fake nostalgia.[15]

Neusner made clear at the beginning of this essay that he was not bitter about being passed over for the HUC presidency. He honestly felt that the Reform movement in America needed, as it had in the past, appropriate leadership at a formative moment if it was to meet successfully the challenges of the coming millennium. It turns out that Neusner was prescient. Rabbi Zimmerman was forced to resign four years later amid accusations of sexual misconduct. In retrospect, however, it was unlikely that the Reform movement—or any other mainstream American Jewish organization—would ever have wanted someone as controversial and opinionated as Neusner to be its leader.

It is perhaps natural that Neusner's attitude to Hebrew Union College would change as his relationship to JTS became increasingly strained during the course of the 1990s. Although Neusner had always had a tense relationship with the Conservative Seminary, it was certainly exacerbated by Neusner's public outrages over the years. In an article published in the *National Jewish Post*, for example, he criticized the seminary for offering an endowed chair—the Saul Lieberman Professorship of Talmud—to a non-Jew, Peter Schaefer, who subsequently declined it. This, of course, fell on the heels of JTS's refusal to award Neusner an honorary degree in 1990 because he was too ill to travel to New York City to receive it in person.[16] Here it is worth noting that Neusner was willing to make a legal challenge to a public university that refused a position in Jewish studies to a non-Jew. Now, however, he argued that a private Jewish seminary should hire only Jews. While this might strike us as contradictory—especially since he was so critical of the makeup of the faculty when he was a student there in the 1950s—the logic nonetheless seems straightforward.

Perhaps this explains Neusner's different reception in Europe and America. In America, Neusner was a very political figure, someone involved in all sorts of debates about the future of Judaism, and the role of education in that future. His opinions and his willingness to share them with others in any variety of media made him, at times, a very controversial figure. This may have been exacerbated by his conservative opinions in both the NEH and the NEA. In Europe, by contrast, Neusner was, quite simply, a scholar, someone who had little at stake in European political culture. Instead, he was someone who had successfully integrated Jewish data into the academic study of religion and, in so doing, had changed the ways we think about the study of religion. In redefining the study of early Judaism, he also redefined the study of the New Testament and early Christianity, the epicenter of the study of religion in the United States prior to the 1960s. Having said this, though, it is clear—at least by looking at Neusner's letters from this period—that he maintains a certain discomfort with the fact that many scholars of religion in Europe, and their students, were not interested in Judaism as a living tradition, but—even in the 1990s, that is, fifty years after the decimation of European Jewry—Judaism remained that which produced Christianity. Jewish history, in other words, ended as Christianity's began.[17] This is not to say that Neusner did not cause controversies abroad. In New Zealand, for example, he created a national scandal when, in a letter to the *Christchurch Press*, he complained about how poorly undergraduates were trained there.[18] In Sweden, he was involved in trying to mediate a public, lengthy, and rather nasty spat between Jan Bergman, a Swedish theologian who expressed anti-Jewish views, and Rabbi Morton H. Narrowe of Stockholm. The debate between the two dated to a court case in 1989 when Bergman defended Sheikh Ahmed Rami, who had denounced Jews on Radio Islam in Stockholm.[19] He was also growing very critical of the inhospitality of his German hosts in Germany who refused to dine with him, interact with him as a colleague, or attend his lectures when he visited there.

Eventually, after an overseas trip to Prague in March 1997, the Neusners decided they would no longer travel to Europe. This decision seems to have been precipitated by a nasty bug that sickened Neusner. This sickness was compounded by his growing disillusionment with European scholarship on the Hebrew Bible and Judaism. Increasingly as Neusner turned away from European universities, he began, as we shall see shortly, to reach out again to Israeli universities, especially to a new generation of scholars who increasingly came to appreciate his work in the field.[20]

Friendship with Andrew Greeley

Much of the 1990s saw Neusner make influential friendships with important theologians that would change the way he thought about things. These friendships seem to have facilitated his interest in theology. Among the first was with Andrew Greeley (1928–2013), the well-known Roman Catholic priest, sociologist, journalist, and novelist. Like Neusner, Greeley was outspoken and never afraid to make confrontational public statements. It was often said of him, as it was of Neusner, that he never had an unpublished thought. Although Neusner and Greeley had different political views—the latter liberal, the former conservative—they developed a deep and profound friendship over the years. Greeley seems to have been the one to encourage Neusner to engage in constructive reading of texts, and in such a way that was in dialogue with those of other traditions. This can be seen in their 1990 *The Bible and Us: A Priest and a Rabbi Read Scripture Together*, whose back cover describes it as "the first book in two thousand years in which a rabbi and a Roman Catholic priest discuss and debate Scripture, tenets of faith, and each other's viewpoints."

Neusner and Greeley contended that since both religions were in the process of reshaping their understanding of the other, such a volume would provide an impetus for talking about substantive issues.[21] Just such an issue, for example, was Jesus. For Greeley, "Jesus' sacrifice of Himself for others and the Father's validation (acceptance) of the sacrifice through the resurrection of Jesus actually do change the existential nature of the human condition, precisely because they drastically transform the possibility of human interpretation of life and death."[22] Neusner, by contrast, argues that such a belief leads to the need to "denigrate and deny to Judaism all salvific promise." Instead, Neusner argues that Christianity must see itself not as reforming Judaism, but as *a* Judaism, like other Judaisms, that seeks to affirm itself.[23]

For Neusner,

The upshot is simple. Among the religious systems of the people, Israel, in the land of Israel, one of which we call Christianity, another of which we call Judaism—and both names are utterly post facto—we find distinct social groups, different people talking about different things to different people. Each had its way of life and world view and definition of itself as "Israel," and all appealed to the Torah. But everyone read the Torah in the way that his or her Judaism insisted it was to be read.[24]

The book proved very popular. It was translated into both Spanish and Portuguese, and was named an "Alternative Selection" at the Jewish Book Club. It was subsequently republished in a second edition in 1996 with a new title: *Common Ground: A Priest and a Rabbi Read Scripture Together*. While the book with Greeley made an important contribution to interfaith dialogue, it was but an initial foray into the topic. Neusner would only later get into a systemic and systematic discussion of the construction of shared theological categories after his conversations with another Christian theologian, Bruce Chilton. It is also worth noting that in the book with Greeley, Neusner referred to himself as an "ordained rabbi in the Conservative movement"; in the books with Chilton he will call himself "unaffiliated"—most likely the result of his growing dissatisfaction with the leadership and policies of Conservative Judaism.

A Rabbi Talks with Jesus (1993)

In 1993 Neusner published what would amount to his best-selling book, *A Rabbi Talks with Jesus: An Intermillennial, Interfaith Exchange*. The stated goal of the work is to provide insight into Christianity from the perspective of Judaism. Why, in particular, Neusner asks, can a Jew not believe in Jesus and the good news of his rule in the kingdom of heaven? The answer for Neusner is simple: Jews believe in the Torah of Moses and, based on that belief, form their own community as a holy people. To show this, Neusner transports himself to the time of Jesus and enters into a dialogue with him to show why he cannot accept his teachings. It is a respectful disagreement, to be sure, and Neusner certainly takes Christian beliefs seriously, just as he hopes that his Christian readers will take his beliefs seriously. The result, as Cardinal Ratzinger, later Pope Benedict XVI, noted, was "by far the most important book for the Jewish-Christian dialogue in the last decade. The absolute honesty, the precision of analysis, the union of respect for the other party with carefully grounded loyalty to one's own position characterizes the book and makes it a challenge especially to Christians, who will have to ponder the analysis of the contrast between Moses and Jesus."[25] It proved so popular that it was eventually translated into Italian (three times), Swedish, German, Russian, French, Hungarian, Czech, and Croatian. He would subsequently write to a friend, "My *Jesus* book is making waves, and benign ones at that; how shall I cope with popularity and acceptance?"[26]

Neusner's goal in the work was not to uncover the historical Jesus, to wade into the scholarship surrounding the early followers of Jesus in first-century CE Palestine, or to engage in Jewish apologetics. Rather, Neusner wanted to articulate how and why Judaism differs from Christianity. In so doing, he hoped to get Jews and Christians to believe more strongly in their own tradition while, at the same time, respecting that of the other. He did not make the case for Christianity. Rather his point of departure was that "by the truth of Torah, Israel's religion in the time of Jesus was authentic and faithful, not requiring reform or renewal, demanding only faith and loyalty to God and the sanctification of life through carrying out God's will."[27] Neusner sought, then, to provide an unapologetic dissent from Jesus by showing Jesus that where he "diverges from the revelation by God to Moses at Mount Sinai, he is wrong, and Moses is right."[28]

A case in point is the following observation that Neusner makes about the violation of the Sabbath by Jesus's disciples. The reason that Jesus gives for this violation is that, in the Temple, the priests perform the rites of the cult on the Sabbath; therefore, it is all right for his followers to do so outside of the Temple. Neusner retorts that "you have to know that the Temple and the world beyond the Temple form the mirror images of one another. What we do in the Temple is the opposite of what we do everywhere else." He then expatiates,

> The Torah is explicit that the sacrifices are to be offered on that day. For example, an additional offering for the Sabbath is prescribed in Numbers 28:9–10, 28:3–8; the show bread of the Temple was replaced on the Sabbath Day (Lev 24:8). So it was clear to everybody that what was not to be done outside the Temple, in secular space, was required to be done in holy space, in the Temple itself. When, therefore, Jesus says that something greater than the Temple is here, he can only mean that he and his disciples may do on the Sabbath what they do because they stand in the place of the priests in the Temple: the holy place has shifted, now being formed by the circle made up of the master and his disciples.[29]

Here Neusner gets to the heart of the differences between Judaism and Christianity. The book is an attempt to articulate their insurmountable differences. However, rather than construct walls between Judaism and Christianity, Neusner seeks to get Christians to respond by showing them exactly how Judaism differs from their tradition so as to engage them in "a heartfelt reaffirmation of the faith" that makes room for a deeper understanding of Judaism. In like manner, his goal is to get Jews, especially American Jews, to realize that there is more to the tradition than the current malaise of secularism. To them, he tries to show that Judaism is about "life with God whom we know in and through the Torah."[30]

Neusner and Cardinal Ratzinger shared a number of correspondences in which they talked deeply about theological differences between Judaism, Catholicism, and Protestantism. As early as December 1992, just as *A Rabbi Talks with Jesus* was about to be released, Neusner articulated to the future pope that "Protestant scholarship draws invidious comparisons between Judaism and Christianity, and it goes without stating, Jesus and Judaism. Catholic scholarship tends not to do so, and, of course, from Vatican II onward, represents Judaism in a very positive way." Neusner went on to state that "the more I reflect on that rather general comparison, the more I reach the conclusion that, if you believe in faith as God's grace, you do not have to find this-worldly validation for it, and if not, you do."[31]

In further correspondences, Neusner and Cardinal Ratzinger shared offprints of their respective writings and discussed, among other things, the differences between "historical" thinking and "paradigmatic" thinking. Cardinal Ratzinger was particularly impressed with Neusner's *The Presence of the Past, the Pastness of the Present: History, Time, and Paradigm in Rabbinic Judaism*, informing him that "your treatment of 'paradigmatic time' finds an echo also in the Church's traditional understanding of the 'Liturgical Year' and her celebration of the Mysteries of salvation and redemption. Yes, indeed, you have permitted much food for thought!"[32]

After Cardinal Ratzinger had spoken in Jerusalem in February 1994, Neusner wrote to him very favorably, saying that "your appeal to mystery, tragedy, and God's intervention allows Christianity to stand on its own foundations, not through comparison with, and denigration of, the Jews and Judaism."[33] Neusner seems to have been particularly impressed with Ratzinger's unwillingness to denigrate Judaism as a way to substantiate the truth of Christianity, which was often presented as the latter's reform of the former. In like manner, Cardinal Ratzinger no doubt appreciated Neusner's willingness to take Christianity seriously and not repudiate it on account of the Holocaust. Typical of Neusner's comments are his remarks in the same letter: "I think that a Christian theology of the Holocaust, out of the resources of Christianity but responsive to the suffering of Holy Israel, has to be formulated. Right now what we are given is repudiations of Christianity because of the Holocaust; this too is a purely secular phenomenon; and it presents the impossible choice of the destruction of Christianity out of worldly guilt or the repudiation of the Holocaust as somehow justified."[34]

Due to his friendship with Cardinal Ratzinger, in addition to that with Andrew Greeley, Neusner became involved in interfaith dialogue with the Catholic Church, appearing regularly at various meetings organized in Italy. Neusner and Cardinal Ratzinger increasingly shared the same position that a strict historicism paralyzes religious thought in the contemporary world, both Jewish and Christian, on account of the desire to reduce all questions to matters of historical fact (for example, the "historical" Jesus). Such reduction, according to Neusner, renders faith "cheap and shallow."[35] It is also worth noting in this context that Pope Benedict XVI invoked Neusner more than any other contemporary scholar in his 2007 book on the life of Jesus.

The correspondence between Neusner and Cardinal Ratzinger, and the friendship that developed out of it, culminated in 2010 when Neusner was awarded the Medal of Pope Benedict XVI. Neusner's visit to the Vatican to receive the medal coincided with Pope Benedict XVI's historic visit to the Synagogue of Rome on January 18.

Judaism's Theological Voice (1995)

At around the same time that Neusner was engaged in his examination of the teachings of Jesus from the perspective of Judaism, Neusner was also engaged in his own constructive reading of Judaism. In *Judaism's Theological Voice*, Neusner explores and represents the theological encounter between God and Israel through the metaphor of music. His premise is that Israel and God meet in the Torah, which functions as God's self-manifestation, through song. When Israel sings the words of the Torah, whether in the context of the synagogue or the yeshiva, Neusner holds that God is made manifest in the congregation of Israel, the very locus in which God has chosen to become known to humanity.[36]

Neusner decides to redescribe this using the language of music because a musical performance is "an event, a happening ephemeral but perfect for its moment, not to be replicated." Neusner refines his understanding of theology in this project, defining it as "rigorous thought about religious truths aimed at forming a systematic and cogent, philosophically valid structure of propositions."[37] Like so much of his earlier, "non-theological" work, Neusner again stresses system and knowability. Theology does not mine the depths of God's mystery, but rationally reflects upon questions of faith for those who believe. Neusner's goal, then, is to set forth, in a sustained and coherent manner, the systematic theological statement of Judaism, which is tantamount to the tradition's rationality.

It is really with this monograph that Neusner acknowledges his foray into theology, a path down which his study of history, literature, and religion—what he had spent the previous thirty-five years elucidating— inevitably led him. This theological work meant that Neusner was no longer interested solely in the facts of history, literature, and religion, but in the rationality that infuses the truth of faith. Although Neusner would continue with his project of description, analysis, and interpretation in the coming years, it is certainly worth highlighting that *Judaism's Theological Voice* signals a new venture, one that seeks to elicit a different logic and rationality.

One example from the work should suffice to demonstrate the novelty of this new project. The difference between the Written and Oral Torahs is not just that the former is sung in the synagogue and the latter in the yeshiva, but that the Written Torah must be translated, not from Hebrew into English, but from the age of the patriarchs to our age. We must enter its melody and let its words transform us. The Oral Torah, by contrast, amplifies the message of the Written Torah, further articulating the law and making it more rational in the process. Its language does not require the same labor of mediation since it transcends particular time or circumstance. The beauty of Judaism, Neusner argues, is that both of these melodies work together to form one coherent song, a song that permits ready access to those who want to listen and to sing. He concludes the book in the following poetic passage that signals a new direction in his thinking about the texts of formative Judaism from a different perspective:

> When God sings to Israel, God lives in the connections between note and note, and we sing in the silences. Ours is the song of words that match the

music, by which I mean, the sense that a perfect rationality governs all creation and its rules; our minds match God's. Our sense of the right fit, the perfect match, the ineluctable connection, corresponds to how things are. There I hear the melody of the oral part of the Torah, that melodic line within the complex voice of that one whole Torah that (in secular language) constitutes the theological voice of Judaism.[38]

Annual of Rabbinic Judaism: Ancient, Medieval, and Modern

Neusner always made it his habit to review every single book and dissertation that was published in his chosen field. This permitted him to keep abreast of the latest scholarship. He would not wait for a journal to ask him for these reviews, but would quickly type them and send them off to what he considered to be an appropriate journal. All of this was to change, however, in 1996 when he wrote a review of a book and sent it to the *Journal for the Study of Judaism in the Persian, Hellenistic, and Roman Period* (*JSJ*), which subsequently rejected the contribution. The editors claimed that the review was too long, that they had not assigned him the book, and that they were not interested in post-70 CE Judaism. Neusner, needless to say, was livid. He accused the editors and the press of censoring him, which, he reasoned, threatened the free exchange of scholarship and instead engaged in politics.[39] He also accused the editors of harboring anti-Semitic views because they refused to consider any Jewish texts produced after the destruction of the Second Temple.

After writing to the editors, editorial board, and publisher (Brill), Neusner decided to establish his own journal. Brill, worried at the thought of losing Neusner as an author—he had been a regular and best-selling author with them since the publication of his first book in 1962—agreed to publish it. This new journal was to be called the *Annual of Rabbinic Judaism: Ancient, Medieval and Modern*, and its stated goal was to be "the first and only journal to focus upon Rabbinic Judaism." Neusner assembled an all-star editorial board (Alan Avery-Peck, Herb Basser, William Scott Green, Mayer Gruber, Ithamar Gruenwald,

Aviezer Ravitzky, and Elliot R. Wolfson), with the aim of refuting the "theological anti-Semitism involved in supersessionism ('Judaism died at Calvary')" witnessed in *JSJ*.[40]

Looking at the editorial board of his new journal, it is important to note that Neusner was now beginning to renew ties with a new generation of Israeli scholars. He still nursed a major grievance from his invitation and subsequent dis-invitation to speak at the celebration of the fifty-year anniversary of *Zion*. In the fifteen years since this event, what he still called "the world famous Jerusalem boycott," he began to enter into correspondence with younger scholars. In 1995, for example, he met Ithamar Gruenwald, a professor of religion and Jewish mysticism at Tel Aviv University, at a conference in Europe. Neusner was so impressed with him that he invited him the following year to a conference that he was running at USF on "Religion and the Political Order: The Ideal Politics of Christianity, Islam, and Judaism." Writing to Anita Shapira in February 1997, he says of Gruenwald, "he did a fine job [at the conference] and made an effort to meet students and relate to them (which we highly value in this country)." Gruenwald returned the invitation, so Neusner and his wife made their first visit to Israel since 1981, where he presented a keynote address, "The Religious Sources of Toleration," at a conference of the same name at Tel Aviv University in 1997.[41]

His correspondence with Gruenwald is among his more philosophical in the archives. They write about everything from Israeli politics to writing schedules, in addition to the usual complaints about students. In a letter from December 1997, for example, Neusner gives him the following guidance on the importance of writing as opposed to just lecturing:

> I want to be the one in your life to encourage you to write it down, write it down, so people can benefit from your thought who are not in the range of your voice or not alive now. The reason I work hard on all public events is that I publish the lectures in books, so what happens on the occasion matters only a bit; what happens intellectually—have I said something interesting and compelling—matters a lot, for that reason.[42]

On his visit to Israel, Neusner was pleased to learn that Israelis not only knew his name, but appreciated his scholarship. This, he writes, "took quite a burden off my shoulders." In the same letter to his friend, Edward Alexander, a professor of English at the University of Washington, he expresses that he was pleased to find in Israel not only a general recognition, but a certain respect among "formidable audiences and response to the public events." Things were beginning to change in terms of not only the Israeli academy's relationship to Neusner but his to it as well. Neusner's writings, it seems, were slowly emerging from under lock and key at the national library. "I would have then to say," he concludes the letter to Alexander, that "what happens in the future doesn't matter so much; this is closure."[43]

Leaving USF (2000)

Ever since Neusner had arrived at USF, he had found a tremendous amount of support and goodwill. His years there seem to have been his most productive in terms of publication and his busiest in terms of almost-annual travel to Europe for extended lengths of stay to lecture and to hold visiting positions. Within four years of his arrival he would accept a temporary, but then permanent, position at Bard College in Annandale-on-Hudson, New York, that would see him teach a semester at each institution over an academic year. Unlike his time at Brown, Neusner's experience at USF provided him with an idyll. There were certainly moments of tension with colleagues, as there are anywhere, based on, among other things, miscommunication, petty jealousies, and the like.[44]

One of Neusner's biggest disappointment there seems to have been the institution's inability to hire the well-known scholar of Islam John Esposito, then of Holy Cross College and now of Georgetown University. In the fall of 1992 everything was pointing to the fact that Esposito would be hired by USF. For some reason, most likely having to do with the sheer cost of bringing him to Florida, the deal fell through. Esposito's proposed hiring was inspired by Neusner's desire to create a new doctorate program in religion at the university. When the Esposito deal collapsed, he took it as a death knell for the proposed program. As was typical of Neusner, his first reaction was to write letters to anyone involved in the process. He wrote to the president of the University, Francis S. Borkowski, and the dean of the College of Letters and Sciences, Rollin Richmond, calling the whole matter a "fiasco," implying that the administration at USF wanted the Religion Department to be little more than a service department to the rest of the university. Neusner, again typically, saw this personal failure as endemic to the structure of the entire university. Since his complaints went nowhere with the administration, he took them to the next level. Writing to his old friend, Bob Johnson, the state senator, he laments, "for a place just thirty years old, USF is amazing for the absence of energy, ambition, and vigor. It should be making history, innovating, infusing its entire community with the power of learning."[45]

In the fall of 1993 Neusner began to enter into negotiations with Bard that would enable him to teach the fall semesters in New York and the spring semesters at USF. The primary reason for this move—in addition to the fact that his children and grandchildren lived in the Northeast— was his close intellectual relationship with Bruce Chilton of Bard. Chilton and Neusner by this point had already begun to collaborate on a number of projects involving the shared theological matrices and categories of early Judaism and Christianity. Neusner's increased interest in theology, the presence of Chilton at Bard, and his disillusionment with the USF administration's incompetent dealing with his desire to establish a doctoral program in the Religion Department seem to have precipitated this part-time move to Bard beginning in the fall of 1994. His teaching there would see him offer one course on his own and one course cotaught with a colleague, either Bruce Chilton or Jonathan Brockopp, the department's specialist in Islam.[46]

Neusner's time at Bard got off to the wrong start when the college was unable to secure housing for Neusner for his first semester there. Halfway through that first semester, he wrote a personal note to its president, Leon Botstein, resigning his position, stating that "I have to protect my time and conserve my energy so that I can complete the life's work in which I am engaged. To have to struggle with the kinds of impediments placed in the way of my work by Bard College is simply not worth my time or effort, and that is why I have decided to end the relationship at the conclusion of this semester."[47] Needless to say, Botstein and others went out of their way to dissuade Neusner. After he finished teaching his first semester there, Bard renewed his position for another three years, and from both schools he was remunerated with an annual salary and half, in addition to ample research funds and benefits. If Neusner had found the undergraduates at USF willing if unprepared, he found the ones at Bard—a highly selective and private liberal arts college—both engaged and serious about learning.[48]

In the fall of 1996, Neusner received a call from Robert Berchman, a professor of religious studies at Dowling College on Long Island, informing Neusner that the college would like to award him an honorary doctorate the following year, and asking him if he would like to teach at Dowling in the fall of 1997. Neusner agreed to both. This would mean that he would spend the fall semester commuting between Annandale and Long Island (a two-and-a-half-hour drive, without factoring in traffic), and the spring semester at USF. Yet although he was awarded the honorary doctorate, the university was not able to arrange the teaching position, so Neusner remained solely at Bard in fall semesters.[49]

In addition to all of his monograph publishing, Neusner was also involved from 1994 to 1999 in a massive encyclopedic project. Along with his former students William Scott Green and Alan Avery-Peck, Neusner coedited the three-volume *Encyclopaedia of Judaism*, which appeared with Brill, in collaboration with the Museum of Jewish Heritage (New York) and Continuum Press in 1999. The project's goal was to provide a detailed account of Judaism the religion—including its diverse history, literature, beliefs both past and present, observances and practices, and their place in the context of society and culture—beginning in ancient

Israelite times until the present. The result was a systematic presentation within each entry that accorded with Neusner's high expectations
of analysis.[50]

In November 2009 Neusner wrote to Leon Botstein, the president
of Bard, declaring his intention to resign from USF and move full-time
to Bard the following year, 2000.[51] Meanwhile, in 1999 Scholars Press,
which had long published Neusner's series, both at Brown and then at
USF, went out of business. Neusner was able to find two other presses to
publish his series. University Press of America, based in Lanham, Maryland, agreed to publish his Studies in Ancient Judaism series, in addition
to taking over the entire backlist of both Brown Judaic Studies and South
Florida Studies. The other press was a small print-run business called
Global Publications that was run out of Binghamton, New York. They
agreed to publish three series under Neusner's editorship: Academic
Studies in the History of Judaism, Academic Studies in Religion and the
Social Order, and International Studies in Formative Christianity and
Judaism. When Global Publications went into receivership in 2002, all
of Neusner's series transferred to University Press of America.[52]

Institute for Advanced Theology, Bard

When Neusner moved to Bard College in 2000, he identified primarily with the Institute for Advanced Theology. The goal of the Institute,
established by Bruce Chilton in 1996, is to foster a critical understanding,
based in careful scholarship as opposed to received opinion, with the
aim of making true religious pluralism possible. Its web page declares,

> The Institute is not interested in making general assertions of the ne-
> cessity for religious tolerance; well-meaning and useful though such im-
> peratives are, they do not address the heart of the challenge of religious
> diversity. To promote genuine dialogue, people must be enticed by hope
> in the possibility of sympathetic acceptance of each other's views and the
> common threads within them. Such an open dialogue needs to be sup-

ported by serious reading, learning, and thinking—for neither the mystery itself nor the evidence is easy. . . . [T]he Institute's work has focused on how religions influence history, society, one another, and are in turn influenced by them. Institute scholars refine the newest critical research methods to pursue a comparative approach to the study of religion. The Institute's recent scholarship on James, the brother of Jesus, has sought to develop a common language of comparison between early Jewish Christianity and Judaism.[53]

The Institute in general, and the work of Chilton in particular, permitted Neusner to put his lengthy reflections on Jewish data into conversation with other data. More explicitly, Neusner and Chilton now began the process of examining the intersection between Judaism and Christianity, especially from the perspective of comparative theology. In a trilogy, titled *Christianity and Judaism: The Formative Categories*, Neusner and Chilton sought to articulate, compare, and contrast the major theological categories of Judaism and Christianity—for example, revelation, faith, the meaning of Israel, God—to show how the two traditions address the same issues, but from their own distinct set of propositions. Although earlier attempts at interfaith dialogue had begun in mutual recriminations and ended in rancor or worse, Neusner and Chilton, as spokespeople for their respective traditions, sought to examine what the classical theological positions of the two traditions are and to show how each tradition is in conversation with that of the other, whether by comparison or contrast. The goal was neither tolerance nor theological negotiation, but conviction in the faith that each is correct and that this can yield respect for those with differing theological positions.[54]

Since both Judaism and Christianity share a similar structure and system, it stands to reason, argue the two authors, that it is possible to compare their theological formulations on the same questions. Using his work with Greeley as a springboard, Neusner argues that it is necessary for Jews to find "friends outside not among militant secularists but in Christians of goodwill—Roman Catholic, Protestant, and Orthodox."[55]

At the beginning of *The Body of Faith*, Neusner and Chilton reveal their aims to the reader:

> Ours is not a relationship of sentimentality or careful avoidance of difference. We do not believe that, at the foundations, we really are the same thing, and neither wants to become like the other or to give up any part that makes him different from the other in the most profound layers of conviction and calling. The one writer is called to the study of the Torah as his way of life and purpose of being; the other is called to understand how God may be embodied within human living. But for the one, the study of the Torah, and for the other, the divine incarnation that Jesus Christ makes possible, carry learning beyond the boundaries of the Torah or of Christ, respectively. Each finds his work possible only through learning more about the religion of the other. And both maintain that sound learning and authentic understanding of their respective faiths demand attention to the near-at-hand religion of the other.[56]

This interest in comparing and contrasting theological categories is predicated on the idea that, for both authors, religions—to be fully understood—must be studied in comparative perspective; moreover, that Judaism and Christianity join together from their shared origin in Scripture, and because of this they never completely part company from one another but share a similar set of concerns. This means that the two religions neither can nor should be studied in isolation from one another. Each sheds light on the other—historically, scripturally, and theologically.

A good example of their discussion may be found in their differing conceptions of Israel. According to Neusner, "for the theology of Judaism, the definition of an 'Israel' takes the form of spelling out the rules of relationship. To define one social entity, an 'Israel,' the sages of the Judaism of the dual Torah not only explain how that entity relates to some other but also compare and contrast that entity to some other." Chilton, by contrast, sees Israel, as preached by Jesus, as undefined: "All the vital aspects of his ministry—his public activity in preaching and helping, his commissioning of disciples to act as his representatives, his shameful death at the hands of the current Roman prefect—imply that Jesus contested the social definition of Israel." This crucial difference—in Judaism "Israel" refers to a distinct socioethnic group, whereas in Christianity "Israel" refers to a more loosely defined category that seeks to understand God's relationship to diverse peoples (the "Church")—is at the heart of theological difference. Without trying to mediate these differences, Neusner and Chilton let them—as indeed they do for other theological categories—sit side by side with the hope that readers will understand the complexity and valences of the category within and between the two traditions.[57]

In addition to his work with Bruce Chilton, Neusner worked with colleagues who specialized in Islam. This permitted him to expand his theological comparison beyond Judaism and Christianity. Neusner and Tamara Sonn (his colleague at USF, now at Georgetown) wrote together an important book titled *Comparing Religions through Law: Judaism and Islam*. Therein, their stated goal was to understand that "religions that aspire to be realized in collective conscience, not only in individual conviction, will frame for themselves public policy through laws that define what is to be done or not done and they will enforce those laws in God's name." This observation permits them to put the two religions in counterpoint, with the aim of showing how the classical statements of both religions generate a set of authoritative legal prescriptions and proscriptions for their followers. Their mode of comparison is based on how the two traditions say similar things about a similar topic (for example, the relationship between individuals and God, and among individuals); areas where they say different things about something similar (for example, the role of sacrifice); and, finally, areas where they do not intersect at all (for example, all of the laws in rabbinical literature that deal with the Temple, for which there is no equivalent in Islam).[58]

This comparison was furthered with a sourcebook that Neusner put together, along with Sonn and Jonathan Brockopp, a scholar of Islam at

Bard (now Penn State). In their *Judaism and Islam in Practice* (2000), they sought to show how the theological categories of these two traditions share certain commonalities because they both "concur that God cares deeply not only about attitudes but actions, not only about what one says to God but how one conducts affairs at home and in the village."[59] Since both Judaism and Islam are monotheisms of law, despite certain differences, they nonetheless have a shared framework of convictions about the social and legal dimensions of theology. Once again, this is not a feel-good book of interfaith dialogue, but an attempt to show historical sources of common responses to divine messages. This does not mean that, at root, Judaism and Islam are the same religion, but it does point to how two different theologies undertake a sustained dialogue on issues believed to be of common concern. One such example they point to is prayer in Judaism and Islam:

> Both Islam and Judaism concur that fixed obligations govern the recitation of prayer, and much law encases the performance of those obligations in set rules and definitions. Prayer confirms to a fixed text. It is carefully choreographed, body movements being specified. It takes place at set times, not merely wherever and whenever the faithful are moved, or indeed, whether they are moved at all. It is an obligation that God has set, because God wants the prayers of humanity. And while Protestant spirituality judges that the letter convicts but the spirit revives, Muslim and Judaic faithful attest to the contrary: the requirement of regular, obligatory prayer provokes piety despite the recalcitrant human spirit.[60]

It was perhaps only natural that Neusner's work with scholars of Christianity and Islam in these individual volumes would lead to larger comparative projects with scholars from other traditions. In 2002, for example, along with Bruce Chilton and William Graham, a scholar of Islam from Harvard, Neusner cowrote a book titled *Three Faiths, One God: The Formative Faith and Practice of Judaism, Christianity, and Islam*. The goal of this volume was to examine, through comparison and contrast, how the three monotheistic religions develop the relationship between God, the Creator of heaven and earth, and their respective faith communities.[61]

Chilton and Neusner, under the auspices of the Institute of Advanced Theology at Bard, further initiated a number of conferences that brought together scholars from different religious traditions—both monotheistic and non-monotheistic—to discuss relevant issues in the contemporary period. Conferences, and subsequent multiauthored volumes, were produced on topics such as tolerance, altruism, and the ethics of reciprocity.

Diagnosis with Parkinson's Disease

Although Neusner took on the entire academic world for much of his life, things would begin to change—at first slowly, and then more dramatically—when he was diagnosed with Parkinson's disease in 2003 at the age of seventy-one. As is typical with Parkinson's, early signs were mild and, for the most part, went unnoticed. Neusner then began to notice a gentle tremor in his hand, especially of the pill-rolling kind (that is, a back-and-forth rubbing of his thumb and forefinger), in addition to tremors when it was relaxed. At first, as was typical, there was little impact on Neusner's daily activities, and, as things got worse, he began to take medication to counter some effects.[62]

As time went on, however, the other and inevitable symptoms began to appear at an increasingly rapid rate: slowed movement, rigidity in the muscles, impaired posture and balance, and the loss of automatic movements. When we spoke at his home in Rhinebeck, he did not want to talk much about his diagnosis or the long-term effects it had on his career. In fact, just the opposite. He avoided the question even though the effects of living with Parkinson's were apparent to all.[63] He still wrote. Though this is not surprising since writing had served as Neusner's raison d'être since he was a teenager. As evident in these conversations, the disease had not touched his intellect or memory. His reflections on the field and his ability to both remember and articulate clearly arguments from the past were impressive to the point of my astonishment.

In the summer of 2013, when I first got to know Neusner, I asked him how he might like to be remembered. He responded that he did not know and that he had really not thought about such a question. Puzzled, I persisted. But he was still unable—or unwilling—to answer. He referred to his corpus of writing, and his instructions say that, after his death, everything is to be placed online for everyone to access free of charge. But I wanted to know how such an important scholar envisaged his legacy. Why had someone who had spent his lifetime engaging in critical and systematic reflection on religion, Judaism, and the place Judaism in America not reflected more on his own mortality?

In the concluding chapter, I reflect on such questions.

Conclusions

A Life Lived

The genre of biography opens before the reader a window onto the enormous complexity of a life lived, providing flesh and context to a set of otherwise rarefied ideas. Where we might expect consistency or even a state of equilibrium, however, we instead often encounter disharmony and even incongruity. Perhaps it cannot be otherwise, and should not. Translated into a literary register, every life represents a multitextured narrative that witnesses—sometimes in equal measure, and sometimes not—periods of character stability, development, and regression, all of which take place against a larger backdrop of cultural, social, and intellectual contexts. A biography must present something of these larger contexts with the aim of illuminating the production of an individual's ideas, while at the same time realizing that the latter cannot simply be reduced to the former. Even if they could be, there is no way that a biographer, or anyone else for that matter, could gain access into the psychological and physiological workings of another. Instead what we are offered is a life into which are subsumed emotions and longings, desires and frustrations, and successes and disappointments that ebb and flow through a finite period of time, and that take place both in and through bodily interactions with others. Since ideas emerge from the spatial and temporal coordinates of an embodied life, they are susceptible to change, development, and even abrogation. It is the goal of biography, then, to open up a set of questions that deepen or nuance, but rarely, if ever, explain the very complexity of being human.

Perhaps more than others, Jacob Neusner engenders all the complexities, messiness, and contradictions of a lived life. The colorful, mercurial, controversial, often bordering on the outrageous, nature of Neusner's personality makes him the perfect candidate for a biography. Although I have tried to let Neusner's impressive contributions and personality emerge by plotting his chronological coordinates on a larger graph, we must not lose sight of the production of ideas over the course of one of the most colorful and prolific careers in the history of the academy. As conservative historian and one of Neusner's fellow finalists for the Library of Congress position, Gertrude Himmelfarb, wrote in 1987, "ideas and events [are] so firmly rooted in their historical context that history, rather than philosophy or nature, becomes the arbiter of truth."[1] If history is indeed the final arbiter, we must also be aware that truth—although I do not think that this is what Himmelfarb had in mind—is more relative and elastic than we might expect since the historian, not unlike the biographer, necessarily approaches the past from the concerns of her present. Biographical truths, like any set of truths, constantly shift and are often at the whims of those doing the telling.

The story that I have chosen to tell here focuses on Neusner's transformation of the American academy through his recalibration of the study of Judaism. It is no understatement to declare that because of Neusner, all of us who work in the field of Jewish studies broadly conceived are able to do what we today do. This book's focus has been on how, through a set of contested entanglements, Neusner was able, virtually single-handedly, to make this field possible. His life has offered a set of interconnections: Neusner's story becomes the story of Jewish studies in America, both of which intersect with the story of American Jews in the second half of the twentieth century.

I was initially drawn to Neusner due to his brazenness and his desire to remove the study of Jews and Judaism from the parochial concerns and identity politics that habitually threaten ethnic and area studies with marginalization. Despite Neusner's pioneering advances, however, we may well have returned to an intellectual ghetto, if in fact we ever left it, one wherein Jews are reified, and Jewish contributions become celebrated without regard to the larger intellectual and social contexts in which Jews lived and to which they contributed. This contextual amnesia, when combined with a certain historical myopia, means, as Neusner so clearly articulated throughout his lengthy career, that Jewish studies will only be for Jews. This return, the atavistic impulse at the heart of any ethnic studies, means that we have to ask ourselves whether or not Neusner was successful. Is it possible, as Neusner wanted, to make Jewish studies less Jewish? If this ultimately proves to be an impossibility, what does this say about Neusner? Does his career represent an anomaly that otherwise proves the rule of Jewish learning in this country? Or is there something more?

In his fight for the normalization and successful integration of his subject matter into larger disciplinary fields of study, Neusner was at the center of pretty much every ideological battle fought over how to study Jews and Judaism that occurred in this country over the past sixty years. Although he exhibited a notoriously mercurial personality, this trait was undoubtedly necessary in order for him to accomplish what he did. While he certainly wore his scars well and with dignity, he systematically alienated many both within and outside of the academy. The flip side of this ability to alienate, however, is that it risks undermining his legacy, at least in the short term.

Neusner's scholarship, especially on rabbinics, was controversial at the time, but has now been accepted, modified, or surpassed. He would have liked it this way. It is safe to say that in terms of academic rabbinics we now live in a post-Neusner world. Within this context, his early studies about how to engage in the history of the rabbinic period and his methods of understanding rabbinic texts remain widely in use even as they are challenged. Yet, unfortunately, Neusner seems to be best known for the length of his publication list and his colorful personality. Being a colorful character or the author of over a thousand books does not necessarily have to translate into a positive, let alone lengthy posthumous, legacy. For this reason it is important that we do not simply reduce Neusner's ideas or his accomplishments to his personality. To return us to the end of the previous chapter, even Neusner himself was uncertain as to his legacy or to how he might like to be remembered. When I spoke with him in the summer of 2013, he summarized his major contribution to the field of rabbinics in the following rather modest manner: "I was able to tear down some walls, and to open the field up to the comparative study of religion."[2] Admittedly, this was the assessment of a frail and ailing Neusner, an individual more concerned with his failing health than with worry about how others would remember him. I pushed him, but he was unwilling to go further. When I asked his wife of over fifty years, Suzanne too was unable to answer the question. I asked his son Noam, and he shared that his father's greatest legacy was his students, whom he pushed to think on their own. I am not fully convinced by these answers, so in what remains of this book I dig a little deeper.

Neusner's earlier correspondences reveal that he was not interested in establishing a legacy. His main goal, especially after the arrival of the Internet, was to have all of his works available for free online for anyone to access. Yet, the very facts that he saved all of his correspondences—in two archives, no less—and that he authorized the present biography show that, as he neared the end of his life, he did want to be remembered. Indeed, and contrary to his above statement, the position he held at Bard College has now become the "Jacob Neusner Professorship in the History and Theology of Judaism" and supports an annual "Jacob Neusner Lecture in Comparative Religion." Perhaps later in his life he was aware that he risked being the punch line for either a joke about writing too much or his infamous "drop dead" letters. The inability or unawareness on the part of Neusner to explain to me his lasting legacy seems to be based on the fact that he regarded his primary contribution to reside solely in his published works. Yet, since he wrote so much before the rise of the Internet, which today functions as our collective conscious, his legacy has not been properly archived therein.

If Martin Heidegger is correct that being is time and that since time is finite we have to confront our finitude, it is perhaps surprising that Neusner never wanted to do so. Perhaps it is safe to assume that his writing is what kept him alive or, framed slightly differently, the means through which he sought to avoid death. The problem for the reader though, and this is exacerbated by the sheer volume of his writings, is that his legacy is by no means on clear display. The quantity of his literary output threatens the quality of his innovations. Again we confront the questions: Is his legacy simply the fact that he was one of the most published authors in history? Or does it reside in his notorious and mercurial personality? While some might well see either of these or a combination of them as his lasting legacy, neither is a particularly positive assessment, and neither engages with the content of his work.

Is there something that we can distill in his writings that transcends the quantity of his publications and the venomous disagreements he had with others? Since so much of Neusner's work involved analysis of and reflection about historical documents, it is important to ask, does his analysis yield insights beyond history or historicism? Can Neusner, framed somewhat differently, be a "primary" source of modern American Jewish thought, or will he be remembered as a "secondary" source, one who helped illumine Jewish texts, but who had little to say about them? Did Neusner's lifework establish a place for him in the canon of great American Jewish thinkers?

In the introduction to this volume I stated boldly that Jacob Neusner was one of the most influential Jewish intellectuals in postwar America, and that a place belongs for him in the pantheon of great American Jewish thinkers. Today we read Joseph Soloveitchik, Abraham Joshua Heschel, and Mordecai Kaplan in courses on modern Jewish thought or philosophy. Some might think that Neusner does not belong among such distinguished company because his contribution resided more in elucidating the technical details of a scholarly approach to rabbinic texts as opposed to developing theoretical ideas about the nature and place of Judaism in the modern world. He was, some might contend, an academician more than a thinker. This assessment is unfortunate because, and as I have tried to show in considerable detail in the previous pages, the scholarly life of Jacob Neusner represents but one of his many intersecting lives.

Neusner's most profound work paradoxically had very little to do with the field that he is known for pioneering in this country, rabbinics. Rather, Neusner, for me, is at his most innovative when he deals with the place of Judaism in the American humanities and in his more theological work, both of which grew out of his journalistic training. Let me address each of these in turn. His work on the place, role, and function of the study of Judaism in the broader context of American higher education represents, to this day, the most astute and important reflection on what it means to study Judaism in the context of the modern university. Whereas many of his contemporaries were content to take up jobs in newly created departments of religious studies, Neusner took this new discipline seriously, and spent his academic career trying to figure out and then show to others the intersections between Judaism and the study of religion on both methodological and theoretical levels. Religious studies did not simply pay his salary, it helped him to rethink the place of Judaism in the academy and simultaneously forced that academy to make room for postbiblical Judaism. This is his bequest to all of us in the field. Moreover, he rethought this relationship not only in academic monographs, but in reflections he placed on full display to readers of Jewish newspapers and magazines. In this respect, Neusner was not just an academician, but very much a public intellectual. This is certainly reinforced by his political career.

I constantly return to these writings in my own work, and submit that the field would be less ethnic or parochial today and would have a rather different set of concerns if more scholars had taken them seriously.[3] Neusner clearly shows in these writings what the stakes are for studying Judaism using entrenched disciplinary methods, and what the pitfalls are when we fail to do so. The study of Judaism, for Neusner, must open itself to larger intellectual conversations, and within this context he spent much of his academic life showing how Jewish data were illustrative of larger issues in the humanities. Neusner argued that Jews and Judaism, both in the university and in society, needed to shed their atavism and their inability to ask why something was important other than the fact that a Jew said or wrote it. In this Neusner the academician and Neusner the Jewish thinker were two sides of the same coin.

Neusner's works are a must-read for anyone who thinks or writes about Judaism within the context of the American academy. Some now over forty years old, they reveal a prescient awareness of a set of issues as relevant today as they were when he first penned them. As we have seen, these include, but are certainly not limited to, what it means to talk about, teach, and think about Judaism in the context of the modern university. In typical Neusnerian fashion, he shows that none of these issues are unique to Judaism, but are representative of any other area or ethnic study. For Neusner, Judaism, or Jewish data, can only ever be exemplary of larger issues. He illumined for so many of us how to grapple with the age-old tensions between the universal and the particular. Problems begin when we forget this and want to make Jews and/or Judaism sui generis or singular. This is why Neusner was so critical of Jewish scholarly organizations, such as the Association for Jewish Studies, which he complained functioned as a halfway house between the yeshivah and the secular university. We pass over Neusner's reflections at our own peril.

Even more important are his works on, for lack of a better term, theology. Within this context, it is important to remember that Neusner was a rabbi as well as a scholar and that he wore the rabbinic hat seriously in many ways. This more theological Neusner was a natural extension of the Neusner who wrote so forcefully about what the study of Judaism must look like in order to be a viable field of study. If the latter reflected on the place of Judaism in the academy, the former concentrated on the place of Judaism in American society. His *Stranger at Home*, for example, remains one of the most original examinations of what it means to be a Jew in America, and by extension an American Jew. He sought to depart from defining American Judaism in terms of the Holocaust and Israel to something more integral to American Judaism itself. Much of this reflection, he argued, now occurred at the secular university as opposed to the synagogue. He thus sought to make space and grant authority to the secular study of Judaism. This work, and those like it, such as *Israel in America: A Too-Comfortable Exile?*, are among Neusner's most important, providing a penetrating analysis of the identity crisis that he believed resided at the heart of American Jewry. In these works we see Neusner's character traits—controversial, entertaining, and informative—on full display. However, we also witness his love of Jewish learning and his desire to see it thrive as the nucleus of the Jewish community. His was a Judaism for adults.

These works belong among the classic texts of American Jewish literature. I use them, for example, in my classes on modern Jewish thought, where students read them along with the likes of Hermann Cohen's *Religion of Reason: Out of the Sources of Judaism*, Franz Rosenzweig's *Star of Redemption*, and Martin Buber's *I and Thou*, in addition to works by American Jewish authors such as Joseph Soloveitchik's *Halakhic Man* and Abraham Joshua Heschel's *The Sabbath*. Like the authors of these other works, Neusner provides a reflection on the intersection of Judaism and modernity. He does so, moreover, within the specific context of the United Sates. I would hope that these works of Neusner will take their place alongside these other modern classics.

Yet, and this is the problem, these non-rabbinic works of Neusner risk being hidden by or subsumed under the sheer magnitude of his other writings. In this respect, Neusner wrote so much that he paradoxically risks writing himself out of a posthumous existence. Neusner was certainly proud of the fact that he wrote over a thousand books and that he was the most published author in history, but we have to face the fact that many of those books have been forgotten already or soon will be. Ironically, had he published less, his oeuvre might well have had a different impact. Despite his best of intentions to take the study of Judaism outside of the parochial wall of the yeshiva and to remove it from ethnic ghetto that he believed threatened it on campus, his most important works are those that deal directly with the experiences of American Jews. While his approach in such works is certainly not overly ecumenical or hackneyed, it nonetheless is directed at a predominantly Jewish reading audience.

I would not be surprised if future generations remember Neusner less as a scholar of rabbinic Judaism and less as the herculean author of over a thousand books, and more as an astute commentator on the affairs and experiences of American Jews. Jews in America have always struggled to form a positive identity, caught as they are between the past in Europe and a perceived future in Israel. This tension will undoubtedly be exacerbated in coming years as young American Jews continue to struggle on an unprecedented level with Zionism and the human rights abuses associated with the Israeli occupation. For many young American Jews the Holocaust risks becoming little more than a historical fact, and Zionism increasingly appears politically and ideologically unfathomable. Neusner recognized this danger, and his most important work both describes and analyzes these problems. His solution: create a positive Jewish identity based not on ethnicity or empty slogans, but on learning from Jewish texts.

When I spoke to him in the summer of 2013, Neusner told me that he was the happiest with his theological work, which is the most recent. It opens up his data to theoretical generalization, which permits higher reflection and comparison with other religions. This work, in many ways at odds with the first half of his career, is more rabbinic than professorial. His work with Bruce Chilton at the Institute for Advanced Theology at Bard showed a much more sanguine Neusner, one trying to work out in his own mind and with others the nature of the relationships between both Judaism and Christianity, and Judaism and other religions. Again, though, this material was written less for an academic audience than for Jews and Christians interested in an informed dialogue between these two religious traditions.

Although Neusner would say that the theological represents only the latest iteration of his scholarly career, I do not think this is entirely correct. He wrote works of Jewish theology, although at the time he would not have used this term, as early as his teen years when he worked at his father's paper. This impulse never left him. Even as a young rabbinical student, he frequently wrote articles and op-eds—

much to the chagrin of his teachers—about what he considered to be the sorry state of most American Jews. This early work in journalism never left him, and it paved the way for his contribution to what became the havurah movement. In this respect, his *Fellowship in Judaism* (1963) represents one of the earliest calls to American Jews that they need to find like-minded individuals to study Jewish texts together. Neusner argued that such an approach, missing in the large and cold congregations wherein people have very little in common other than a shared ethnicity, had the ability to re-create a vibrant and dynamic Judaism. Again, though, since Neusner wrote so much, such early gems risk being concealed by the sheer quantity of his later publications. While most know of the literally hundreds and hundreds of monographs and other studies that he wrote on rabbinic Judaism, very few are aware of these other, less rushed and, I would argue, much more profound writings.

Then there is the political dimension of Jacob Neusner's life. While his political and ideological views might make more liberal-leaning individuals uncomfortable, they are not completely incongruous with his academic life. Like many Republicans, he thought that because he had succeeded based on his own hard work and sheer determination, others could and must do the same. Framed somewhat differently, if he could make the case for the successful integration of the academic study of Judaism within the secular academy, then others—women, African Americans, Latinos, and so on—ought to be able to do the same. While there is certainly something to be said for this attitude, one could undoubtedly make the case that it was the very Christocentric, male, and Western categories that were responsible for the marginalization of minority voices in the first place. While Neusner believed that these categories could be forced to change in response to minorities' narratives when they are framed and articulated properly, others would certainly disagree. Yet, the alternative is not particularly appealing. If area and ethnic studies simply become insider clubs that revel in victimhood and refuse to ask certain hard questions, the university risks losing its raison d'être. Neusner was acutely aware of this threat, and resisted it whenever he had the opportunity. Here I agree with Neusner, and submit that this resistance cannot simply be written off as old-fashioned or conservative.

Regardless, it is difficult to understand how one of the most astute commentators on American Jewish life, someone who sought to create a new type of Judaism based on books and learning as opposed to atavism or special-pleading, could end up holding political beliefs that were so beyond the mainstream of American Jews. This is one of several incongruities of Neusner's life. Perhaps he thought that the Republican Party took religion more seriously than the Democrats. Perhaps it had more to do with his urge to be difficult and set himself up as the opposite of mainstream opinion (whether intellectual or communal). A right-wing Jew and a right-wing academic certainly go against the grain of expectations, a feature that we should not at all be surprised to encounter in Neusner's life and career. But, once again, his active involvement with right-wing politics at a time of the great cultural wars in the United States risks further obscuring his intellectual accomplishments. In this Neusner was his own worst enemy in potentially undermining his own legacy.

Neusner always felt like an outsider, and this feeling seems to be what motivated him and drove him forward. He was not an Old World Jew, a *yeshiva bokher*, or a Jewish leader who was part of the mainstream status quo. He was a proud American, someone who was critical of traditional methods of Jewish learning, and he despised the status quo in its leadership of the American Jewish community. Much of his literary output is an attempt to critique and undermine all of these. His work, then, can appear to be as reactionary as it is transformative. Yet, despite all of this, he was—perhaps paradoxically, perhaps not—uncommonly and deeply committed to Jewish learning and Jewish values. Right-wing values and difficult personality aside, Neusner is one of the most important voices that sought to transmit the beauty of Judaism and its truths for the postwar generation of American Jews.

His "American" translations of the entire canon of rabbinic works, his theological works trying to nudge American Jews out of their complacency, and his constant op-eds in a variety of Jewish (and non-Jewish) magazines and newspapers all attest to his deep concern for the fate of American Jews. It is my hope that his tremendous accomplishments—less having to do with the sheer quantity of his publications and more having to do with the quality of those few truly transformative works—will ascend to the place that they deserve.

* * *

I began this conclusion with the claim that a lived life is an infinitely complicated phenomenon, one full of vibrancy, contradiction, and incongruences. It cannot be otherwise. A life examined in its rich texture and entangled contexts reveals more than just its subject matter; it also reveals a great deal about the age in which that life was lived. Set against this broader context, Neusner lived at a formative moment in American Jewish history. It was the time of increased suburbanization, of a generation trying to understand itself in the aftermath of one of the largest atrocities of the twentieth century, the Holocaust. Neusner emerged from and responded to these contexts. In so doing, he became perhaps the most important American-born Jewish thinker this country produced.

In the final analysis, I maintain that it is his theological work that ought to attain for him the status of a great American Jewish thinker. The great paradox is that if one reads only the work produced in the first half of his career—the historical and the literary material—one might not realize the import of this other body of work that shadows the work on rabbinics. It is important, however, that this not be overlooked. For it is through this work that Neusner sought to transmit Judaism to American Jews, Jews, like himself, who did not grow up in the Old World and who did not have a traditional Jewish education.

More than a scholar of rabbinics, Neusner was monumental in the formation of contemporary Jewish studies and helped to integrate it into the American academy. His life story is the story of Jewish integration and acceptance in the intellectual world of the United States. This story represents triumph over anti-Semitism and the concomitant Christo-centric categories that followed in its wake, and the desire to study Judaism not on its own terms (as was done, for example, in the yeshiva), but using and transforming existing paradigms. The place of Judaism in the American academy today, a place that we all take for granted, was virtually unheard of when Neusner walked onto the scene. He single-handedly, with the force of both his intellect and his personality, made this happen.

His writings, especially, those on American Judaism and the place of the study of Judaism in American culture, represent the most original and creative reflections we possess. It is these works that will stand the test of time and ensure that Neusner will take his rightful place as a great American Jewish thinker. He is truly an American Jewish iconoclast.

NOTES

ABBREVIATIONS

AJA   American Jewish Archives, Manuscript Collection No. 0890

A   Correspondences and Writing

B   Scrapbooks

C   Memorabilia

AWH/IN   Aaron W. Hughes interview with (followed by name and date)

JN   Jacob Neusner

NCH   Neusner Collection, Widener Library, Harvard University

The chief source for reconstructing Neusner's life was my series of interviews with him in the summer of 2013. These interviews are cited as AWH/IN JN, followed, where possible, by the date in question. Another major source is the correspondences found in the Neusner Collection at Harvard's Widener Library, which I abbreviate as NCH (that is, Neusner Collection Harvard). These, however, are more problematic because, frequently, Neusner often saved only his own letters in these files, and rarely the letter to which he is responding. This becomes somewhat easier to reconstruct in the late 1990s when he switches many of his correspondences over to email. This means that, while it is often clear by the address to whom he is writing, on occasion it is not. Sometimes there is a letter to, for example, "Greg," and that is it (i.e., no surname or institutional affiliation). When this happens, and it rarely does, I simply put "letter to Greg." Citations to NCH include box number, binder number within that box, and cumulated binder number, a brief description, and, where available, date (e.g., NCH 5.6.40, letter to Lawrence Schiffman, 3/27/1984).

Neusner has also deposited many of his files at the American Jewish Archives at the Hebrew Union College–Jewish Institute of Religion in Cincinnati. When citing these correspondences I use the following formula: AJA A (Correspondences and Writing), box number and folder number, description, and date (e.g., AJA A 40.6, Fred Neusner to JN, 11/9/2007). Or, they are AJA B (Scrapbooks), followed by the book number and, if possible, the date (e.g., AJA B, book 2).

Interviews with other sources are cited as AWH/IN, followed by the name of the person interviewed, together with the date of the interview (e.g., AWH/IN Suzanne Neusner, July 15, 2013).

Full bibliographic citations may be found in the bibliography.

INTRODUCTION

1 On the rise of Jewish studies in America and the role of various institutions in its growth, see Ritterband and Wechsler, *Jewish Learning in American Universities.*

2 Neusner, "Introduction" to *New Humanities and Academic Disciplines,* xxiii.

3 Ibid., xxi.

4 Neusner summarizes these approaches in *Three Questions of Formative Judaism,* xvi–xxii.

CHAPTER 1. AFLOAT IN A SEA OF WORDS

1 This is certainly not the place to give an overview of this subject matter, but a convenient point of departure may be found in Holtz, *Back to the Sources.*

2 See, e.g., Yerushalmi, *Zakhor;* and, more recently, Brenner, *Prophets of the Past.*

3 See the aptly named article by Ismar Schorsch, "Scholarship in the Service of Reform," in his *From Text to Context,* 303–333.

4 Leopold Zunz, "On Rabbinic Literature," in Mendes-Flohr and Reinharz, *Jew in the Modern World,* 222. My goal here is certainly not to tell the story of this movement, *Wissenschaft des Judentums,* the precursor to the modern field of Jewish studies. Relevant literature may be found in, for example, Schorsch, *From Text to Context;* Myers, *Re-inventing the Jewish Past;* Brenner, *Prophets of the Past;* and Hughes, *Study of Judaism.*

5 See, e.g., Heschel, *Abraham Geiger and the Jewish Jesus;* and, more recently, Erlewine, *Judaism and the West.*

6 Again, see the important study in Schorsch, "Scholarship in the Service of Reform."

7 See the comments in Bland, *Artless Jew,* 13–36.

8 See Wiese, *Challenging Colonial Discourse,* 77–83.

9   On the general context of American Jews at this time, see Sarna, *American Judaism*, 272–306.
10 AWH/IN Suzanne Neusner, July 15, 2013.
11 See Sarna, *American Judaism*, 282–293.
12 Hoffman, *Jewish West Hartford*, 23.
13 See, for example, AJA A 1.3, Harvard Class of 1954 Sexennial Report (1960).
14 Neusner, *Life of Yohanan ben Zakkai*, 2nd ed., xvi.
15 AWH/IN JN, July 14, 2013.
16 Ritterband and Wechsler, *Jewish Learning in American Universities*, 10.
17 This and the following three paragraphs rework my *Study of Judaism*, 64–67.
18 This example builds on Hughes, *Study of Judaism*, 65–66.
19 Qtd. in Ritterband and Wechsler, *Jewish Learning in American Universities*, 47.
20 Wolfson, "Needs of Jewish Scholarship in America," 32–33.
21 From Barbara DeConcini's interview of JN on November 12, 2002 (p. 3).
22 AJA A 17.11, JN to Mr. Phillips, May 3, 1990.
23 AJA A 41.2, Eli Neusner to JN, June 22, 2012.
24 Neusner, "Struggle and Success: Story of a Newspaper," *Connecticut Jewish Ledger*, June 25, 1959, in AJA B, book 2.
25 Silverman, *Hartford Jews*, 231.
26 Neusner, "Struggle and Success."
27 Ibid.
28 Although eventually sold, the paper still thrives. See its website at http://www.jewishledger.com.
29 Silverman, *Hartford Jews*. On the cause of death, see NCH 17.5.113, JN to Eddie, October 15, 1995.
30 NCH 20.4.133, JN to Klaus, November 19, 1997.
31 AJA A 39.13, Fred Neusner to JN, March 28, 2007.
32 NCH 16.3.104, JN to Marvin Fox, March 24, 1994.
33 NCH 20.4.133, JN to Klaus, November 19, 1997.
34 AJA A 40.6, Fred Neusner to JN, November 9, 2007.
35 On his mother's keeping kosher, see NCH 20.3.132, JN to Klaus, October 14, 1997; and on the episode at McDonald's, see NCH 20.4.133, JN to Klaus, November 19, 1997.
36 NCH 16.3.104, JN to Marvin Fox, March 24, 1994.
37 AJA A 40.6, Fred Neusner to JN, November 19, 2007.
38 AWH/IN JN, July 14, 2013.
39 NCH 22.5.149, JN to Millie Neusner, May 13, 1999.
40 AJA A 3.1, Fred Neusner to JN, October 28, 1981.
41 Ibid.
42 AJA B, book 15.
43 AJA A 39.13, Fred Neusner to JN, March 27, 2007.

44 This autobiographical account may be found in Neusner and Neusner, *Price of Excellence*, 60.

45 Ibid., 59.

46 Neusner, "Speaking of Jewish Books," *Connecticut Jewish Ledger*, December 6, 1951 in AJA B, book 2.

47 Neusner, "'Man Is Not Alone' Develops Rational Approach to Religion," *Connecticut Jewish Ledger*, November 8, 1951, in AJA B, book 2.

48 Neusner quotes this response from Heschel in his "Speaking of Jewish Books."

49 These were subsequently saved and can be found in either the Harvard collection or the collection at the American Jewish Archives in Cincinnati.

50 Neusner, "Cincinnati Archives Hold Key to American Jewish Past," *Connecticut Jewish Ledger*, July 16, 1953.

51 NCH 20.3.132, JN to Ithamar Gruenwald, October 14, 1997.

52 Neusner and Neusner, *Price of Excellence*, 37–38.

53 Feuer, "Recollections of Harry Austryn Wolfson," 48–49.

54 Though Neusner did insist that the rabbis of the Mishnah were "philosophers" and that their system ought to be contextualized within the larger trends of contemporaneous Greco-Roman philosophy.

55 AWH/IN JN, July 15, 2013.

56 As Neusner writes in his *How to Grade Your Professors*, 154, "When I was a freshman in college, I went out for the fencing team, for two ghastly days, and for the soccer team for one more. Then I discovered God wanted me to be a writer, not a fencer. So I took a creative writing course. My classmate, John Updike, got an A, and I got a B. So I decided God wanted Updike to be a writer. I was meant for something else. I can't remember just now what I thought it was. It does not seem important anymore."

57 On his appointment by Lynne Cheney, see NCH 9.2.61; on his lobbying for Updike, see NCH 10.2.66. John Updike did not receive the award that year, but he did the following year, 1989.

58 DeConcini interview with JN, September 12, 2002 (p. 7).

59 AWH/IN JN, July 13, 2013. See also Neusner and Neusner, *Price of Excellence*, 64.

60 The copy of the interview appears in AJA A 5.4 (this quotation is from p. 19). The interview appeared in the January 1985 issue of *New Traditions*.

61 In his Personal Statement in his Harvard Class of 1954, 40th Anniversary Report, he writes, "I remember only one course at Harvard that kept the promise to educate, which was Leonard Nash's and Thomas S. Kuhn's general education course in the area of the history of science, later on yielding the classic, *The Structure of Scientific Revolutions*." See NCH 16.4.105.

62 In NCH 1.3.3, May 1953.

63 Neusner later defines what it means to be a Zionist in an op-ed "Why I Am a Zionist," *Connecticut Jewish Ledger*, January 26, 1961, AJA B, book, 4.

64 AJA A 1.2.

65 AJA A 1.6.

66 Neusner and Neusner, *Price of Excellence*, 65.

67 Ibid., 65.

68 Neusner would subsequently go on to write the foreword to the 1995 edition of the work.

69 AWH/IN JN, July 14, 2013.

70 Neusner and Neusner, *Price of Excellence*, 66.

71 AWH/IN JN, July 14, 2013.

72 See, for example, Neusner, "Why the Republicans?," *Brown Banner Forum*, October 18, 1984.

73 Neusner and Neusner, *Price of Excellence*, 67.

74 Ibid., 68.

75 AWH/IN JN, July 14, 2013.

76 The quotation is reproduced in Aidan Stowe, "Theology Dons Calm in Face of Major Affront," *Oxford Times*, August 20, 1983, 20. It may be found in NCH 4.8.34.

77 Stowe, "Theology Dons Calm in Face of Major Affront," 20.

CHAPTER 2. FROM RABBI TO SCHOLAR

1 Shore, "Jacob in the Lion's Den," in NCH 3.7.25.

2 See Diner, "Like the Antelope and the Badger: The Founding and Early Years of JTS, 1886–1902," in Wertheimer, *Tradition Renewed*, 1:13. See also Sarna, *American Judaism*, 184–193.

3 Diner, "Like the Antelope and the Badger," 1–43.

4 Scult, "Schechter's Seminary," in Wertheimer, *Tradition Renewed*, 2:59.

5 On Kaplan more generally, see the important biography in Scult, *Radical American Judaism of Mordecai Kaplan*.

6 On the tensions between JTS and the Conservative movement, see Wertheimer, "JTS and the Conservative Movement," in Wertheimer, *Tradition Renewed*, 2:403–442.

7 See Greenbaum, "The Finkelstein Era," in Wertheimer, *Tradition Renewed*, 1:161–232.

8 Ibid., 1:165–167.

9 A biography of Lieberman may be found in Schochet and Spiro, *Saul Lieberman*.

10 Ibid., 31.

11 Ibid., 62.

12 See Shapiro, *Saul Lieberman and the Orthodox*, 15–18.

13 Qtd. in ibid., 29.

14 Ibid., 35.

15 On Neusner's reminiscences of Lieberman's pedagogical ability, see AWH/IN JN, July 14, 2013. For Lieberman's "infamous" review of Neusner's work, see Lieberman, "Tragedy or a Comedy?," 315–319. Neusner commemorated the ten-year anniversary of this publication with his own *Why There Never Was a*

"Talmud of Caesarea": Saul Lieberman's Mistakes (1994). I will discuss this, and other debates, in chapter 5.

16 AJA C, book 18, Saul Lieberman to JN, December 4, 1972.

17 Qtd. in Golinkin, "Was Professor Saul Lieberman 'Orthodox' or 'Conservative'?," 13–29.

18 AJA A 8.4, Bernard Mandelbaum to JN, August 23, 1986. Neusner's footnote in that volume reads as follows: "I am inclined to think that historical perspectives have clouded the vision of those who attempt them for exegesis of Talmudic literature. The most ambitious, and, consequently, the most unsuccessful such effort at a kind of historical exegesis of the Talmud and its law is in Louis Finkelstein. . . . But in this regard he merely carried forward the perfectly dreadful approach of Louis Ginzberg. . . . I am able to point to the underlying and generative errors in their approach to the interpretation of the legal materials for historical purposes and in their claim to interpret the legal materials from a historical perspective as well (a totally confused work)." See Neusner, "Talmud as Anthropology," 65n8.

19 AWH/IN JN, July 14, 2013.

20 Shore, "Jacob in the Lion's Den," NCH 3.7.25.

21 Ibid.

22 AWH/IN JN, July 14, 2013. See also Neusner and Neusner, *Price of Excellence*, 70–71.

23 Neusner and Neusner, *Price of Excellence*, 71–72.

24 Neusner, "Review Essay," 323–324.

25 On his relationship to Heschel, see also Neusner and Neusner, *Price of Excellence*, 112n11. On being Heschel's research assistant, see AWH/IN JN, July 14, 2013.

26 AWH/IN JN, July 13, 2013.

27 Neusner wrote about this a lot. Perhaps one of his most pointed criticisms may be found in his review of the work of Eliezer Segal, someone whom Neusner turns into a metaphor for the entire Israeli system. See Neusner, *Documentary Foundation of Rabbinic Culture*, 47–72. Although it is important to note that Neusner published Segal's work in his *Brown Judaic Studies*.

28 On his self-confessed unsuitability for the rabbinate, AWH/IN JN, July 14, 2013. A selection of his sermons may be found in NCH 1.9.9.

29 NCH 1.9.9, Yom Kippur sermon in Oneonta, NY, September 24, 1958.

30 Ibid.

31 AWH/IN JN, July 14, 2013.

32 AJA A 10.3, Ismar Schorsch to JN, March 19, 1987. For JN's acceptance, see AJA A 10.3, JN to Ismar Schorsch, March 27, 1987.

33 Neusner, "The Next Chancellorship at JTS: Some Hopes," in AJA A 11.3.

34 Ibid.

35 AJA A 11.12, Ismar Schorsch to JN, August 27, 1987.

36 AJA A 11.13, letter from JN to Ray Scheindlin, September 14, 1987. The telegram JN sent to the seminary may be found in the same box.

37 AJA A 11.14, JN to colleague, October 6, 1987.

38 AJA A 17.11, Ed Greenstein to JN, May 3, 1990.

39 AJA A 41.8, JN to Arnold Eisen, July 5, 2010.

40 AJA A 41.8, Arnold Eisen to JN, July 6, 2010.

41 AWH/IN JN, July 14b, 2013.

42 Jacob Neusner, "Returning to Reform," *Forward*, December 4, 2009, http://forward.com/articles/119646/returning-to-reform/#ixzz2rKJKfJH8.

43 See Ritterband and Wechsler, *Jewish Learning in American Universities*, 36–44.

44 24 Pa. Stat. 15–1516, as amended, Pub. Law 1928.

45 Online at http://en.wikisource.org/wiki/Abington_School_District_v._Schempp_ (374 _U.S._203)/Opinion_of_the_Court.

46 See Ritterband and Wechsler, *Jewish Learning in American Universities*, 189–199.

47 Levy, "American University and *Olam Ha-Ba*," 15.

48 Neusner and Neusner, *Price of Excellence*, 73.

49 Ibid., 73.

50 See, for example, Moore, *Judaism in the First Centuries of the Christian Era*. Neusner would be fairly critical of his approach for its lack of an overtly critical methodology. See his criticism in, among other places, *Judaism: The Evidence of the Mishnah*, 2nd ed., 8.

51 Neusner and Neusner, *Price of Excellence*, 74.

52 AWH/IN JN, July 14, 2013.

53 Ibid.

54 Neusner, *Life of Yohanan ben Zakkai*, 2nd ed., xviii.

55 AJA C, book 6, Morton Smith to JN, January 21, 1963.

56 AWH/IN JN, July 14, 2013. E.g., Neusner, *Documentary Foundation of Rabbinic Culture*, 13.

57 Neusner, *Life of Yohanan ben Zakkai*, 1st ed., 2.

58 AWH/IN JN, July 14, 2013.

59 Spicehandler, "Review of *A Life of Yohanan ben Zakkai*," 364.

60 Ibid., 365.

61 Ibid., 365.

62 Zeitlin, "A Life of Yohanan ben Zakkai."

63 Ibid., 146.

64 Ibid., 147.

65 Neusner, *Judaism: The Evidence of the Mishnah*, 2nd ed., 424.

66 Ibid., 151.

67 Neusner and Neusner, *Price of Excellence*, 75.

68 Ibid., 76.

69 Online at http://www.svhe.org/ourhistory.html. In 1973 the organization underwent another name change, to the Society for Values in Higher Education (SVHE), in which form it exists to this day.

70 AWH/IN JN, July 14, 2013.

71 NCH 20.5.134, JN to Leon Botstein, December 12, 1997.

72 Neusner and Neusner, *Price of Excellence*, 115.

73 AWH/IN JN, July 14, 2013.

CHAPTER 3. COMMUNITY TENSIONS

1 A general sociological survey of the rise of Jewish studies in America may be found in Ritterband and Wechsler, *Jewish Learning in American Universities*, 216–236. See also my *Study of Judaism*.

2 This section builds upon my *Study of Judaism*, 64–76.

3 Ritterband and Wechsler, *Jewish Learning in American Universities*, 35.

4 Ibid., 65.

5 The quotation comes from Cyrus Adler (1863–1940), a Jewish leader and educator, and is quoted in Ritterband and Wechsler, *Jewish Learning in American Universities*, 67.

6 Ritterband and Wechsler, *Jewish Learning in American Universities*, 89.

7 Schwarz, *Wolfson of Harvard*, 1–8. See also Ritterband and Wechsler, *Jewish Learning in American Universities*, 108–110.

8 The details of the establishment of the chair may be found in Ritterband and Wechsler, *Jewish Learning in American Universities*, 120.

9 Branscomb, "A Note on Establishing Chairs of Jewish Studies," in Jick, *Teaching of Judaica in American Universities*, 97.

10 AWH/IN JN, July 14, 2013.

11 Ibid.

12 On the AAJR, consult their webpage for a description: "fellows are nominated and elected by their peers and thus constitute the most distinguished and most senior scholars teaching Judaic studies at American universities" (http://www.aajr.org/about/). Neusner's characterization of the organization and his encounter with Halkin is based on AWH/IN JN, July 15, 2013.

13 Part of this is made difficult because his archives (at least the NCH) do not deal with this period. His later attempt to situate himself, *Price of Excellence*, which he cowrote with his son, Noam, is too stylistic and more in the genre of *apologia pro vita sua* as opposed to raw reflection.

14 AJA C, book 5, p. 2. The article was subsequently published as "Jewish Studies in the American University."

15 AJA C, book 5, p. 3.

16 Ibid., p. 5.

17 Ibid., p. 5.

18 Ibid.

19 The lectures were subsequently published in *Judaism: A Quarterly Journal of Jewish Life and Thought*.

20 The integration of Jewish studies into the humanities would subsequently become the major preoccupation of Neusner. His reflections on this topic may be found

in, for example, Neusner, *Judaism in the American Humanities* and *Judaism in the American Humanities*, second series.

21 Neusner and Neusner, *Price of Excellence*, 125.
22 AJA C, book 11.
23 AJA C, book 7.
24 Ibid.

CHAPTER 4. FINDING HIS WAY

1   AWH/IN JN, July 15, 2013.
2   Ibid. On Neusner's own reflections on Frye, see *Price of Excellence*, 130.
3   See Hughes, *Study of Judaism*, 93–95.
4   See Schwartz, "Historiography on the Jew in the 'Talmudic Period' (70–640 CE)," 98–99.
5   For Neusner's comments on Goodenough, see AWH/IN JN, July 15, 2013; Neusner and Neusner, *Price of Excellence*, 132–135.
6   NCH 20.5.134, JN to Ithamar Gruenwald, December 10, 1997.
7   On Goodenough and his death, see Mattes, *Myth for Moderns*. Bibliographic reference to the edited volume may be found in the bibliography.
8   AWH/IN JN, July 15, 2013.
9   AWH/IN Suzanne Neusner, July 14, 2013.
10 A review of one of her gallery showings in the Rina Gallery in Jerusalem from the *Jerusalem Post*, undated, is collected in AJA C, book 8.
11 AWH/IN JN, July 14, 2013. See also the comments in Neusner and Neusner, *Price of Excellence*, 139–140.
12 The engagement notice, titled "Suzanne Richter and a Professor Will Be Married," may be found in AJA C, book 7.
13 AWH/IN JN, July 14, 2013. See also the comments in Neusner and Neusner, *Price of Excellence*, 139–140.
14 On Suzanne "doing it all," see NCH 21.7.145, JN to Ithamar Gruenwald, January 1, 1999. On his diet prior to meeting Suzanne, see Neusner and Neusner, *Price of Excellence*, 126.
15 NCH 4.3.29, memo from JN, president, to guests of the Max Richter Foundation's Fifth Richter Conversation, June 23, 1980.
16 On "The Max Richter Conversation on Ancient Judaism," see AJA A 1.33; and on "Judaic Studies and the University," see AJA A 1.49, including the letter from President Marver H. Bernstein of Brandeis thanking JN on November 16, 1979.
17 AJA A 40.7, JN to Dimitri Papadimitriou (vice president of Bard College), January 2, 2008.
18 AWH/IN JN, July 14, 2013.
19 There is a joke told of Neusner. Someone calls his office and, depending upon the variant, either his secretary or wife answers. "He can't come to the phone right now," she says, "he's working on a new book." "It's okay," the voice on the other end shoots

back, "I'll wait." This joke disgusted Neusner. He thought, and rightly so, that it reduced his entire corpus to a set of simplistic and nondeliberative acts. He terminated friendships over this joke. In a letter to a former friend, Rabbi Jack Reimer, Neusner wrote, "I first heard that story about [Robert] Gordis, then about [Salo Wittmayer] Baron, and about [Martin] Buber, and about anybody that has published more than three books. It is an ugly, hateful story, which denigrates hard and good work and does not show appreciation or respect for the life's work of another person." See NCH 23.4.159, JN to Rabbi Jack Reimer, June 16, 2000; see also NCH 25.5.172, JN to Ms. Hanisch, an editor at Rowman & Littlefield, August 8, 2001.

20 Shore, "Jacob in the Lion's Den."

21 AJA C, book 15, letter from S. D. Goitein to Suzanne Richter, April 17, 1971.

22 NCH 20.1.130, JN to Ithamar Gruenwald, July 7, 1997.

23 On Avery-Peck's recollection, see AWH/IN Alan Avery-Peck, August 26, 2013. The quotation from Neusner comes from Shore, "Jacob in the Lion's Den," 18.

24 NCH 17.6.114, JN to Mark, November 9, 1995.

25 AJA A 5.6 (p. 22).

26 Neusner, "Preface," in *History of the Mishnaic Law of Purities*, x.

27 AWH/IN Suzanne Neusner, July 14, 2013. See the comments in AWH/IN Alan Avery-Peck, August 20, 2013.

28 NCH 14.3.98, letter to Larry Tisch, October 31, 1991.

29 Neusner, *Fellowship in Judaism*, 63.

30 Ibid., 67.

31 Ibid., 74. It is worth pointing out that in the 1960s, it was customary to say "men" when referring to "humanity." When Neusner uses "men" in the above quotation, then, he does not mean that the havurah should be solely a masculine enterprise (even if it was in antiquity).

32 For Jewish Renewal more generally, see Magid, *American Post-Judaism*.

33 Neusner, *History of the Jews of Babylonia*, 1:ix.

34 Ibid., 2:xi.

35 AWH/IN JN, July 14, 2013.

36 Ibid.; an allusion to the event may be found also in NCH 26.3.176, JN to Fred Berthold, May 13, 2002.

37 On Neusner's recognition of Smith's place in the field, see AWH/IN JN, July 15, 2013.

38 On Neusner's relationship to Smith, see AWH/IN JN, July 14b, 2013. On Smith's relationship to Neusner, see Smith, *Relating Religion*, 4–9. The quotation at the end of the paragraph comes from p. 9.

39 As Neusner himself remarks in a footnote in his important article "Map Without Territory," written the year after Smith's own collection titled *Map Is Not Territory* (1978),

> The entire theoretical framework of this paper, from this point to the end, forms a detailed, concurring response to the brilliant essays of Jonathan Z.

Smith, collected in *Map Is Not Territory*. . . . I *do* claim that when I answer questions raised by historians of religions, and when I do so in the framework of interpretive issues set forth in history of religions, then, even though I address said questions and speak in said framework only in the context of the data of a small part of a single, itself kaleidoscopic, religious tradition, I commit history of religions. (111n10)

Neusner here is clear that what he is engaging in is the history of religions in the manner that Smith understands this term.

40 On the episode at the University of Chicago, see NCH 13.4.84; on Neusner's critique of Smith, seemingly inspired by the imbroglio at Chicago, see NCH 14.2.88.

41 NCH 14.2.88, JN to Jonathan Z. Smith, August 14, 1991.

42 AWH/IN JN, July 13, 2013.

43 On his positive assessment of both Meeks and Childs, consult AWH/IN JN, July 14, 2013. On the question from Childs, see Neusner, *Documentary Foundation of Rabbinic Culture*, 13–14.

44 E.g., AWH/IN JN, July 14, 2013.

45 Neusner, *Life of Yohanan ben Zakkai*, 2nd ed., xiv.

46 On the acknowledgment to Lieberman in the first edition, see *Life of Rabban Yohanan ben Zakkai*, ix. On the acknowledgment to Smith in the first, see also *Life of Rabban Yohanan ben Zakkai*, ix, and on the new thank-you in the second edition, see *Life of Yohanan ben Zakkai*, 2nd ed., xviii.

47 Neusner, *Development of a Legend*, xi.

48 Neusner, *Rabbinic Judaism*, 25.

49 Neusner, "The Scandal of the Jewish College Student," in the B'nai B'rith–published *National Jewish Monthly* (December 1964), found in AJA C, book 9.

50 AJA A 3.5, JN to colleagues at Brown, February 21, 1982.

51 Neusner, "Unearned Dividends," in AJA C, book 11.

52 AJA C, book 11.

53 His starting salary effective July 1, 1968, would be sixteen thousand per year. See AJA A 2.4, Morton P. Stolz, provost of Brown to JN, March 13, 1967.

CHAPTER 5. INSTITUTIONAL ACCEPTANCE

1 See chapter 2.

2 There exists a fairly extensive bibliography on the inherent Christian and Protestant biases in the academic study of religion. Foremost are McCutcheon, *Manufacturing Religion*; Fitzgerald, *Ideology of Religious Studies*; Dubuisson, *Western Construction of Religion*; Masuzawa, *Invention of World Religions*.

3 See Ritterband and Wechsler, *Jewish Learning in American Universities*, 189–199.

4 On Neusner's fear of this, see AWH/IN JN, July 15, 2013. This is also a topic that he wrote about frequently, both academically and in the popular media. See, for example, his *How Not to Study Judaism*.

5 Neusner, "Reflections on Jewish Studies in Universities," in AJA C, book 13.

6 Ibid.

7 Ibid.

8 Ibid.

9 Parts of this section rework and build upon my *Study of Judaism*, 69–75.

10 From the AAJR's website at http://www.aajr.org/history/.

11 Loveland, "Association for Jewish Studies," 3. See also Robinson, "American Academy for Jewish Research (AAJR)."

12 This and the following three paragraphs rework material in my *Study of Judaism*, 69–72.

13 Band, "Jewish Studies in American Liberal-Arts Colleges and Universities," 3.

14 Jick, *Teaching of Judaica in American Universities*, 1–3.

15 See, for example, the comments in the inaugural *Association for Jewish Studies Bulletin* 1.1 (1970): 1–2. It is worth noting that Neusner was eventually elected to the AAJR. He resigned after Lieberman's review because he did not see much reason for belonging. As a quick perusal of the AAJR fellows will show—http://www.aajr.org/officers-fellows/—he is now no longer affiliated with them.

16 Blau, "A Proposal for a Professional Association," in Jick, *Teaching of Judaica in American Universities*, 90.

17 Greenberg, "Scholarship and Continuity: Dilemma and Dialectic," in Jick, *Teaching of Judaica in American Universities*, 116.

18 Meyer, "Toward a Definition of Jewish Studies," 2.

19 AJA C, book 16, JN to "Colleagues of AJS," December 22, 1971.

20 Neusner, "An American Journal of Jewish Studies?," 1–2.

21 Loveland, "Association for Jewish Studies," 7.

22 AWH/IN JN, July 14, 2013.

23 Neusner, "Two Modes of Jewish Learning," 5.

24 Neusner, *Judaism in the American Humanities*, second series: *Jewish Learning and the New Humanities*, 40.

25 AWH/IN JN, July 14, 2013. He would, however, engage in the occasional book review in the various publications of the AJS. On his participation at a roundtable panel on "The Nature and Structure of Jewish Studies in Graduate School," at the AJS annual meeting in College Park, MD, on November 13, 1972, see his contribution titled "Autodidacts in Graduate School," *Association for Jewish Studies Newsletter* 4.1 (1973): 4.

26 AJA A 2.11, JN to Mike, September 15, 1980.

27 Ibid.

28 AJA A 2.11, JN to doctoral alumni of Brown, September 3, 1980.

29 See DeConcini interview with JN, September 12, 2002 (p. 17).

30 Ibid. (p. 18).

31 AJA A 1.8.

32 AJA A 1.8. Cf. DeConcini interview with JN, September 12, 2002 (pp. 23–25).

33 DeConcini interview with JN, September 12, 2002 (p. 25).

34 AWH/IN JN, July 14b, 2013.

35 AJA A 1.9.

36 AWH/IN JN, July 14b, 2013.

37 NCH 3.3.21, letter to the Board of the Study of Judaism Section, July 16, 1978.

38 AWH/IN JN, July 15, 2013.

39 This was based on a conversation that I had with Norbert Samuelson at the 2014 annual meeting of the AAR in San Diego.

40 NCH 20.8.137, JN to Barbara DeConcini, executive director of the American Academy of Religion, August 8, 1998. In his *How Not to Study Judaism*, he writes of the Study of Judaism Section at the AAR:

> What it signals is the confusion between Jewish ethnicity and Judaic religiosity, and between expressing the preoccupations of the stylish left-wing culture and the academic study of a subject or a problem. . . . Don't get me wrong. Scholarship on Judaism the religion thrives. But that is not the AAR section. There the study of Judaism is certainly not carried on as is scholarship on Islam or Christianity or Buddhism or Hinduism. Rather, when Judaism the religion is studied, it is as a mere detail of ethnic culture, with nothing much to say to someone who is not Jewish—let alone to anyone who is an academic scholar of religion with specialization in Judaism. (160–161)

41 DeConcini interview with JN, September 12, 2002 (pp. 47–48).

42 Ibid. (p. 22).

43 AWH/IN JN, July 14, 2013; AWH/IN JN, July 15, 2013.

44 AJA A 1.13, JN to Donald Hornig, December 7, 1973.

45 Neusner, *How Adin Steinsaltz Misrepresents the Talmud*, xi. For less overt criticisms of Brown, see, for example, Neusner, *Judaism States Its Theology*, xiii; Neusner, *Are the Talmuds Interchangeable?*, viii.

46 AWH/IN JN, July 14, 2013.

47 Neusner, *How to Grade Your Professors*, 106.

48 Religious Studies 3600, "Introduction to Judaism," taught at the University of South Florida. In NCH 14.7.93.

49 Bryan Walpert, "When Profs Go Too Far," *Brown Daily Herald*, October 3, 1986, 1. Found in NCH 10.2.65.

50 Neusner, *How to Grade Your Professors*, 106.

51 Ibid., 106.

52 On Neusner's criticism of Beiser, see AJA A 13.2, JN to Peter Richardson, chairman of the Faculty Executive Committee (FEC) at Brown, April 1, 1988.

53 See NCH 6.6.48.

54 Neusner, *Way of Torah*, xix.

55 NCH 15.4.98, JN letter to editor of the *National Jewish Post*, June 14, 1993.

56 See Schochet and Spiro, *Saul Lieberman*, 41.

57 NCH 17.4.112.

58 Ibid.

59 NCH 14.7.93, "Introduction to Judaism" syllabus, 1992.

60 Ibid.

61 NCH 16.6.107, "Introduction to Judaism" syllabus, fall 1994.

62 See Neusner, "The Scholar's Apprentice," *Chronicle of Higher Education*. The essay was reproduced in his *Formative Judaism, New Series*. A list of all of his graduate students over the years: David Goodblatt, Chuck Primus, Robert Goldenberg, William Scott Green, Gary Porton, Richard Sarason, Baruch Bokser, Shamai Kanter (became a pulpit rabbi), Jack Lightstone, Joel Gereboff, Tzee Zahavy, Irving Mandelbaum, Martin Jaffee, Alan Avery-Peck, Peter Haas, Louis E. Newman, Roger Brooks, Paul Flesher, Judith Romney Wegner, and Howard Eilberg-Schwartz.

63 AWH/IN JN, July 14, 2013.

64 AWH/IN Alan Avery-Peck, August 26, 2013.

65 AWH/IN William Scott Green, March 2, 2014; AWH/IN Alan Avery-Peck, August 26, 2013.

66 AWH/IN Alan Avery-Peck, August 26, 2013.

67 Shore, "In the Lion's Den," 19. See also AWH/IN JN, July 14, 2013.

68 AWH/IN Alan Avery-Peck, August 26, 2013.

69 AWH/IN JN, July 14, 2013; AWH/IN Alan Avery-Peck, August 26, 2013.

70 AWH/IN Alan Avery-Peck, August 26, 2013; AWH/IN William Scott Green, March 2, 2014.

71 NCH 9.4.63, JN to Stuart Eizenstat, March 4, 1988. Nothing came of this. Paul Flesher now teaches Judaic studies in the Department of Religious Studies at the University of Wyoming. On the Flesher affair, also see AWH/IN JN, July 14, 2013. Neusner also wrote a letter of protest to the president of Dartmouth when another of his students, Roger Brooks, was denied a job there. See NCH 5.8.42, JN to President McLaughlin, April 2, 1984.

72 AJA A 1.33.

73 AJA A 9.4, Howard Eilberg-Schwartz to JN, December 18, 1986.

74 AWH/IN JN, July 15, 2013; AWH/IN Alan Avery-Peck, August 26, 2013.

75 His best example of the documentary hypothesis in action may be found in his 1984 *Judaism: The Evidence of the Mishnah*. On his use of the documentary hypothesis in general, see Neusner, *Rabbinic Judaism*, 24.

76 Neusner, *Documentary Foundation of Rabbinic Culture*, 6.

77 AWH/IN JN, July 14b, 2013. In addition to his *History of the Mishnaic Law of Purities*, Neusner also produced multivolume translations and commentaries of other Orders of the Mishnah. These may be found in Neusner, *A History of the Mishnaic Laws of Holy Things*, 6 vols. (1978–1979); *A History of the Mishnaic Law of Women*, 5 vols. (1979–1980); *A History of the Mishnaic Law of Appointed Times*, 5 vols. (1981); *A History of Mishnaic Law of Damages*, 5 vols. (1982). Neusner's

translation of the complete document may be found in *The Mishnah: A New Translation* (1988). For Danby's translation, see Danby, *The Mishnah* (1933).

78 Levey, "Neusner's Purities," 338.

79 Ibid., 356.

80 Fox, "Review of *A History of the Mishnaic Law of Women* by Jacob Neusner," 6.

81 Ibid., 6.

82 AWH/IN JN, July 14b, 2013. On his translation of the two Talmuds, see Neusner, *Talmud of the Land of Israel*; Neusner, *Talmud of Babylonia*.

83 The Proposal for a European Consultative Conference on Judaic Studies and related materials associated with the founding of the EAJS may be found in NCH 4.4.30.

84 AWH/IN JN, July 14, 2013; see also AWH/IN Alan Avery-Peck, August 26, 2013. On Tisch as the "silent partner," see NCH 16.2.103, JN to Thomas Tisch, January 1, 1994.

85 A list of the projects and editors may be found on the second page of every book in the series. One of the best examples of a work that Neusner is critical of is Segal's *Case Citation in the Babylonian Talmud* and *Babylonian Esther Midrash*. Despite publishing the volumes, Neusner responds extremely negatively to them in Neusner, *Documentary Foundation of Rabbinic Culture*, 47–72.

86 NCH 22.11.155, JN to Thomas Tisch, November 23, 1999.

87 See, for example, Neusner and Neusner, *Price of Excellence*, 233–236; his introduction to *Documentary Foundation of Rabbinic Culture*, xiv, n. 2.

88 AWH/IN JN, July 15, 2013.

89 *Judaism: The Evidence of the Mishnah*, 1st ed. A second edition appeared as *Judaism: The Evidence of the Mishnah*, 2nd ed., xiii. Unless noted, quotations are from this second edition. In this edition, Neusner not only connects this work to his intellectual growth as a scholar, but also conveniently collects numerous critical reviews of the original edition and responds to them in considerable detail. Hebrew translation: *Hayyahadut le'edut hammishnah* (Tel Aviv: Sifriat Poalim, 1987); Italian translation: *Il Giudaismo nella testimonianza della Mishnah*, trans. Giorgio Volpe (Bologna: Centro editoriale Dehoniane, 1995).

90 AJA A 2.7, J. Z. Smith to Alan N. Fitchen, humanities editor, University of Chicago Press, May 1, 1980.

91 Neusner describes it as one of his favorite books in AWH/IN JN, July 14, 2013. On the "what we cannot show we do not know" slogan, see Neusner, "*The Mishnah*: Methods of Interpretation," 42. This is also repeated by his students; see, for example, AWH/IN Alan Avery-Peck, August 26, 2013.

92 Neusner, *Judaism: The Evidence of the Mishnah*, 3.

93 Ibid., 3.

94 Ibid., 7.

95 On the work of his predecessors, see Moore, *Judaism in the First Centuries of the Christian Era*; and Urbach, *Sages*.

96 Neusner, *Judaism: The Evidence of the Mishnah*, 18. Neusner subsequently goes on to elaborate five qualifications to this proposition, which need not detain us here. For those interested, see ibid., 18–22.

97 Ibid., 124. Neusner had already worked out the details earlier in an article published in the University of Chicago Press's *History of Religions*. It provides a convenient expression. See his "Map Without Territory," 103–127.

98 See the comments in Cohen, "Jacob Neusner, Mishnah, and Counter-Rabbinics," 54–55.

99 Neusner, *Judaism: The Evidence of the Mishnah*, 283.

100 AWH/IN JN, July 15, 2013.

101 Cohen, "Jacob Neusner, Mishnah, and Counter-Rabbinics," 62.

102 Maccoby, "Jacob Neusner's Mishnah," 25.

103 Elman, "Judaism of the Mishna," 17 (his italics).

104 Maccoby, "Jacob Neusner's Mishnah," 26.

105 His major criticism can be found in Sanders, "Jacob Neusner and the Philosophy of Mishnah," 309–331.

106 Ibid., 317.

107 Ibid., 317.

108 Ibid., 319.

109 Maccoby, "Jacob Neusner's Mishnah," 31.

110 Ibid., 26.

111 Cohen, "Jacob Neusner, Mishnah, and Counter-Rabbinics," 59.

112 Neusner, *Judaism: The Evidence of the Mishnah*, 420, 424.

113 Ibid., 425.

114 In *Documentary Foundation of Rabbinic Culture*, ix, he writes that his approach is "now dictating the agenda for future scholarship and especially debate, and, it is now clear, work ignoring that method and approaching matters in complete isolation from it no longer appears in Western academic scholarship in formative Judaism (whether in English, German, French, Spanish, Italian, Scandinavian)." Indeed, as the subtitle of this work indicates, all that remains, according to him, is "to mop up isolated pockets of resistance."

115 For this volume I am using the following version: Neusner, *Stranger at Home*, 33. Here I also follow the lead of Magid, *American Post-Judaism*, 199–209.

116 Neusner, *Stranger at Home*, 3.

117 Ibid., 7.

118 Ibid., 31.

119 AWH/IN JN, July 15, 2013.

CHAPTER 6. "ORWELL'S 1984—AND MINE"

1 See, for example, Neusner and Neusner, *Price of Excellence*, 7–13; on Brown, in particular, see ibid., 149–172.

2   For Neusner, the ringleader of these changes was Ira Magaziner, later vice chairman and CEO of the Clinton Health Access Initiative and chairman of the Clinton Clean Energy Initiative, both of which he cofounded with former president Bill Clinton. See Magaziner, "New Order."

3   See the 1972 article on him in the *Brown Daily Herald* titled "Neusner Criticizes Minority Quotas," in NCH 2.6.17.

4   Neusner, *Are the Talmuds Interchangeable?* On his critique of JTS and its offering a chair to Peter Schaefer, see NCH 15.4.98, JN letter to editor, *National Jewish Post*, June 14, 1993; and on his criticism of Rabbi Sheldon Zimmerman, the new president of Hebrew Union College, who subsequently resigned because of a sex scandal, see NCH 17.4.112, "The Wrong Man, in the Wrong Job, at the Wrong Time," July 25, 1995.

5   NCH 6.6.48, JN to Zev Garber, May 15, 1985. Numerous variations on the Orwellian motif may be found in NCH 6.5.47 and AJA A 5.1.

6   AJA A 5.1.

7   Neusner, "A Commencement Speech You'll Never Hear," *Brown Daily Herald*, May 1, 1981, in NCH 4.5.31. The "speech" is reprinted in Neusner and Neusner, *Price of Excellence*, 199–201.

8   The *Donahue* transcript may be found in NCH 4.6.32. See also the various letters, mostly supportive of Neusner, in AJA A 2.19–20. More generally on the response, see Charles E. Claffrey, "Brown Professor Speaks Out—and the Grades Are Mixed," *Boston Globe*, June 27, 1981, in NCH 4.6.32. The faux commencement speech was followed by many others in the coming months and years that were critical of colleagues and administrators at Brown. See, for example, Neusner, "Brown: 'Best' at What?," *Brown Daily Herald*, January 19, 1982, 2, in NCH 4.7.33. See also AWH/IN Alan Avery-Peck, August 26, 2013.

9   On Neusner's reaction to the events, see *Price of Excellence*, 200–202.

10 It seems that Neusner's relationship to his department was becoming increasingly strained as of the summer of 1978. See NCH 4.4.30, letter to John Giles Milhaven, September 4, 1980. See also the memo from Maurice Glicksman, the provost, to Neusner in NCH 4.6.32 and Neusner's response in AJA A 2.23, September 15, 1981.

11 NCH 4.6.32, JN to Sumner B. Twiss, September 25, 1981. On his final break with Twiss, see NCH 4.7.33, JN to Sumner B. Twiss, November 19, 1981.

12 See AJA A 2.23, JN to Howard Swearer, president of Brown, September 8, 1981.

13 On his criticisms of "ghettoization" and Jewish studies programs, see NCH 4.4.30, letter to Mr. Giametti of Yale, December 9, 1980. He writes in reference to Yale's newly formed "Jewish Studies Major" that "[i]n my view Yale's department of religious studies has never done a good job with the study of Judaism, because it has treated the subject as essentially 'special'; it has treated the religious study of Judaism as an intellectual ghetto, in which no outsider enters, from which no insider escapes, and that is why this further, natural development can take place."

14 AJA A 3.2, JN to Sumner B. Twiss, November 19, 1981.

15 AJA A 3.5.

16 NCH 5.1.35, September 10, 1982.

17 On his resignation, see NCH 5.4.38, JN to President Swearer, June 3, 1983. On Religious Studies' refusal to cross-list courses, see NCH 5.2.36.

18 NCH 9.4.63, JN to Stuart Eizenstat, March 4, 1988.

19 Though in AJA A 4.5, November 3, 1983, Judith Baskin, not one of his students, writes to him telling him she is grateful "for your concern for younger scholars." See also NCH 19.6.127, JN to Dr. Meadows, March 3, 1997: "So far as I am able, I am always happy to help serious scholars in their work."

20 NCH 7.1.50, David Sorkin to Leah Niederman (director of faculty personnel), July 8, 1985.

21 Neusner even defended the program's decision not to rehire Sorkin in a letter to the editor, *Brown Daily Student*, November 6, 1986.

22 On CONFRAT's decision, see Andrew Skoler, "CONFRAT Overrules Judaic Studies Decision," *Brown Daily Herald*, November 14, 1985. See Neusner's letter to the upper administration about this in NCH 7.2.51, JN to President Swearer and Provost Glicksman, November 5, 1985.

23 NCH 7.2.52, JN to President Swearer, referred to as "colleague," January 8, 1986.

24 It may be found in NCH 11.2.70. It seems that until the troubles with Cohen, the Neusner archives at Harvard were open to all—this is how Cohen was able to write his dossier. Neusner had assumed that his papers were closed, and when he found out that they were not, he immediately made them restricted. In this regard, see AJA A 14.12, JN to Harvard University Libraries, December 15, 1988.

25 AJA A 15.12, JN to Brown President Swearer, May 19, 1989.

26 The FEC Memo may be found in NCH 10.2.65, January 1, 1988. Several of the files in NCH pertaining to Richard Cohen in 11.1.69 had been removed because of "legal reasons."

27 NCH 10.4.67, George Landow to JN, November 15, 1988.

28 Neusner, "When a Presidency Changes," *Brown University Faculty Bulletin* 1.5 (1988): 16–17, in NCH 11.1.69.

29 NCH 10.3.66, JN to Joseph, June 30, 1988.

30 Even his critics at Brown challenged him to leave. Edward Beiser, a professor of political science, wrote a letter to the editor, titled "Neusner a Disruptive Force in Brown Community," *Brown Daily Herald*, November 12, 1985, stating that "I think the time has come to ask in public whether Brown would be better off without Neusner. It is an open secret that Neusner has abused colleagues, graduate students, and undergraduates over the years."

31 NCH 6.3.45, JN to John Strugnell, January 16, 1984.

32 Ibid.

33 AJA A 5.7.

34 NCH 6.3.45, JN to Peter Stansky, December 12, 1984.

35 NCH 8.5.59, JN to President Arnold Webber, February 19, 1987.

36 Neusner, "Quality Control in the Humanities Endowment," *Chronicle of Higher Education*, April, 23, 1979, in NCH 3.7.25.

37 Neusner, "Defining the Humanities: A Circular Letter," to Colleagues on the National Council on the Humanities, January 9, 1981, in NCH April 5, 1931. See also his lecture "From Many, One," originally presented to the Rhode Island Alpha of Phi Beta Kappa, at Brown University, on March 24, 1980.

38 Neusner, "Defining the Humanities."

39 Neusner, *Judaism in the American Humanities*, xi. His thinking on the place and role of the study of Judaism and the larger humanities goes back at least to 1975 when he published *Academic Study of Judaism*.

40 Neusner, *Judaism in the American Humanities*, 22.

41 See his "The Humanities, Public Policy, and Organized Jewry," in *Judaism in the American Humanities*, 51.

42 On his criticism of the Jewish community, see NCH 16.7.108. On his goal as a scholar of Jewish studies who wrote books, see NCH 20.7.136.

43 Baumgarten, "Name of the Pharisees." On Neusner's reaction to this, see his many letters devoted to the subject in NCH 5.8.42.

44 AJA A 4.6, JN to Daniel Schwartz, December 29, 1983.

45 Neusner, "Methodology in Talmudic History," 101.

46 NCH 57.41, Zvi Yekutiel to JN, March 5, 1984.

47 NCH 5.8.42, JN to Lawrence Schiffman, April 14, 1984.

48 On the détente, see NCH 7.1.50, letter to editor, *New Traditions*, September 6, 1985. On the "world famous Jerusalem boycott," see his letter to Lee Levine in NCH 22.4.148, unknown date (but its placement in the box puts it some time in 1999).

49 AJA A 4.12, Menahem Stern (chairman of the Historical Society of Israel) to JN, May 3, 1984.

50 Ibid.

51 AJA A 4.12, JN to M. Stern, May 11, 1984.

52 AJA A 4.12, JN to M. Stern, May 12, 1984.

53 Ibid.

54 Ibid. Neusner subsequently published a version of the lecture for the conference from which he was uninvited as "Methodology in Talmudic History," to which he appended the following note at the beginning of the essay: "Written for the Historical Society of Israel. Conference in celebration of its journal, *Zion*, on the occasion of its fiftieth volume. Jerusalem, Israel. Scheduled for July 2, 1984. This paper was mailed to Jerusalem on January 27, 1984, and the invitation to present it was withdrawn in a letter dated March 5, 1984. The facts speak for themselves but I prefer not to suggest what they say."

It is also worth noting that this issue of *Biblical Theology Bulletin* was devoted to the work of Jacob Neusner and titled "Jacob Neusner: Expositor of the Rabbinic Canon." It consisted of an introductory essay by James A. Sanders, Ancient

Biblical Manuscript Center (Claremont, CA), four essays by Neusner, and a bibliography indicating his major scholarly works.

55 On the theme of his work being "under lock and key" at Hebrew University, see, for example, Neusner, *Documentary Foundation of Rabbinic Culture*, xv.

56 Neusner, *Documentary Foundation of Rabbinic Culture*, xv.

57 Katz, "Issues in the Separation of Judaism and Christianity," 43–76.

58 AJA A 5.1.

59 On Neusner's desire to respond, see NCH 7.5.54, a scathing letter to William Hallo, a leader in the American Oriental Society who had just sent Neusner several of his offprints, May 5, 1986. See also AWH/IN JN, July 14, 2013.

60 Lieberman, "Tragedy or a Comedy?," 315.

61 Ibid., 316, 316, and 318, respectively.

62 Ibid., 319.

63 Neusner, *Judaism: The Evidence of the Mishnah*, 425n5.

64 See NCH 6.5.47, Norman G. Orodenker of Levy, Goodman, Semonoff, and Gorin to Prof. Wolf Leslau, March 11, 1985.

65 Neusner, *Why There Never Was a "Talmud of Caesarea,"* 2.

66 NCH 6.2.44, Kent Harold Richards to JN, February 9, 1984.

67 NCH 6.2.44.

68 AWH/IN JN, July 14, 2013. See also AWH/IN Alan Avery-Peck, August 26, 2013.

69 On the nadir of his career, see AWH/IN JN, July 14, 2013. On Smith's "discovery" and the affair surrounding it, see Jeffery, *Secret Gospel of Mark Unveiled*. Some have certainly implied that Smith created a homoerotic portrait of Jesus—a portrait based on a forged manuscript no less—because of his own sexual proclivities.

70 Hershel Shanks, "Annual Meetings Offer Intellectual Bazaar and Moments of High Drama," 16. On Neusner's response to the editors of *BAR*, see NCH 6.4.46, letter to editor of *BAR*, February 20, 1985.

71 NCH 6.5.47, Norman G. Orodenker to Prof. Morton Smith, March 15, 1985. The apology appears in *Biblical Archaeology Review* 11.3 (May/June 1985): 8.

72 See Neusner, "Foreword" to Gerhardsson, *Memory and Manuscript*, xxvi–xxvii.

73 E.g., Neusner, *From Literature to Theology in Formative Judaism*, 14–15.

74 Ibid., 48–50. The quotation is from p. 48.

75 Neusner, *Theology of Rabbinic Judaism*, 21.

76 E.g., ibid., ix–x.

77 AJA A 5.1.

CHAPTER 7. POLITICAL INTRIGUE

1 Patrick J. Buchanan, "1992 Republican National Convention Speech," August 17, 1992, http://buchanan.org/blog/1992-republican-national-convention-speech-148.

2 See, for example, Hunter, *Culture Wars*.

3 NCH 1.2.2, for example, has several examples of articles that he wrote for the *Oxford Tory*.

4 AJA C, book 2.

5 NCH 2.6.17.

6 The October 4, 1978, announcement of the eight persons President Carter nominated to the National Council of the Humanities may be found on AJA A 1.35.

7 AJA A 1.31.

8 Neusner, "The Difference William Bennett Made."

9 See AWH/IN Bruce Chilton, August 27, 2013.

10 Schwardon, "Neusner Criticizes Minority Quotas."

11 Ibid.

12 Neusner and Neusner, *Reaffirming Higher Education*, 146–147.

13 Neusner, "Why the Republicans?," in NCH 6.2.44. The positive description comes from the NEH website.

14 Neusner, "Why the Republicans?"

15 NCH 8.5.59, JN to Sidney R. Yates, February 16, 1987.

16 NCH 12.7.80, JN to William Kristol, July 30, 1990.

17 NCH 14.3.89, JN to William Kristol, September 29, 1991.

18 NCH 12.4.77, JN to Lynne Cheney, chair of NEH, February 21, 1990.

19 NCH 12.4.77, JN to Lynne Cheney, March 2, 1990.

20 NCH 14.2.88, JN to Lynne Cheney, August 22, 1991.

21 AWH/IN JN, July 15, 2013. See also NCH 12.7.80, JN to William Kristol, July 30, 1990.

22 See, for example, Nea, "Content Restrictions and National Endowment for the Arts Funding," 165–184.

23 Michael Oreskes, "Senate Votes to Bar U.S. Support of 'Obscene or Indecent' Artwork," *New York Times*, July 27, 1989, http://www.nytimes.com/1989/07/27/arts/senate-votes-to-bar-us-support-of-obscene-or-indecent-artwork.html.

24 Ibid.

25 This comes from the testimony of Henry R. Wray, the senior associate general counsel, Office of the General Counsel. See "Legal Analysis of Section 304(a) of Public Law No. 101–121 and NEA's Actions Under Section 304(a)," p. 1, and released as part of the "National Endowment for the Arts' Compliance 304(a) of the 1990 Interior Department Appropriate Act," June 6, 1990, https://play.google.com/store/books/details?id=e_bktopXwkoC&rdid=book-e_bktopXwkoC&rdot=1.

26 NCH 12.6.79, JN to John O'Sullivan, June 27, 1990.

27 Stephan Salisbury, "NEA Panel Votes Against Funds for 2 ICA Projects," *Philadelphia Inquirer*, May 15, 1990; Allan Parachini, "NEA Advisers Nix Grants after Mapplethorpe," *Los Angeles Times*, May 15, 1990.

28 "NEA Panel Rejects Broad Restrictions," *Seattle Times*, August 7, 1990.

29 NCH 12.5.78, JN to John Frohnmayer, May 17, 1990. Frohnmayer's letter had been published in a variety of media, including the conservative *Human Events*.

30 NCH 12.6.79, JN to John O'Sullivan, June 27, 1990.

31 NCH 12.7.80, JN to William Kristol, July 30, 1990; see also NCH 12.4.77, JN to John Frohnmayer, May 2, 1990.

32 Neusner, "We Won," in NCH 13.1.81.

33 http://www.chroniclesmagazine.org/rockford-institute/about-the-rockford-institute/. On Neusner's involvement, see NCH 14.6.92.

34 Online at http://www.cornwallalliance.org/articles/read/a-renewed-call-to-truth-prudence-and-protection-of-the-poor/.

35 Neusner and Neusner, *Reaffirming Higher Education*, 58–59.

36 Ibid., 59.

37 Ibid., 59.

38 Ibid., 59.

39 Ibid., 71.

40 Ibid., 73.

41 Ibid., 73.

42 Ibid., 151.

43 On Washington as an escape, see AWH/IN Suzanne Neusner, July 15, 2013. On the application to the Bornblum Chair at Memphis, see NCH 8.2.56, letter of application, September 9, 1986.

44 On his supporters, see NCH 8.4.58, JN to Judy, December 26, 1986.

45 NCH 8.4.58, JN to Judy, December 26, 1986; see also NCH 8.4.58, JN to Sidney Yates, January 2, 1987.

46 NCH 8.5.59, JN to William F. Buckley, Jr., March 16, 1987.

47 On his appointment by Lynne Cheney, see NCH 9.2.61.

48 Neusner and Neusner, *Price of Excellence*, 159, 160.

49 On Brown's failures, see his "Brown 'Best'? At What?," *Brown Daily Herald*, January 19, 1981, in NCH 4.7.33.

50 Neusner and Neusner, *Price of Excellence*, 161, 163.

51 Ibid., 163.

52 Neusner saved a lot of clippings from the *Brown Daily Herald* that were highly critical of Swearer and Glicksman. These may be found in NCH 11.1.69.

53 AJA A 8.5, JN to Rabbi Korff, September 1, 1986.

54 AJA A 8.11 (his italics).

55 Neusner and Neusner, *Price of Excellence*, 221.

56 Ibid., 222.

57 On Neusner's assessment of Vidal, see ibid., 221. On his response to Gregorian, see NCH 11.1.69, JN to Vartan Gregorian, March 9, 1989.

58 AJA A 14.9, JN to Vartan Gregorian, November 10, 1984.

59 AJA A 14.12, JN to Vartan Gregorian, January 25, 1989.

60 See NCH 11.5.73, letter to his son ("Prince Charming"), August 12, 1989.

61 On his arrangement with Brown, see NCH 12.1.74, Provost Glicksman to JN, September 28, 1989. On Gregorian's counteroffer, see NCH 12.1.74, President Gregorian to JN, September 11, 1989.

62 AWH/IN JN, July 15, 2013.

63 NCH 12.3.76, JN to Richard Scheuer, February 20, 1990.

64 This is a recurring theme of his in the mid-1990s. See the letters found in NCH 20.2.131.

65 NCH 12.1.74, JN to Marvin Goldberger, September 25, 1989.

66 Ibid.

67 NCH 12.1.74, JN to Elliot Schor, September 18, 1989.

68 NCH 12.1.74, JN to Marvin Goldberger, November 7, 1989.

69 NCH 12.3.76, JN to Elihu Richter, January 29, 1990.

70 Neusner and Neusner, *Price of Excellence*, 239.

71 NCH 12.5.78, JN, letter of application to be director of the Institute of Advanced Studies, Princeton, June 30, 1990.

72 NCH 14.7.93, JN to Anthony DePalma, June 8, 1992.

73 NCH 15.2.96, JN to Dr. Morna Hooker, February 22, 1993.

74 Neusner and Neusner, *Price of Excellence*, 240.

75 AJA A 16.10, January 14, 1990.

76 NCH 13.6.86, JN to Fred Neusner, June 23, 1991.

77 The official letter rescinding his emeritus status was sent by Frank G. Rothman, the new provost at Brown, on January 12, 1991. It may be found in AJA A 18.9.

78 NCH 12.6.79, JN to Ernest Frerichs, June 13, 1990; NCH 12.6.79, JN to Tom Anton, June 13, 1990.

79 NCH 12.6.79, letter to chairman, Board of Directors, Scholars Press, via James Wiggins, June 14, 1990. Later that summer, Neusner all but acknowledged that he had no legal recourse and says to James Wiggins at Scholars Press, "If in your judgment Brown University owns Brown Judaic Studies, let them own it." See NCH 12.7.80, JN to James Wiggins (CC to Ernest Frerichs and Provost Frank Rothman at Brown, the successor to Maurice Glicksman), July 18, 1990. On Tisch's involvement, see NCH 12.3.76, JN to President Frank Borkowsky and Provost Gerry Meisels, University of South Florida, January 13, 1990.

80 NCH 13.4.84, JN to Ernest Frerichs and Wendell Dietrich, March 18, 1991.

81 See further NCH 13.4.84, JN to Ernest Frerichs and Wendell Dietrich, March 18, 1991: "The two of you are answerable not to me, but to twenty people who trusted you, who believed in you, and whom you have now repudiated. Now go and invite them back for your 'annual alumnus lecture.'"

CHAPTER 8. SUCCESS AND WINDING DOWN

1 This comes from the blurb that Pope Benedict XVI wrote to the revised edition of the text—Neusner, *A Rabbi Talks with Jesus*. On Neusner on Chilton, see AWH/

IN JN, July 15, 2013. Once Neusner retires from his position at Bard, it will become known as the Jacob Neusner Professor of the History and Theology of Judaism. See AWH/IN JN, July 15, 2013.

2 E.g., Neusner and Chilton, *Religion and Economics*; Neusner and Chilton, *Altruism in World Religions*; Neusner and Chilton, *Religious Toleration in World Religions*; Neusner, Chilton, and Tully, *Just War in Religion and Politics*.

3 This comes from Neusner's Personal Statement in his Harvard Class of 1954, 40th Anniversary Report, in NCH 16.4.105.

4 AWH/IN JN, July 15, 2013.

5 Neusner, *Theology of Rabbinic Judaism*, 25.

6 Ibid., 29.

7 Ibid., 29.

8 AWH/IN JN, July 14, 2013. The quotations come from Neusner, *Theology of Rabbinic Judaism*, 29.

9 Neusner, *Theology of Rabbinic Judaism*, 29.

10 On Neusner's admission that he would have been uncomfortable with the phrase "theologian of Judaism," see AWH/IN JN, July 14, 2013.

11 Jacob Neusner, "Returning to Reform," *Forward*, December 4, 2009, http://forward.com/articles/119646/returning-to-reform/#ixzz2rKJKfJH8.

12 Ibid.

13 On his candidacy, see NCH 17.2.110, JN to Mr. Stanley Gold, April 18, 1994.

14 Neusner, "The Wrong Man, in the Wrong Job, at the Wrong Time," in NCH 17.4.112.

15 Ibid.

16 See, for example, NCH 15.4.98, JN to the editor of the *National Jewish Post*, "Should a Catholic Teach at a Rabbinical School?," June 14, 1993. See also NCH 18.6.121, JN to Jonathan Mahler, August 14, 1996. Further letters indicating his increasingly problematic relationship to JTS may be found, for example, in his correspondence with Rabbi Joel Meyers, the executive vice president of the Rabbinical Assembly, the organization that supports and serves the professional and personal needs of Conservative rabbis worldwide. See NCH 17.2.110, JN to Rabbi Joel Meyers, March 24, 1995, and NCH 17.4.112, JN to Rabbi Joel Meyers, August 25, 1995. This might also explain his support, in 1986, for the creation of the Ziegler School of Rabbinic Studies, the first independent ordaining rabbinical school in the western United States at the University of Judaism, now known as American Jewish University (see NCH 17.5.113, letter to Daniel Gordis, September 27, 1995).

17 See, for example, NCH 18.2.117, JN to Prof. Martin Hengel in Germany, December 31, 1995; see also NCH 18.2.117, JN to Mr. J. Jakobovitz in Stockholm, April 20, 1996.

18 See NCH 16.6.107.

19 See the various letters that Neusner wrote to both parties in NCH 15.3.97. For relevant background of the case, see Israeli, *Fundamentalist Islam and Israel*, 187–195.

20 The major reason behind his "turn" on German universities stems from his negative experiences he had while a Von Humboldt Research Fellow and Professor at the University of Göttingen in 1995. See the numerous letters collected in NCH 18.2.117.

21 Greeley and Neusner, *Bible and Us*, xiv.

22 Ibid., 192.

23 Ibid., 209.

24 Ibid., 218.

25 This comes from the pope's blurb to the revised edition of the book.

26 Neusner, *A Rabbi Talks with Jesus* (1993). It underwent a second, revised and expanded, edition, in which the subtitle was dropped: Neusner, *A Rabbi Talks with Jesus* (2000). The quotation from Cardinal Ratzinger/Pope Benedict XVI comes from his blurb of the book, which appears on back. See his letter in NCH 15.2.96, JN to Elisabeth, February 15, 1993.

27 Neusner, *A Rabbi Talks With Jesus* (1993), xiii.

28 Ibid., xii.

29 Ibid., 68–69.

30 Ibid., 153.

31 NCH 15.1.95, JN to Cardinal Ratzinger, December 30, 1992.

32 NCH 15.4.98, Cardinal Ratzinger to JN, June 22, 1993.

33 NCH 16.3.104, JN to Cardinal Ratzinger, February 17, 1994.

34 Ibid.

35 On these interfaith meetings, see, for example, NCH 16.5.106, JN to Cardinal Ratzinger, August 5, 1994. It is, however, worth noting that Ratzinger and Greeley did not see eye to eye when it came to politics. On their criticism of historicism, see NCH 18.3.118, JN to Dom Ambrogio Spreafico, January 22, 1996.

36 Neusner, *Judaism's Theological Voice*, xi–xii.

37 Ibid., xv.

38 Ibid., 207.

39 On reading and reviewing everything that came out in his field, see NCH 19.6.127, JN to Steven Katz, March 5, 1997. On his criticisms of the "new editorial policy" of the *Journal for the Study of Judaism in the Persian, Hellenistic, and Roman Period*, see NCH 19.5.126, JN to Günther, January 29, 1997.

40 See NCH 19.5.126, letter announcing the new journal.

41 On the "the world famous Jerusalem boycott," see NCH 22.4.148, JN to Lee Levine (Hebrew University), no date, but its placement in the file puts it at the end of 1998 or beginning of 1999. See also NCH 19.5.126, JN to Anita Shapira (Tel Aviv University), February 19, 1997.

42 NCH 20.5.134, JN to Ithamar Gruenwald, December 7, 1997. See also NCH 20.1.130, JN to Ithamar Gruenwald, July 7, 1997.

43 NCH 19.4.125, JN to Edward Alexander, January 24, 1997.

44 On his experiences with petty politics, see, for example, NCH 16.6.106, memo from Darrell Fasching, chair, to the rest of the department complaining about Neusner, February 9, 1994; and Neusner's response of February 10, 1994. This really was, however, the exception to the norm.

45 NCH 15.1.95, JN to President Francis S. Borkowski, December 11, 1992; JN to Rollin Richmond, December 14, 1992; JN to Senator Bob Johnson, January 8, 1993.

46 The earliest mention of Bard occurs in NCH 16.2.103, JN to Dean Robert Neville, Boston University, December 24, 1993.

47 NCH 16.6.107, JN to President Leon Botstein, September 17, 1994.

48 On his renewal at Bard, see NCH 17.1.109.

49 NCH 19.8.129, JN to James Caraway, dean of Dowling College, June 17, 1997.

50 Neusner, Avery-Peck, and Green, *Encyclopaedia of Judaism*. Also published were three supplements, in 2002, 2003, and 2004, respectively, also with Brill.

51 NCH 22.10.154, JN to Leon Botstein, November 7, 1999.

52 See NCH 22.11.155, JN to Thomas Tisch, November 23, 1999.

53 On Neusner's desire to have the institute as his primary affiliation, see the documents surrounding his appointment in NCH 25.1.168. The Institute for Advanced Theology's website may be found at http://www.bard.edu/iat/about. shtml.

54 The three volumes of the series are Neusner and Chilton, *Revelation* (1995); Neusner and Chilton, *Body of Faith* (1996); Neusner and Chilton, *God in the World* (1997).

55 Neusner and Chilton, *Body of Faith*, ix.

56 Ibid., x.

57 Ibid., 26, 94.

58 Neusner and Sonn, *Comparing Religions through Law*, vii, 16–18.

59 Neusner, Sonn, and Brockopp, *Judaism and Islam in Practice*, vii.

60 Ibid., 1.

61 Neusner, Chilton, and Graham, *Three Faiths, One God*.

62 AWH/IN JN, July 14, 2013.

63 Ibid.; AWH/IN Bruce Chilton, August 27, 2013.

CONCLUSIONS

1 Himmelfarb, *On Looking into the Abyss*, 131–135.

2 AWH/IN JN, July 15, 2013.

3 I think, in particular, of Neusner, *Academic Study of Judaism* (1975); *Academic Study of Judaism*, second series (1977); *Academic Study of Judaism*, third series (1980); *Judaism in the American Humanities* (1981); *Judaism in the American Humanities*, second series (1983).

BIBLIOGRAPHY

BY NEUSNER

Greeley, Andrew M. and Jacob Neusner. *The Bible and Us: A Priest and a Rabbi Read Scripture Together*. New York: Warner Books, 1990.

Neusner, Jacob. *The Academic Study of Judaism: Essays and Reflections*. New York: Ktav, 1975.

———. *The Academic Study of Judaism: Essays and Reflections*. Second series. New York: Ktav, 1977.

———. *The Academic Study of Judaism: Essays and Reflections*. Third series. New York: Ktav, 1980.

———. "An American Journal of Jewish Studies?" *Association for Jewish Studies Newsletter* 2.1 (1971): 1–2.

———. *Are the Talmuds Interchangeable? Christine Hayes's Blunder*. Atlanta: Scholars Press, 1995.

———. *Development of a Legend: Studies on the Traditions Concerning Yohanan ben Zakkai*. Leiden: Brill, 1970.

———. "The Difference William Bennett Made." *National Review* 35.19 (September 30, 1983): 1208–1209.

———. *The Documentary Foundation of Rabbinic Culture: Mopping Up after Debates with Gerald L. Bruns, S. J. D. Cohen, Arnold Maria Goldberg, Susan Handelman, Christine Hayes, James Kugel, Peter Schaefer, Eliezer Segal, E. P. Sanders, and Lawrence H. Schiffman*. Atlanta: Scholars Press, 1995.

———. *Fellowship in Judaism: The First Century and Today*. London: Valentine and Mitchell, 1963.

———. "Foreword." In Birger Gerhardsson, *Memory and Manuscript: Oral Tradition and Written Transmission in Rabbinic Judaism and Early Christianity with Tradition and Transmission in Early Christianity*, xxv–xlvi. Grand Rapids, MI: Eerdmans, 1998.

———. *Formative Judaism, New Series: Current Issues and Arguments*. Vol. 1. Lanham, MD: University Press of America, 1996.

———. *From Literature to Theology in Formative Judaism: Three Preliminary Studies*. Atlanta: Scholars Press, 1989.

———. *A History of the Jews of Babylonia*. 5 vols. 1965. Reprint, Leiden: Brill, 1969.

———. *A History of the Mishnaic Law of Appointed Times*. 5 vols. Leiden: Brill, 1981.

———. *A History of Mishnaic Law of Damages*. 5 vols. Leiden: Brill, 1982.

———. *A History of the Mishnaic Laws of Holy Things*. 6 vols. Leiden: Brill, 1978–1979.

———. *A History of the Mishnaic Law of Purities*. 20 vols. Leiden: Brill, 1977.

———. *A History of the Mishnaic Law of Women.* 5 vols. Leiden: Brill, 1979–1980.

———. *How Adin Steinsaltz Misrepresents the Talmud: Four False Propositions from His "Reference Guide."* Atlanta: Scholars Press, 1998.

———. *How Not to Study Judaism: Examples and Counter-Examples.* Vol. 2: *Ethnicity and Identity versus Culture and Religion; How Not to Write a Book on Judaism, Point and Counterpoint.* Lanham, MD: University Press of America, 2004.

———. *How to Grade Your Professors: And Other Unexpected Advice.* 1984. Reprint, Eugene, OR: Wipf and Stock, 2006.

———. "Introduction." In *New Humanities and Academic Disciplines: The Case of Jewish Studies,* edited by Jacob Neusner, ix–xxvii. Madison: University of Wisconsin Press, 1984.

———. "Jewish Studies in the American University." *Journal of General Education* 13.3 (1961): 160–166.

———. *Judaism: The Evidence of the Mishnah.* 1st ed. Chicago: University of Chicago Press, 1981.

———. *Judaism: The Evidence of the Mishnah.* 2nd ed. Atlanta: Scholars Press, 1988.

———. *Judaism in the American Humanities.* Chico, CA: Scholars Press, 1981.

———. *Judaism in the American Humanities.* Second series. *Jewish Learning and the New Humanities.* Chico, CA: Scholars Press, 1983.

———. *Judaism States Its Theology: The Talmudic Re-presentation.* Atlanta: Scholars Press, 1993.

———. *Judaism's Theological Voice: The Melody of the Talmud.* Chicago: University of Chicago Press, 1995.

———. *A Life of Rabban Yohanan ben Zakkai, Ca. 1–80 CE.* Leiden: Brill, 1962.

———. *A Life of Yohanan ben Zakkai, Ca. 1–80 CE.* 2nd ed. Leiden: Brill, 1970.

———. "Map Without Territory." *History of Religions* 19.2 (1979): 103–127.

———. "Methodology in Talmudic History." *Biblical Theology Bulletin* 14.3 (1984): 9–109.

———. "*The Mishnah*: Methods of Interpretation." *Midstream.* 32 (October 1986): 38–42.

———. *The Mishnah: A New Translation.* New Haven: Yale University Press, 1988.

———. *A Rabbi Talks with Jesus.* 2nd ed. Montreal: McGill-Queens University Press, 2000.

———. *A Rabbi Talks with Jesus: An Intermillennial, Interfaith Exchange.* New York: Doubleday, 1993.

———. *Rabbinic Judaism: Structure and System.* Atlanta: Scholars Press, 1999.

———, ed. *Religions in Antiquity: Essays in Memory of Erwin Ramsdell Goodenough.* Leiden: Brill, 1968; second printing, 1970; third printing, 1972. Reprint, Eugene OR: Wipf and Stock, 2004.

———. "Review Essay." *Review of Rabbinic Judaism* 11.2 (2008): 316–324.

———. *Stranger at Home: "The Holocaust," Zionism, and American Judaism.* Atlanta: Scholars Press, 1981; fourth printing, 1997.

———. "The Talmud as Anthropology." In *The Samuel Friedland Lectures, 1975–1980,* 61–96. New York: Jewish Theological Seminary of America, 1980.

———. *The Talmud of Babylonia: An American Translation.* 36 vols. Chico, CA/Atlanta: Scholars Press, 1984–1995.

———. *The Talmud of the Land of Israel: A Preliminary Translation and Explanation.* 35 vols. Chicago: University of Chicago Press, 1982–1993.

———. *The Theology of Rabbinic Judaism: Prolegomenon.* Atlanta: Scholars Press, 1997.

———. *Three Questions of Formative Judaism: History, Literature, and Religion.* Leiden: Brill, 2002.

———. "Two Modes of Jewish Learning: Pedagogical Differences." *Association for Jewish Studies Newsletter* 2.3 (1971): 5.

———. *The Way of Torah: An Introduction.* 7th ed. Belmont, CA: Thomson Wadsworth, 2004.

———. *Why There Never Was a "Talmud of Caesarea": Saul Lieberman's Mistakes.* Atlanta: Scholars Press, 1994.

Neusner, Jacob, Alan J. Avery-Peck, and William Scott Green, eds. *The Encyclopaedia of Judaism.* 3 vols. Leiden: Brill, 1999.

Neusner, Jacob and Bruce D. Chilton, eds. *Altruism in World Religions.* Washington, DC: Georgetown University Press, 2005.

———. *The Body of Faith: Israel and the Church.* Valley Forge, PA: Trinity Press International, 1996.

———. *God in the World.* Valley Forge, PA: Trinity Press International, 1997.

———, eds. *Religion and Economics: New Perspectives.* Binghamton, NY: Global Publications, 2000.

———, eds. *Religious Toleration in World Religions.* Philadelphia: Templeton Foundation Press, 2008.

———. *Revelation: The Torah and the Bible.* Valley Forge, PA: Trinity Press International, 1995.

Neusner, Jacob, Bruce Chilton, and William Graham. *Three Faiths, One God: The Formative Faith and Practice of Judaism, Christianity, and Islam.* Leiden: Brill, 2002.

Neusner, Jacob, Bruce D. Chilton, and R. E. Tully, eds. *Just War in Religion and Politics.* Lanham, MD: University Press of America, 2013.

Neusner, Jacob and Noam M. M. Neusner. *The Price of Excellence: Universities in Conflict during the Cold War.* New York: Continuum, 1995.

———. *Reaffirming Higher Education.* With an epilogue by William Scott Green. New Brunswick, NJ: Transaction, 2000.

Neusner, Jacob and Tamara Sonn. *Comparing Religions through Law: Judaism and Islam.* London: Routledge, 1999.

Neusner, Jacob, Tamara Sonn, and Jonathan E. Brockopp, eds. *Judaism and Islam in Practice: A Sourcebook.* London: Routledge, 2000.

BY OTHERS

Band, Arnold J. "Jewish Studies in American Liberal-Arts Colleges and Universities." *American Jewish Yearbook* 67 (1966): 3–30.

Baumgarten, Albert I. "The Name of the Pharisees." *Journal of Biblical Literature* 102.3 (1983): 411–428.

Bland, Kalman P. *The Artless Jew: Medieval and Modern Affirmations and Denials of the Visual.* Princeton: Princeton University Press, 2000.

Brenner, Michael. *Prophets of the Past: Interpreters of Jewish History.* Translated by Steven Rendall. Princeton: Princeton University Press, 2010.

Cohen, Shaye J. D. "Jacob Neusner, Mishnah, and Counter-Rabbinics: A Review Essay." *Conservative Judaism* 37.1 (1983): 48–63.

Danby, Herbert. *The Mishnah: Translated from the Hebrew with Introduction and Brief Introductory Notes.* Oxford: Oxford University Press, 1933.

Dubuisson, Daniel. *The Western Construction of Religion: Myths, Knowledge, and Ideology.* Translated by William Sayers. Baltimore: Johns Hopkins University Press, 2003.

Elman, Yaakov. "The Judaism of the Mishna: What Evidence?" *Judaic Book News* 12.2 (1982): 17–25.

Erlewine, Robert. *Judaism and the West: From Hermann Cohen to Joseph Soloveitchik.* Bloomington: Indiana University Press, 2016.

Feuer, Lewis S. "Recollections of Harry Austryn Wolfson." *American Jewish Archives*, April 1976, 25–50.

Fitzgerald, Timothy. *The Ideology of Religious Studies.* New York: Oxford University Press, 2000.

Fox, Marvin. "Review of *A History of the Mishnaic Law of Women* by Jacob Neusner." *Association for Jewish Studies Newsletter*, no. 29 (June 1981): 6–8.

Golinkin, David. "Was Professor Saul Lieberman 'Orthodox' or 'Conservative'?" *Conservative Judaism* 65 (Summer 2014): 13–29. http://seforim.blogspot.com/2014/12/was-professor-saul-lieberman-orthodox.html.

Heschel, Susannah. *Abraham Geiger and the Jewish Jesus.* Chicago: University of Chicago Press, 1998.

Himmelfarb, Gertrude. *On Looking into the Abyss: Untimely Thoughts on Culture and Society.* New York: Vintage, 1995.

Hoffman, Betty N. *Jewish West Hartford: From City to Suburb.* Charleston, SC: History Press, 2007.

Holtz, Barry, ed. *Back to the Sources: Reading the Classic Jewish Texts.* New York: Touchstone, 1984.

Hughes, Aaron W. *The Study of Judaism: Identity, Authenticity, Scholarship.* Albany: State University of New York Press, 2013.

Hunter, James Davison. *Culture Wars: The Struggle to Control the Family, Art, Education, Law, and Politics in America.* New York: Basic Books, 1991.

Israeli, Raphael. *Fundamentalist Islam and Israel: Essays in Interpretation.* Lanham, MD: University Press of America, 1993.

Jeffery, Peter. *The Secret Gospel of Mark Unveiled: Imagined Rituals of Sex, Death, and Madness in a Biblical Forgery.* New Haven: Yale University Press, 2006.

Jick, Leon, ed. *The Teaching of Judaica in American Universities: The Proceedings of a Colloquium*. New York: Ktav, 1970.

Katz, Steven T. "Issues in the Separation of Judaism and Christianity." *Journal of Biblical Literature* 103.1 (1984): 43–76.

Levey, Samson H. "Neusner's Purities: Monumental Masterpiece of Mishnaic Learning." *Journal of the American Academy of Religion* 46.3 (1978): 337–359.

Levy, Richard N. "The American University and *Olam Ha-Ba*." *Religious Education* 69 (1974): 11–27.

Lieberman, Saul. "A Tragedy or a Comedy?" *Journal of the American Oriental Society* 104.2 (1984): 315–319.

Loveland, Kristin. "The Association for Jewish Studies: A Brief History" (2008). http://www.ajsnet.org/ajs.pdf.

Maccoby, Hyam. "Jacob Neusner's Mishnah." *Midstream* 30.5 (1984): 24–32.

Magaziner, Ira. "A New Order." *Brown Alumni Magazine*, May/June 2014. http://www.brownalumnimagazine.com/content/view/3671/32/.

Magid, Shaul. *American Post-Judaism: Identity and Renewal in a Post-ethnic Society*. Bloomington: Indiana University Press, 2013.

Masuzawa, Tomoko. *The Invention of World Religions: Or, How Universalism Was Preserved in the Language of Pluralism*. Chicago: University of Chicago Press, 2005.

Mattes, Eleanor Bustin. *Myth for Moderns: Erwin Ramsdell Goodenough and Religious Studies in America, 1938–1955*. Lanham, MD: Scarecrow Press, 1997.

McCutcheon, Russell T. *Manufacturing Religion: The Discourse on Sui Generis Religion and the Politics of Nostalgia*. New York: Oxford University Press, 1997.

Mendes-Flohr, Paul and Jehuda Reinharz, eds. *The Jew in the Modern World: A Documentary History*. 2nd ed. New York: Oxford University Press, 1995.

Meyer, Michael A. "Toward a Definition of Jewish Studies." *Association for Jewish Studies Newsletter* 24 (1979): 2.

Moore, George Foot. *Judaism in the First Centuries of the Christian Era: The Age of the Tannaim*. 2 vols. Cambridge, MA: Harvard University Press, 1927.

Myers, David L. *Re-inventing the Jewish Past: European Jewish Intellectuals and the Zionist Return to History*. New York: Oxford University Press, 1995.

Nea, Courtney Randolph. "Content Restrictions and National Endowment for the Arts Funding: An Analysis from the Artist's Perspective." *William and Mary Bill of Rights Journal* 2.1 (1993): 165–184.

Ritterband, Paul and Harold S. Wechsler. *Jewish Learning in American Universities: The First Century*. Bloomington: Indiana University Press, 1994.

Robinson, Ira. "American Academy for Jewish Research (AAJR)." In *Jewish-American Voluntary Associations*, edited by Michael Dobkowski, 7–11. New York: Greenwood, 1986.

Sanders, E. P. "Jacob Neusner and the Philosophy of Mishnah." In *Jewish Law from Jesus to Mishnah: Five Studies*, 309–331. London: SCM Press, 1990.

Sarna, Jonathan. *American Judaism: A History*. New Haven: Yale University Press, 2004.

Schochet, Elijah J. and Solomon Spiro. *Saul Lieberman: The Man and His World*. New York: Jewish Theological Seminary of America, 2005.

Schorsch, Ismar. *From Text to Context: The Turn to History in Modern Judaism*. Hanover, NH: University Press of New England, 1994.

Schwardon, Steven. "Neusner Criticizes Minority Quotas." *Brown Daily Student*, November 6, 1972, 1–2.

Schwartz, Seth. "Historiography on the Jews in the 'Talmudic Period' (70–640 CE)." In *The Oxford Handbook of Jewish Studies*, edited by Martin Goodman, 79–114. Oxford: Oxford University Press, 2002.

Schwarz, Leo W. *Wolfson of Harvard: Portrait of a Scholar*. Philadelphia: Jewish Publication Society of America, 1978.

Scult, Mel. *The Radical American Judaism of Mordecai Kaplan*. Bloomington: Indiana University Press, 2014.

Segal, Eliezer. *The Babylonian Esther Midrash: A Critical Commentary*. 3 vols. Atlanta: Scholars Press, 1994.

———. *Case Citation in the Babylonian Talmud: The Evidence of Tractate Neziqin*. Atlanta: Scholars Press for Brown Judaic Studies, 1990.

Shanks, Hershel. "Annual Meetings Offer Intellectual Bazaar and Moments of High Drama." *Biblical Archaeology Review* 11.2 (March/April 1985): 12–16.

Shapiro, Marc B. *Saul Lieberman and the Orthodox*. Scranton, OH: University of Scranton Press, 2006.

Shore, Debra. "Jacob in the Lion's Den." *Brown Alumni Monthly*, March 1979, 17–23.

Silverman, Morris. *Hartford Jews, 1659–1970*. Hartford: Connecticut Historical Society.

Smith, Jonathan Z. *Map Is Not Territory: Studies in the History of Religion*. Chicago: University of Chicago Press, 1978.

———. *Relating Religion: Essays in the Study of Religion*. Chicago: University of Chicago Press, 2004.

Spicehandler, Ezra. "Review of *A Life of Yohanan ben Zakkai*." *Journal of the American Oriental Society* 83.3 (1963): 363–365.

Urbach, Ephraim E. *The Sages: Their Concepts and Beliefs*. Translated by Israel Abrahams. Jerusalem: Magnes Press, 1975.

Wertheimer, Jack, ed. *Tradition Renewed: A History of the Jewish Theological Seminary*. 2 vols. New York: Jewish Theological Seminary of America, 1997.

Wiese, Christian. *Challenging Colonial Discourse: Jewish Studies and Protestant Theology in Wilhemine Germany*. Translated by Barbara Harshav and Christian Wiese. Leiden: Brill, 2005.

Wolfson, Harry Austryn. "The Needs of Jewish Scholarship in America." *Menorah Journal* 7.1 (1921): 28–35.

Yerushalmi, Yosef Hayim. *Zakhor: Jewish History and Jewish Memory*. Seattle: University of Washington Press, 1982.

Zeitlin, Solomon. "A Life of Yohanan ben Zakkai: A Specimen of Modern Jewish Scholarship." *Jewish Quarterly Review* 62.3 (1972): 145–155.

INDEX

94, 110, 111, 115, 123, 132, 136, 137, 156, 164, 181, 189, 228, 233, 240, 243; brief history of, 40–42; center of Jewish research, 41–42; leadership of Louis Finkelstein, 41–43, 52; Neusner at, 46–52; Neusner's criticism of, 45, 51, 52–56, 115; and relationship to Conservative movement, 40–41; Saul Lieberman at, 43–46. *See also* Conservative Judaism; Lieberman, Saul

Jewish Week, 55
Jick, Leon, 120, 129
Johns Hopkins, 74, 144
Johnson, Bob, 226, 255
Johnson, Lyndon, 212
Journal of the American Academy of Religion (JAAR), 146
Journal of the American Oriental Society (JAOS), 63, 189, 191
Journal of Biblical Literature (JBL), 182, 185, 188

Kant, Immanuel, 10
Kaplan, Mordecai, 1, 41, 51, 52, 269
Karp, Abraham, 55
Katz, Steven T., 187–188
Kennedy, Edward, 34, 205, 207
Kennedy, John, 207
Kent, Charles Foster, 66
Kent Fellowship, 65–68, 69
Klutznick Chair (Northwestern), 178
Knesset Yisrael Yeshiva (Slobodka), 42, 76
Koshland Chair (Stanford), 177–178
Kraabel, A. T., 193
Kristol, Irving, 210, 221
Kristol, William, 210–211
Kuhn, Thomas S., 28
Küng, Hans, 53, 54

Labour Party (Britain), 33–34
Landow, George, 174

Lasch, Christopher, 28
Leslau, Wolf, 191
Levey, Samson H., 146–147
Leviticus Rabbah, 145. *See also* rabbinics
Library of Congress, 220–222, 266
Lieberman, Saul, 42–46, 51, 52, 55, 64, 76, 110, 137, 148, 182, 189–192, 194, 195, 199, 243; dean of rabbinical school (JTS), 44; Neusner's criticisms of, 44–46, 52, 55, 137, 191–192; review of Neusner, 45–46, 64, 148, 189–192; tensions with Orthodox world, 43, 44. *See also* Jewish Theological Seminary of America; Smith, Morton
Lipshutz, Robert J., 205
List Professorship (Harvard Divinity School), 175–177
Los Angeles Times, 214
Loveland, Kristen, 120

Maccoby, Hyam, 156–159
Mapplethorpe, Robert, 1, 207, 213, 214
Marx, Alexander, 41
Max Richter Foundation, 96–97, 125, 140, 148, 228
McMahon, Senator Brian, 19
Meeks, Wayne, 106, 109–110, 112–113
methodology, 2, 64, 128, 141, 150, 156, 183, 186, 192
Meyer, Michael, 122, 125, 127
Midrashim, 49, 63, 144, 152, 197, 198. *See also* rabbinics
Milhaven, Giles, 168
Milwaukee, 71, 73, 81–88, 90, 93, 133, 226
Mishnah, 14, 49, 60, 100, 139, 140, 144, 145, 146, 147, 151–159, 193, 197–198, 199, 205, 233. *See also* Babylonian Talmud (Bavli); rabbinics; Yerushalmi Talmud
Moore, George Foot, 61, 129, 153, 182

Narrowe, Morton H., 244
Nash, Leonard, 28

ABOUT THE AUTHOR

Aaron W. Hughes holds the Philip S. Bernstein Chair of Jewish Studies at the University of Rochester.